Searching for a Better Life

Searching for a Better Life

Growing Up in the Slums of Bangkok

Sorcha Mahony

berghahn
NEW YORK • OXFORD
www.berghahnbooks.com

First published in 2018 by
Berghahn Books
www.berghahnbooks.com

First paperback edition published in 2019

Library of Congress Cataloging-in-Publication Data

Names: Mahony, Sorcha, author.
Title: Searching for a better life : growing up in the slums of Bangkok / Sorcha Mahony.
Description: New York : Berghahn Books, 2018. | Includes bibliographical references and index.
Identifiers: LCCN 2017053715 (print) | LCCN 2017056444 (ebook) | ISBN 9781785338595 (ebook) | ISBN 9781785338588 (hardback ; alk. paper)
Subjects: LCSH: Youth--Thailand--Bangkok--Social conditions. | Poor--Thailand--Bangkok--Social conditions. | Slums--Thailand--Bangkok.
Classification: LCC HQ799.T52 (ebook) | LCC HQ799.T52 B35 2018 (print) | DDC 305.23509593--dc23
LC record available at https://lccn.loc.gov/2017053715

British Library Cataloguing in Publication Data

A catalogue record for this book is available from the British Library

ISBN 978-1-78533-858-8 hardback
ISBN 978-1-78920-535-0 paperback
ISBN 978-1-78533-859-5 ebook

[L]est we forget: the reading, the reflecting, and the writing are as nothing in comparison with the cost to those who have lived the stories told here … I trust I have done them no further violence in the rough and impressionistic strokes I have left on this canvas.

—Nancy Scheper-Hughes, *Death without Weeping*

Contents

Figures

Preface

On my laptop there is a collection of photographs that are programmed to run as a slideshow when the keyboard has not been activated for a while. Sometimes when I am struggling to find the words to articulate an idea, I sit and look at the pictures and find myself momentarily transported to a slum in Bangkok, where I lived about a decade ago conducting ethnographic fieldwork with young people.

It is joyful and painful to look at these photographs. They remind me of my friends, neighbours and acquaintances in the slum and inspire me to make contact with those I can, and this usually results in a flurry of emails or Facebook messages in which we exchange news of our families, friends and life events. But they signify too the profound hardship and suffering faced by the urban poor day in, day out, not just in this slum or in Bangkok, or even just in Thailand, but everywhere.

The photographs are in black and white, and I watch as the corrugated tin roofs, stray dogs, smiling faces and abandoned vehicles fade in and out on the screen. Ahhh, there is the main street cutting through the upgraded community where I lived, with its tall concrete rental houses and street food stalls dotted about. There are the wooden huts backing onto the railway line that passed through one of the slum communities, and the children playing on the tracks among the litter. Next come the lorries, captured as they thundered past on the expressway, underneath more houses crammed tightly together. And the strange slum jungle, the community that had been cleared to make way for property development but then abandoned, leaving some residents to return and the trees and plants to run wild. And there is Gee, my little friend with the sweetest smile I had ever seen, who would run to hug me every time I visited, always prompting her grandmother to joke (or not) that I should stay and adopt them both.

And then two pictures in succession that make me pause every time. They are of Boo, a girl of about ten, taken during a neighbourhood walk with her friends around one of the more remote slum communities. In the first photograph, Boo stands in the foreground, an expanse of dusty concrete and gravel around her, a decrepit looking hut behind her to the right and piles of rubbish to the left (there was a recycling centre in the community, where slum dwellers could sell the rubbish they picked from the streets in exchange for cash, and the piles would build up outside people's homes until they had enough to warrant a trip to sell it). Boo stands there, her arms hanging down at either side. She is wearing a sleeveless top with a teddy bear on the front and raggedy trousers that reach just below her knees. Her feet are bare. I do not know what she was feeling at the time, but she does not look particularly happy, maybe a bit bored.

In the next photograph, Boo's face appears close up. She is holding a flower and looking at it with her mouth agape and a sparkle in her eyes. She had seen the flower just as I was about to take a picture of her and her friend, had run off to pick it and stood staring at it in wonder.

After I took these photographs, Boo and her friends borrowed my camera and they scurried away, talking and arguing excitedly about who would get to operate it as they disappeared through a narrow passageway between two blocks of huts. They were gone for a few minutes and came back with no pictures, but with three short videos they had recorded instead. The first video was of toilets – close-up shots of the fetid contents of the shared, squat latrines that the girls and their fellow slum residents used. The second video was of a man from their community, performing a magic trick with a length of string – turning two short pieces into one long one with a sleight of hand, to the utter delight of the children watching. The third video was of flowers. In between the wooden slats of the residential huts the camera goes, down onto the discarded tyres, underneath the body of a disused train carriage, seeking out all the flowers it can and moving in close when it finds one, focusing on the delicate pink and purple petals.

I am embarrassed to admit it, but when I first watched these videos I felt disappointed. I was hoping they might (peer to peer, Hecht-like[1]) provide some great insight into the children's lives, and in my naivety I did not see that they had. It was only much later that I would come to realize that the videos and their sequencing, along with the two photographs of Boo that preceded them, signified with absolute clarity one of the most powerful forces to shape everyday life for young people growing up in the slums of Bangkok: the search for something better and the need for a little bit of magic to turn the tough reality of everyday life into something of beauty.

It has been over ten years since I took Boo's photograph, and I do not know what has become of her in that time. Even during fieldwork, her situation was one of the more precarious that I knew of, with frequent movement between family in one of the Bangkok slum communities and her grandparents in the rural – impoverished – north-east of the country. From the very few snippets of conversation I managed to have with or about her, I gathered that she attended school sporadically, that her mother had passed away a number of years earlier, that her father was in prison, that her paternal grandmother was ostensibly her main carer and that she split her time in the slum between various aunts, cousins and neighbours. To me, Boo seemed to float about like a leaf in the wind, with little in the way of anchorage and even less in the way of real support. Although she had a social network, and although non-governmental organization (NGO) presence was prevalent and effective in many slum communities, Boo somehow drifted past them, her situation epitomized by the perpetual shifting of ground beneath her feet. This made researching with her during fieldwork difficult and keeping in touch with her afterwards impossible, and spoke volumes about the precariousness that already marked her young life and would inevitably shape her ability to create a better one.

Although I do not know what has become of Boo, I do know that in the decade since she posed in those photographs, surrounded by litter and looking in awe at the flower she cupped carefully in her hand, the context in which her life will have unfolded has been marked by a multitude of profound and protracted instabilities. From 2006 to the present day, the political terrain in Thailand has been nothing less than tumultuous. Coups, periods of military rule, anti-government protests and counter protests, corruption and fraud charges against those at the top of the Thai political apparatus, imprisonment of political figureheads, assassination attempts, snap elections, constitutional amendments, the storming and seizure of government buildings, bomb attacks, repeated states of emergency and the shooting to death of government dissenters: these and a long list of related events make for a broad political context that is surely less stable than it was when I lived there in 2005–06. At best, they seem to reveal a preoccupation among those in power with the political machinery itself rather than with the plight of those faring badly on its watch, and at worst they speak of a conscious unwillingness to address the growing inequality in the country or to support those who feel its injustice most keenly.

These political uncertainties have left their mark on the economic stability of the country. Income from tourism, foreign investment and consumption are mainstays of the Thai economy, and these plummeted in the wake of the political upheavals (Sethapramote 2014). And as if that was not enough, the Thai stock, currency and export markets took further blows in the fallout from the 2008 global economic crisis (Kritayanavaj 2008). These, along with the floods that devastated parts of Bangkok in 2011 and the fire that swept through one of the slum communities in 2013, destroying a number of houses and disrupting many lives, alongside the more distant ongoing insurgency in the south of Thailand and the 2008 conflict over territory on the Thai-Cambodian border, function to render even more precarious the circumstances in which the urban poor struggle.

I conducted the fieldwork on which this book is based in 2005–06 and completed an original manuscript in 2010. Life then took over, and work and bringing up young children left little room for sharing what I had found in the field. But through the multitude of turbulences that have been visited on Thailand in these intervening years, one thing is certain: the search for a better life will not have been made easier for people like Boo already living in conditions of considerable hardship and uncertainty.

I offer this book as a small contribution towards understanding the plight of marginalized youth in the developing world. While the core concern is to document and make sense of the lives and dreams of a particular group of young slum dwellers in Bangkok, it will reflect too some of the concerns, experiences and struggles of a broader group; of other young people living in other contexts of urban poverty and rapid development, for whom the search for a better life is neither straightforward nor stable and where guarantees are in very short supply. The book also reflects on issues of methodology and theory as these relate to young people growing up in urban poverty in a context that is changing rapidly and markedly as they find their way in the world.

Boo, I guess you will never read this. If you could, I would tell you that while this story is not directly about you, it is about the precariousness that has prevented me from knowing you more than fleetingly. And it is for you: wherever you are and whatever you are doing, I hope that your life now is full of flowers, that you have managed, with a little bit of magic, to find something better, make it yours and hold it close to you.

Note

1. Hecht, in his 1998 study of street children in Brazil, drew on peer to peer methods to brilliant effect, learning more about the children's lives through allowing them to ask each other questions – in their own space and on their own terms – than he would otherwise have done.

Acknowledgements

While the final text in this book is mine, I would not have been able to write it without the help and support of many, many others. And so my sincerest thanks go to: the Economic and Social Research Council for funding the research on which the book is based; Dr Sarah White, for her inspiration and unfailing support, for her critical engagement and expert guidance, for her apparently unending patience, and for believing in my potential and encouraging me to fulfil it; all of the participants in the study, for sharing their lives with me and letting me share mine with them; my friends at Bath University, for making the research experience a rich and rewarding one, and for their fantastic support, calm reassurance and companionship through the good times and the more challenging ones; the WeD team at Bath for their administrative help, support and encouragement, intellectual stimulation and kindness; the WeD team at Khon Kaen University, for their assistance during my stay in the north-east of Thailand, and for their friendship; Dr Heather Montgomery, for all her support prior to fieldwork and for encouraging me to share this story more widely; my host family in Bangkok, for their hospitality and kindness and for helping to facilitate access to wealthy participants; Am, for her brilliant organization of the wealthy component of this research, for her excellent interpreting skills and for her companionship throughout my stay in Bangkok; the staff at the schools where Am and I conducted interviews, for facilitating access to young people there; Nit, for her excellent Thai language lessons in Bangkok; Dr Judith Ennew, for her kindness, hospitality and intellectual support, and for the delicious food and Earl Grey tea; Helen Veitch and her family, for providing me with respite from data collection during fieldwork; Ganya, for her excellent interpreting and networking skills and for helping to make my stay in Khlong Toey slum such a rewarding one; Note, for his help accessing participants and conducting interviews; the staff at the Duang Prateep Foundation, SCD, Heart's Home and Khlong Toey community school for their insights into life in Khlong Toey slum;

Loong Ajaan Preecha for his kindness and hospitality, and for helping me to gain access to the library at Chulalongkorn University; Ajaan Thianthai, for providing me with reading material; Loong Kanok and his family, for their kindness and hospitality during my time in Bangkok; my friends back home, for the visits during the fieldwork, for their engagement with my research, for helping to look after my children so I could write, and for being rocks during the most difficult times; my family, for their interest and encouragement every step of the way and for helping to look after my children so I could write; my managers and colleagues at The Children's Society, for accommodating the writing of this book.

A special thanks to my mother, Pat Mahony, for… well, far too many things to list here in a way that could ever do justice to them or to her. But for starters, thank you for the roof over my head throughout the writing of the initial product of this research, for all your help with the children, for lending your incisive mind to the testing of my ideas, for casting your critical eye over earlier chapter drafts (even if your red pen did drive me crazy), for facilitating access to many of the things – people, technology, literature – that have made the production of this book easier than it would otherwise have been, for all the laughter, and for going the extra hundreds of thousands of miles in making the life you have given me a happy, healthy and fulfilling one. Also for the advice that 'striving for perfection is the road to madness – go for good enough'.

Finally, I would like to thank my children, Maya and Jakey, for the gift of motherhood and for keeping my feet firmly on the ground (among the nappies and the plastic toys) in the writing of this book. May your lives too be long, happy, healthy and fulfilling ones, and may you learn to appreciate the gifts bestowed on you in your journey through it. I love you both to infinity and beyond.

Introduction

Fieldnotes

The slum, Bangkok. 4.30 p.m. 6 July 2006

I am on my way to the community gym that takes place in the forecourt of a large NGO located in the city's biggest slum. I step into the fierce blaze of the sun and walk under a massive concrete expressway that roars and shakes under the weight of the container trucks transporting goods to and from the port. Lorries are strewn everywhere, rusty skeletons of their former selves that now provide beds for those who do not have them and climbing frames for the young children who live nearby. I cross a railway line littered with rubbish and walk under a second expressway, past an old man sitting on a broken sofa, his ribs sticking out, his back as bent as the top of a coat hanger. Behind the sofa is an outdoor living room that has no walls or ceiling. The space is demarcated by rickety wooden cabinets that run along three sides. A television blares out and about ten people gather around to watch. I walk on, past a young man who is laughing hysterically, one arm inside his zipped-up jacket, holding a plastic bag and sniffing from it. I walk on. A man approaches and asks for five baht, and follows me up the road, barefoot, clutching at my wrist. I get to the main intersection at the centre of the slum and see P[1] Jok making fruit shakes for her customers. She nods towards a group of young couples sitting on motorbikes opposite her stall. 'Look', her nod says, 'I told you the teenagers around here are no good'. The mid-afternoon lull – those hours after lunch when the sun beats hard, the streets are quieter and daily life seems to move in slow motion – gives way to the hustle and bustle of early evening. Barbecue coals are lit and stoked and smoke billows out across the tin rooftops. Woks hiss, dirty water splashes into the gutters, announcements from the community leader crackle through the loudspeakers that are tied to the lamp posts, and motorbikes, bicycles, push carts, pickup trucks, pedestrians and stray dogs compete for space on the dusty lanes. I arrive at the gym and it is deserted except for Som, a young man of seventeen who sits on a weightlifting bench under a plastic awning waiting for his friends.

Som is wearing an NYC baseball cap, a pair of bright orange sunglasses and three chunky metal chains around his neck. Hanging from each chain is a pendant: from one a miniature statue of Buddha, from another a letter from the Japanese alphabet with the word JAPAN inscribed underneath, and from the third a diamante dollar sign. He is dressed in a vest, into which he has cut a deep V shape at the neck, and a pair of baggy jeans scarcely held up by a belt emblazoned with the word BLING, clearly worn for ornamental rather than functional purposes. Som sits with his elbows resting on his knees, his hands clasped together, his head hung low. I sit beside him, and he tells me that he is not feeling so good. When I ask why, he says he has not slept properly for three nights because he has so many problems. What problems? I ask. And he tells me of the troubles that the dark nights intensify in their own cruel way.

Som's mother recently told him that she and Som's sister would be moving up country, because a family feud following the death of Som's grandmother means that they are no longer welcome in the small wooden hut where they live with Som and Som's aunt, uncle and cousins. Som has been told to leave and has three weeks to find somewhere to live. He does not earn a reliable or adequate income: some weeks he gets casual labouring work at the port for one or two nights, he helps a friend's mother at her market stall for a couple of hours on weekday afternoons, and sometimes he gets extra work on Saturday evenings packing away the tables and chairs at a local street cafe. While these sources of income are indispensable for Som, they provide him with no security – nothing with which to weather the storm that has come his way.

Som was born just outside Bangkok and lived in a rented apartment in a low-income neighbourhood with his mother, father and older sister until he was eight years old. His father came from the north-east of Thailand and worked as a telephone repair man, and his mother comes from a family who settled in Khlong Toey slum in the 1950s, and worked in a garment factory. When Som was eight, his father died from cancer of the liver, and an ensuing conflict between his mother and his father's family left Som's mother with no inheritance and insufficient means with which to raise her two children. She moved back to Khlong Toey slum with Som and his sister, and into her mother's house, which was already home to Som's grandmother, aunt, uncle and four cousins. During this time, Som attended the local community school but left at thirteen, before completing compulsory schooling, because he was no longer prepared to suffer the beatings he received at the hands of his teachers (punishments for falling asleep in class, a result of working in the early mornings to help his mother make ends meet). For the next three years, Som worked in a variety of informal jobs: at a toy shop, at market stalls and food stalls, and running errands for neighbours. He continued to live in his grandmother's house with his mother and sister and extended family, but relationships within the household grew increasingly strained, as poverty, overcrowding and gruelling work took their toll on family members, and as Som's mother and sister became increasingly dependent on alcohol and prone to bouts of violence. When Som was fourteen, he moved out to live with a girlfriend who was considerably older than him and rented her own room, but when that relationship broke down he moved back to the family home where he has been ever since, although he stays frequently at friends' houses.

Som has his heart set on a better life than the one he knows today. When he was sixteen, he decided to return to school in order to increase his earning potential, and enrolled on a course at the local community college to prepare for his lower secondary exams. Since then he has been studying part time and working as a casual labourer, but he dreams of doing a nine to five job in an office, of wearing a suit and of earning enough money to support his family and leave the slum.

About this Book

This book is about Som, his friends and his peers growing up in the slums of Bangkok, at a moment in their lives and a moment in national and global history marked by a series of profound and interlocking transitions. It offers an account of an ethnographic study I undertook between 2005 and 2006 in an inner-city slum, first undertaking participant observation and engaging in everyday conversations, then conducting interviews, focus group discussions and a range of other qualitative, participatory research activities. It also draws on fieldwork undertaken in the homes and schools of relatively wealthy Thai families, although these remain in the background, referred to as a means of drawing out some of the issues and concerns particular to those living in slum communities.

The book is about *the search for a better life* – what this means for those struggling to get by in a rapidly developing and globalizing economy, how they try to fulfil their dreams, and the outcomes and side effects of their endeavours. It is not a book about the most destitute or otherwise troubled slum dwellers whose stories may be more familiar; it does not focus on the issues of housing, drug addiction, alcoholism, prostitution, HIV-AIDS, gambling, orphaned children, teenage pregnancy or suicide – although these issues are certainly present and form a crucial part of the backdrop against which Som and his peers were growing up. Instead, this book tells a story about a group of slum dwellers who are trying to create a better life for themselves and their families, with the odds stacked against them.

In this, it focuses on three key spheres of everyday practice: *living the teenage life*, or engagement in global cultural practices; *doing the right thing*, or engagement in local cultural practices; and *forging the future*, or engagement in educational and economic activity designed to reduce hardship and improve material standards of living. It explores the key activities involved in each of these spheres of activity, the meanings that participants attach to them, the pertinent elements of the contexts in which those activities take place and the unintended consequences that can ensue from them.

Theoretically the book reflects on the issue of agency, as exercised by young people living in conditions of severe structural constraint, showing how the exercise of agency can have negative outcomes for those who struggle to survive the daily grind of slum life yet dare to dream of something better. In particular, the book demonstrates that when studying the agency of the urban poor, a holistic approach is important: action in one sphere of life can have 'spill-over' effects in other spheres, and without acknowledging the existence of these multiple spheres and the connections between them, we cannot properly understand the ways in which agency operates when severely constrained, often bumping up against itself in different realms of practice and interacting with multiple structures to produce counterproductive outcomes.

This theoretical approach sits alongside that of scholars writing within the interdisciplinary and expanding global youth studies literature, in particular those whose work takes a critical approach to the study of marginalized agency. Many of these scholars are influenced by Bourdieu's notion of cultural production and reproduction, identifying the mechanisms through which young people living in conditions of socio-economic disadvantage around the world come to reinforce their positions of marginalization through everyday cultural practice. In this book I take a slightly different approach, analysing not how the exercise of marginalized agency can reproduce socio-economic structures of oppression, but instead how exercising marginalized agency within one realm or sphere of cultural practice can engender counterproductive outcomes within other spheres, bringing in its wake a host of unintended, negative outcomes.

The critical scholarship within the global youth studies literature has informed the theoretical framework in this study, which I developed through the iterative process of data analysis and reading. This framework is represented visually in Figure 0.1. Each circle represents a sphere of action and appears porous to represent the insecurity and

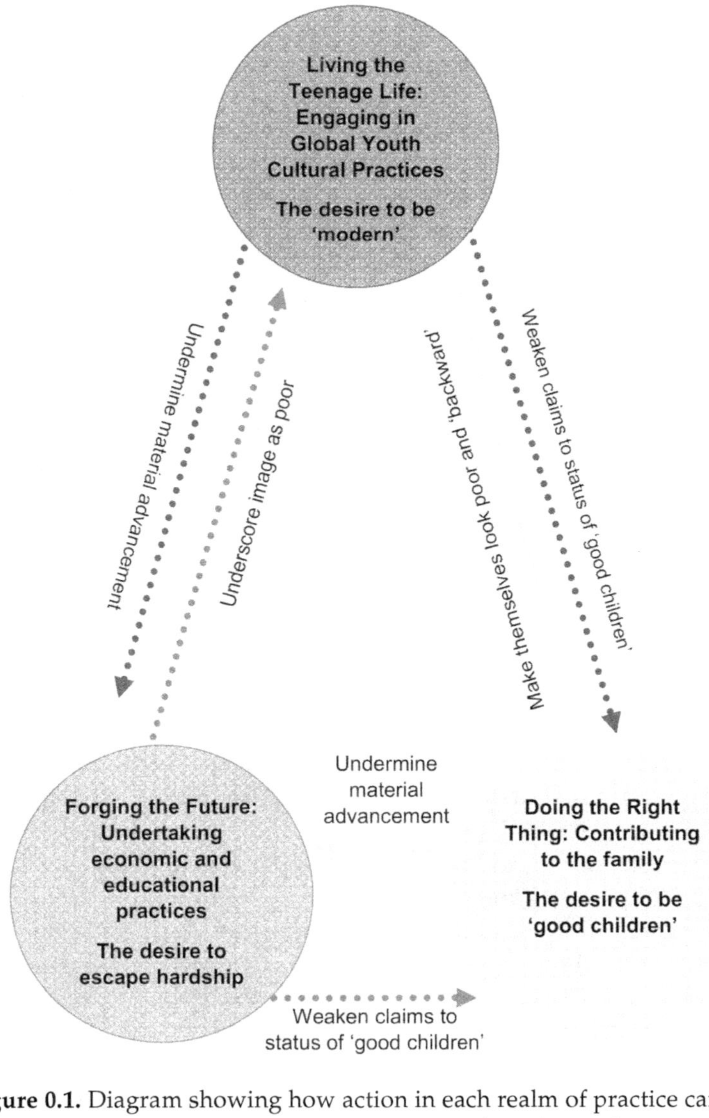

Figure 0.1. Diagram showing how action in each realm of practice can be precarious and have unintended consequences for other realms.

complexities attendant in each set of endeavours (each of these circles forms the basis of discussion in one of the empirical chapters in Part II of the book). The dotted arrows between the circles represent the spill-over effects emanating from and destined towards the other spheres of activity. The diagram provides a way of understanding how action within one realm of practice is itself fraught with tension and can have disabling effects in other realms when exercised by those in positions of structural disadvantage.

The remainder of this book sets about elucidating the central argument – that for young people growing up in urban poverty, the multifarious pursuit of a better life can have profoundly negative consequences. It is divided into three parts. Part I provides the background to the study. Chapter 1 sets the scene: it outlines the key terms used throughout the book, introduces Theravada Buddhism and some of its salient aspects as these relate to the central concerns of the study, then recounts Thailand's story of rapid development and the history of slum proliferation in the country, briefly surveying the socio-economic context in which the search for a better life has come to such prominence and introducing the slum in which fieldwork took place. Chapter 2 goes on to survey and critique the existing literature that deals with young people in Thailand – either explicitly or by implication – and to highlight the theoretically informed, critical studies that have influenced my interpretation of empirical data and the development of my conceptual framework. Chapter 3 describes the fieldwork journey, offering a personal and reflexive account of the processes of research design, data collection and analytical interpretation.

Part II details the main findings of the study. Chapter 4 focuses on young slum dwellers' endeavours to 'live the teenage life', to engage with the products and images of the global youth culture industry, and through these to construct images of wealth, global connection and modernity and present these to others, especially their peers. The chapter explores the complex and contradictory context in which these practices take place and some of their unintended consequences, especially those relating to the other two spheres explored in the book. Chapter 5 discusses young slum dwellers' attempts to 'do the right thing' by their families, to provide much-needed support in the form of money and labour, and through this to construct themselves as 'good' children. The chapter pays attention to the unintended consequences of these endeavours, focusing on those that spill over into the other two spheres of everyday practice. This chapter also investigates young slum dwellers' attempts to make *living the teenage life* and *doing the right thing* compatible, once again focusing on the unintended outcomes of action in this regard. Chapter 6 discusses young slum dwellers' attempts to secure a better standard of living in the future. It explores the key ways in which they work towards their dreams of material advancement, focusing on the unintended side effects that can ensue from the fragility of the support available to them. It explores participants' own understandings of the struggle to get ahead, and notes the irony that it is precisely by thinking and acting in accordance with widely revered norms in the local, national and global contexts that their endeavours can be so fraught.

Part III comprises a short concluding chapter that summarizes the key findings and discusses their implications for the literatures discussed in Chapter 2 and relevant policy arenas.

The search for a better life could not be more central in today's geopolitical and socio-economic climate. Global migration figures from 2015 (International Organisation for Migration 2016) show the highest number of international migrants in recorded history, as people from all over the world – and for very different reasons – attempted to secure a better life for themselves and their families, whether as economic migrants, refugees or asylum seekers. At the same time, the discourse of well-being has moved from the annals of history, philosophy and the periphery of certain academic disciplines, to become a prominent feature of contemporary scholarly, political, organizational, community and individual endeavour, as people the world over wrestle with what it means in contemporary times to live a good life and with how to best attain – and sustain – it.

It is an opportune moment to pause and reflect on some of the more nuanced and problematic processes that can make the search for a better life so precarious for those who begin their journeys on a shaky footing. In so doing, we may be better positioned to support our less fortunate contemporaries to weather the storms that visit them in their search for a better life, to support them in bracing themselves for the potential pitfalls along the way.

Note

1. P is the designation given to older siblings, but can also be – and is often – used for slightly older friends and acquaintances. It denotes respect.

PART I

1

Setting the Scene

This chapter is divided into four sections. In the first, I offer an account of the key terms used in the book, with brief explanations of the reasons behind choosing the more contentious ones. In the second section, I briefly survey some of the key features of the religious context in which young slum dwellers endeavour to build a better life, highlighting some of the prevalent assumptions therein about the means of achieving it. In the third section, I describe the socio-economic context in which the notion of a better life has flourished, focusing on Thailand's economic development during the second half of the twentieth century. Again, I point to the prevalent assumptions within this context about the means of achieving a better life. In the fourth section, I give a historical overview of the growth of slum settlements in Bangkok and introduce the slum in which this study took place. Through the chapter, I demonstrate that the notion of a better life has been embedded in Thai consciousness for many years, albeit with varied meanings attached to it, and that ideas about the way in which it can be achieved imply certain assumptions about the capacity of individuals to break through structures of constraint.

Key Terms

Young People and Youth

The majority of young people who form the core of this study were between fifteen and twenty-two years of age at the time of fieldwork.

I also conducted research with slightly younger people (thirteen years old), but the focus is on those between fifteen and twenty-two. I refer to these participants as 'young people' and 'youth'. It is widely recognized that defining 'youth' (and children or adults for that matter) solely in terms of chronological age provides an insufficient understanding of the ways in which lives are socially constructed. What it means to be a person of a particular age varies across space and over time, and what it means to be a person of a certain age living in a particular place and time varies according to, for example, the prevailing norms surrounding inter-generational and gender relations, and socio-economic positioning.

It is also recognized that the selection of labels with which to write about particular groups of people, not least young people, can be a far from neutral process (see Hall and Montgomery 2000; Bucholtz 2002). The terms we choose to write with carry meaning – the writer's and the reader's – which in turn reflect the broader connotations that prevail at a particular time in a particular culture. Labels can be used to strategic effect, to engender certain associations and emotions and invoke a reader's sympathy – or otherwise – for the people about whom one writes. For example, labelling people in their teenage years or even in their early twenties as 'street children' (a category applied to young people living on the streets in the developing world) functions to construct them as innocent victims in need of support (see Hecht 1998), while the term 'homeless youth' (a category more readily applied to young people living on the streets in developed countries) carries connotations of delinquency and does not invoke the same sympathetic concern (Hall and Montgomery 2000). Furthermore, it has been argued that the term 'child' suggests a need for intervention, while the label 'youth' suggests an element of self-will and an absence of need for assistance (Ansell 2005).

In this book, I use the term 'young people' (or young woman, man or slum dweller) as this is the most neutral one available, and because it encompasses participants at the younger end of the age range as well as those in their early twenties. I use this interchangeably with the term 'youth', and employ the latter because this is widely used in the literatures with which this book connects. There are other terms employed in these literatures to refer to people of the same age as those discussed here, such as 'adolescents' and 'teenagers', but I refrain from using these because each of them carries associations that are not appropriate for this research. 'Adolescent' is associated with an emphasis on biological and psychological development and with related claims to universalism, while this study explores socio-economic, cultural and moral aspects of young people's lives and recognizes these as products of history. The term 'teenager' technically refers to those between the ages of thirteen and nineteen and not those in their early twenties, who form an important element in this study. While I do discuss the phenomenon of the 'teenage life', and while participants use the Thai term *wairoon* (which is translated as 'teenager') to refer to people in their teens and early twenties, using this term may be misleading to English language readers.

Adult Carers

At the outset of this research, I worked with the term 'parents' when referring to those with responsibility for young people. However, this label took insufficient account of the multiple systems of care and forms of cohabitation that young slum dwellers experience. I settled on the term 'adult carer' because it points to generational differences between the two main groups of participants, and to one of the defining features of the ideal-type relationship between adults and the young people in their charge.

Although I use the term 'adult carer' and do so because, after considerable deliberation, it transpired to be the most appropriate, I use the term with some caution. At times during fieldwork, I questioned whether, and to what extent, some of those with responsibility for young people actually 'cared' for them at all, in a practical sense. Furthermore, there were cases where those caring for young participants, such as older siblings or cousins, were themselves not much older than the young people in their charge. Moreover, attaching the term 'carer' only to older generation participants and not to young people – many of whom had a significant duty of care for elders – is perhaps misleading given the bidirectionality of support between adults and young people. However, I have retained the term 'adult carer' because it appears to be the most suitable given what is available.

Slums, Slum Dwellers and the Urban Poor

The United Nations Centre for Human Settlements (UNCHS) defines 'slum' and 'squatter' settlements in the following ways:

> Slum settlements usually consist of run-down housing in older, established, legally built parts of the city proper. Slum buildings are mostly old and poorly maintained. Most of the residents rent their accommodation, although owners occupy some space or detached structures. In some cases, many of the buildings have more than one floor and house

> several families. (UNCHS 1982, cited by Viratkapan and Perera 2006: 158)
>
> Squatter settlements are mainly uncontrolled low-income residential areas with ambiguous legal status regarding land occupation. They are to a large extent built by the inhabitants themselves using their own means and are usually poorly equipped with public utilities and community services. The usual image of a squatter settlement is of a poor, under serviced, overcrowded and dilapidated settlement consisting of make-shift, improvised housing areas. The land occupied by squatter settlements is often, but not always, located further from the city centre than is the case with slums. Often, but not always, the houses are built and occupied by their owners. The land is often occupied illegally. (Ibid.)

Viratkapan and Perera (2006) note that in the context of Thailand, the label 'slum' is used to refer to what the UNCHS separately labels 'slum' and 'squatter' settlements. Pornchokchai (2003) notes that the National Housing Authority (NHA) and Bangkok Metropolitan Authority (BMA) define slums in the following ways:

> A dirty, damp, swampy or unhealthy area with overcrowded buildings and dwellers [*sic*] which can be harmful for health or lives or can be a source of unlawful or immoral actions. (NHA, cited in Pornchokchai 2003: 13)
>
> An overcrowded, unorderly [*sic*] and dilapidated community with unample [*sic*] environment which can be harmful for health and lives. The minimum number of housing units per rai is 15. (BMA, cited in Pornchokchai 2003: 13)

In 1982, Thai government ministers in the Department for Public Welfare suggested that the label '*chumchorn ae at*' ('crowded community') should replace 'slum' in an attempt to diminish the negative connotations and prejudice experienced by residents. However, the term '*salum*' (slum) continued to be widely used and the government continued to define the 'crowded communities' in the same way as they had previously defined 'slums', as communities that are:

> … full of people with bad quality houses. People there lack money and assets, public utilities and food, have poor sanitation, low education, and have family problems and distorted behaviour. (Anon-DPF 2006)

Slums do not necessarily house the poorest of the poor in urban areas; indeed, it is argued that the poorest of the poor are not housed at all, they are homeless, or are itinerant workers on construction sites (Pornchokchai 2003). In Thailand, the NHA divides the urban poor into three levels: the 'lowest', which comprises homeless people and those who beg for a living; the 'middle', which comprises slum dwellers who earn low incomes; and the 'highest', which comprises those who rent low-cost housing that is not in slum communities and who earn more than those at the middle level (Anon-DPF 2006). Clearly, such rigid categorization breaks down once it is recognized that some homeless people live on the streets in slum communities, that some slum dwellers earn relatively large incomes (for example through money lending, drug trafficking or pimping), and that some who rent low-cost housing outside of designated slum areas earn less than some living in slums.

However, while slum communities are marked by considerable internal diversity (Askew 2002), and while there may be blurred boundaries between slums and non-slum communities, there are common characteristics within them. Incomes in slum communities tend to be very low, as does educational and occupational status. They are densely populated,[1] tenure insecurity is a significant issue and housing and other physical infrastructure is of low quality. Social problems such as substance abuse, violence and family breakdown are common. House fires are a constant threat, as many dwellings are packed closely together and made of wood, and the cooking oil used is highly flammable. Pornchokchai (2003) identifies four overriding characteristics uniting the settlements labelled 'slums': overcrowding, limited privacy, substandard housing and a substandard environment.

In this book, I use the terms 'slum' and 'slum communities' and refer to participants as 'slum dwellers' for several reasons. First, 'slum' is the label that many of the participants used when referring to themselves, each other and their neighbourhoods – sometimes with mocking self-deprecation, sometimes with a painful awareness of how it signified their low social status, and sometimes with no obvious connotations at all. While their use of this label could arguably be a result of my identity as an outsider and someone they expected to perceive them in certain ways, it became a familiar term and did not seem to cause offence to the people who shared their stories and their lives with me. Second, it is a label commonly used by NGOs and their staff working in the slum. Third, the term 'slum' and its various permutations remains commonplace in the literature by Thai and foreign academics writing about low-income urban communities in Thailand, albeit sometimes with acknowledgement that there may be more appropriate labels.

Throughout the book, I also use the phrase 'urban poor' to refer to participants living in slum communities. In doing so, I have not measured them against an official, absolute poverty line, but take a relative approach, defining them as 'poor' on the basis that their incomes are significantly lower than the average in Bangkok (see Chestnut et al. 1997) and, from the data collected in this research, they have significantly less savings and fewer assets, and higher levels of unmanageable debt, than their wealthy counterparts. I also use the term 'marginalized' because this is widely employed within other studies of urban poverty (see, for example, Bourgois 1995) and speaks of the structural processes at work in its production and reproduction.

'Wealthy' Participants

The fieldwork for this study included research with wealthier families in Bangkok, and while the focus of this book is on the young people living in urban poverty, I do refer to wealthier youth and their parents throughout. Initially I used the term 'middle class' to refer to these participants, but it became apparent that the differences in material wealth between the two groups was vast, and that I had probably bypassed a middle stratum. I use the term 'wealthy' in order to convey the affluence of non-slum participants.

Agency, Culture and Structures

The focus in this book is mainly empirical, its emphasis being on the experiences of young slum dwellers in their attempts to create a better life, but I use the concepts of agency, culture and structure in order to analyse those experiences, and so it is worth outlining my understanding of them here. The literatures on agency, culture and structures are vast; they represent some of the core concepts in the social sciences, with which sociologists and anthropologists have grappled since the emergence of their respective disciplines.

I take 'agency' to refer to the capacity of individuals to make choices and act in the world, and importantly I recognize that this does not always entail positive or emancipatory outcomes. I take 'structures' to refer to the social systems – norms, values and institutions that persist over time – that determine and are determined by the exercise of agency. One of my key interests in this study is in the outcomes of agency as exercised by those in positions of material disadvantage, and in particular as exercised through cultural practice.

I take a broad approach to conceptualizing culture, understanding the term to refer to the way of life, practices and beliefs of a particular group of people in a particular place at a particular time. I use the phrase 'cultural practice' to refer to the everyday practices that people engage in, which are both manifestations of and constitutive of the beliefs and way of life of the broader culture. I refer to 'youth cultural practice' to denote the particular activities and related objects and meanings that young people engage with on an everyday basis.

The following sections turn to the prominent features of the Thai context in which the notion of a better life has gained such a foothold in the popular imagination.

Theravada Buddhism

The vast majority of people in Thailand practise Theravada Buddhism.[2] While a minority follow other religions, notably Islam and Christianity as well as Hinduism, Sikhism, Judaism and some Chinese indigenous religions, over 95% of the Thai population are Theravada Buddhists. In a certain sense, the notion of a better life is central to Theravada Buddhism, albeit with a very particular conceptualization of what it means.

According to Theravada Buddhist thought, the starting point of the *dhamma* – the Buddha's teachings, or 'that which is true' – is the recognition of four Noble Truths:

1. The first Noble Truth is that life is unsatisfactory and painful. This is known as *dukkha* and is commonly – and some argue misleadingly – translated as 'suffering' (L.K. Mills 1999). For Theravada Buddhists, the entirety of life, including past, present and future lives, is *dukkha*: to be born is a traumatic experience; to inhabit a physical body that constantly craves is miserable; to grow old, get sick and die are experiences that involve pain, sorrow and loss. Life is *dukkha*.

2. The second Noble Truth is that *dukkha* has its origins in desire, or the attachment to things and states that are actually impermanent, and this attachment keeps us locked in an endless cycle of rebirth.

3. The third Noble Truth is that it is possible to extinguish the desire that causes *dukkha* – to reach *Nibbana*, or true happiness/enlightenment/liberation from perpetual rebirth.

4. The fourth Noble Truth is that the way to extinguish the desire that causes *dukkha* and reach *Nibbana* is to follow the Eightfold Path, also known as the Middle Way. This entails 'right view, right resolve, right speech, right action, right livelihood, right effort, right mindfulness and right concentration'.

Central to the four Noble Truths, and to the eightfold path towards the cessation of *dukkha*, is the concept of *kamma*. *Kamma* is intentional action and the thoughts and words that accompany it, which produces results. 'Wholesome' actions produce 'wholesome' results and 'unwholesome' actions produce 'unwholesome' results. *Kamma* and its results span past, present and future lives – that is, past actions can manifest in one's past, present and future lives, and actions in the present can manifest in present and future lives.

Linked with the concept of *kamma* is the notion of *merit* (*boon* in Thai), or *merit-making* (*tam boon*). By engaging in wholesome *kamma* or actions, one accumulates *merit*, which in turn cleanses and purifies the mind and opens opportunities, such as getting a good education, obtaining wealth and being open to the *dhamma* (L.K. Mills 1999).

As a young person born in Thailand and following the Theravada Buddhist tradition, one grows up with the notion of a better life as both a spiritual and material concept. A better life is freedom from *dukkha* (the inherent suffering of life) and the gradual path towards that freedom, which may take many lifetimes, and it is the fruits of one's wholesome actions that might manifest as financial wealth, educational status and the elevated social status these bring. One also grows up with the understanding that one's *kamma* – one's intentional actions, thoughts and words – is what brings about certain results and a certain stock of *merit*, both in this life and in subsequent lives. In this sense, the means of achieving a better life – either in a worldly sense in terms of achieving education and wealth, or in a spiritual sense in terms of liberation from *dukkha* – is the actions one takes, the thoughts one thinks and the words one utters. L.K. Mills (1999: 33) puts it thus:

> It is true that we must experience the fruits of past kamma which certainly limits and influences our choice in the present. But it is in the present when we make our decisions, wholesome or otherwise and when if we take matters in hand instead of allowing them to overpower us, we can for instance decide to train ourselves this or that way. The religious life in Buddhism is not one for sitting down and resignedly letting whatever must be, happen. There is no room here for concepts of fate, doom or destiny. The Buddha urged his followers many times to make an effort, to strive diligently and this can be done only in the present moment.

While Theravada Buddhism does not explicitly employ the concept of agency, it is clear that the concepts of *kamma* and *merit-making* in the pursuit of freedom from *dukkha* and accruing *merit*, respectively, imply something akin to agency. There are distinctions; *kamma* refers to actions, thoughts and words that are intentional and it is only these intentional actions that produce results, whereas the relationship between agency and intentionality within social theory is both less prescriptive, with agency potentially encompassing unintentional as well as intentional actions and choices, and less explicit about the 'results' of exercising agency, even if there are implicit assumptions about its positive potential in the current political climate.

But despite these differences, the fundamental conceptualization of people as beings with the capacity to think and act in the world in such a way that produces outcomes that one has control over is common to both understandings of agency on the one hand and *kamma* and *merit-making* on the other. Thus, the notion of striving for a better life and the central role of the individual in achieving it has, in a certain sense, been a part of Thai culture and belief for many hundreds of years.

The Birth of the Tiger

In addition to its long history within Theravada Buddhist thought, the notion of a better life has enjoyed particular prominence – and a particular conceptualization – in the Thai context in more recent history.

From the middle of the nineteenth century, under the rule of the Chakri kings, there was an explicit orientation towards 'modernization' in Thailand (Peleggi 2002). But it was over the second half of the twentieth century, as Thailand underwent deep macroeconomic restructuring and experienced phenomenal rates of economic growth, that the notion of a better life took on new meanings and moved firmly to the centre of public and private discourse. By the beginning of the twenty-first century, not only had 'development' become a key fixture on the political, economic and social landscape, but the notion of a better life had rippled out from the centre of power, through the burgeoning luxury housing estates, into the rice fields of the impoverished north-east and deep into the slums of Bangkok.

For centuries, Thailand's economy has been primarily agricultural, based on wet rice farming in rural areas, but from the mid twentieth century, agriculture as a percentage of GDP and exports began to shrink, and the manufacturing industries expanded significantly, as did the marketing and advertising industries that promoted their products to internal and external markets (Slagter and Kerbo 2000). This shift away from an economy based on agricultural production mainly for the domestic market to one based on industrial manufacturing for export was part of a broader programme of economic development that entailed increasing financial openness and foreign investment, trade liberalization and export orientation (ibid.).

These changes in the second half of the twentieth century saw Thailand leapfrog its way from the bottom of the World Bank's global development rankings to a much-coveted place alongside other Asian 'success' stories. Prior to the 1960s, the country had been one of the poorest in the world, but by the 1990s it had been reclassified as a middle-income economy and in the space of one generation had completely reinvented itself and joined the ranks of the Asian tigers (Parnwell and Arghiros 1996).

Boom

During the boom years, business magnates became 'fabulously wealthy' (Hewison 1999: 22), capitalizing on investment opportunities and bolstering the ranks of Thailand's elite. The middle classes also prospered, populating a growing number of luxury townhouses and suburban housing estates, living lifestyles characterized by Western-style consumption that were increasingly promoted throughout the country via the evermore ubiquitous medium of television (Baker and Phongpaichit 2005). But the benefits of Thailand's phenomenal economic growth did not accrue equally to all. Many were 'left behind, and even marginalized, in the scramble for self improvement' (Parnwell and Arghiros 1996: 1). Slum families continued to struggle for subsistence, let alone prosperity, doing so in a context where material wealth was widely revered and – importantly – represented as achievable through individual effort (Baker and Phongpaichit 2005).

Bust

Following Thailand's economic boom (and a minor downturn in the mid 1980s) was a crisis of severe proportions. In the mid 1990s, increasing economic instability resulting from unsupervised financial liberalization led to over-investment, which in turn prompted increasing speculation on the Thai baht and huge foreign reserve spending on the part of the Bank of Thailand (Kittiprapas 2001). In 1997, the Thai government, with external debts of more than $70 billion, unpegged the baht from the currencies to which it had been tied and its value plummeted. This triggered a national, then regional crisis. The Thai economy all but ground to a halt; major infrastructure projects ceased mid build, factories closed their doors and investments fell dramatically (ibid.). Bankruptcy rates doubled, unemployment reached the highest levels on record and education dropout rates soared (Hewison 2000). During the crisis, it was the poor who felt the impact most keenly. The cost of living rose while their incomes fell, debts increased, savings were in short supply (if there at all), and social security nets were grossly inadequate, making the business of everyday survival an extremely difficult one (ibid.). For many slum children, this meant having to steal food when they needed to eat and having to work before and after school to earn money to support parents who had lost jobs, alongside the continuing belief that they were responsible for finding their own way out of the financial difficulties they faced.

Bailout

Following the 1997 crisis, Thailand's economy was like a heavily listing ship – badly in need of ballast if it was to continue on course with its development trajectory. The Thai government accepted a bailout package from the International Monetary Fund (IMF) in the form of a Structural Adjustment Programme (SAP) – a set of macroeconomic policy reforms adhered to as a condition of an IMF loan, and seen by many as a tool of ideological and economic control, vehemently discredited for inflicting pain and suffering on millions throughout the developing world (Abouharb and Cingranelli 2007). Thailand accepted this SAP even though adhering to the type of neoliberal policies that comprised it had been at the root of the country's economic downfall in the first place (LaRocco 2011).

Under the IMF conditions imposed on Thailand, the privatization, deregulation and trade liberalization that had previously been etched more cautiously into the country's macroeconomic policy documents became enshrined in its plans for recovery. Public spending cuts were initiated, interest rates rose and plans to improve the health and education systems were abandoned. The neoliberal agenda, with all that this entailed in terms of assumptions of personal responsibility for one's lot (Trnka and Trundle 2014), looked set to be the order of the day.

Throughout boom, bust and bailout, families living in urban poverty in Bangkok – along with their counterparts in other cities and the rural poor – struggled to gain a foothold from which to benefit from their country's economic success, weather the storm of its crisis and survive the period of structural adjustment. But the notion that things could get better was never far away, and the idea that this could – and should – happen through individual determination remained ever-present.

'Thaksinomics' and Its Fall from Grace

In 2001, Thaksin Shinawatra became the Prime Minister of Thailand. Under the Thaksin government, the post-crisis neoliberal reforms were undermined (LaRocco 2011), as he proceeded to implement a range of macroeconomic policies – dubbed 'Thaksinomics' – aimed at redistributing wealth in the country. Through the 'million baht village fund', microfinance was made available in 77,000 villages; under the '30 baht healthcare scheme', every citizen who registered was afforded access to universal health coverage; and under the 'One Tambon One Product' (OTOP) programme, rural enterprise was stimulated and supported in every region. Thaksin oversaw the subsidizing of fuel, the lowering of electricity tariffs, the direct government financing of infrastructure projects such as railway improvements and airport expansion programmes, debt forgiveness for farmers and low-interest loans for small businesses (LaRocco 2011). Despite the widespread and derogatory references to these policies as 'populist', and despite some studies showing that the outcomes of these schemes were variable (see, for example, Kaboski and Townsend 2012), during Thaksin's administration Thailand repaid its debt to the IMF two years ahead of schedule, saw an increase in the rate of economic growth, and momentarily gave a new lease of life to the idea of effective government support for the most vulnerable (LaRocco 2011).

However, during Thaksin's tenure – which covered the period of research for this book – the poor still struggled, albeit with a little more government support than they had previously enjoyed. Although the notion of supporting the populace in their efforts to improve their lot arguably gained increased purchase, the idea of achieving success through individual effort persisted; the narrative of personal responsibility resounded loud and clear throughout the slum communities in which I conducted this study.

And then came the military coup of 2006, which took place towards the end of my fieldwork. This threw Thaksin from power, the potential for government intervention to reduce socioeconomic inequality into question, and the question of personal responsibility for improving one's lot firmly into the maelstrom of political struggle. The newly formed 'red shirt' movement, which comprised the rural and urban poor, demanded a more democratic and transparent political system, government support for the poor and a less fervent adoption of free market policies, while the government continued with a policy agenda that favoured individual responsibility for achieving a better life.

The Birth of the Bangkok Slum

Bangkok lies at the heart of Thailand's development story. Despite the continuing importance of the rural sector to the Thai economy, despite the sheer volume of land taken up by rice farming and other agricultural activities, and despite moves to stimulate regional development, the city remains the nerve centre of economic development in the country and the multitude of changes that have accompanied this (Ruland and Ladavalya 1996). What began hundreds of years ago as a small water hamlet had, within a few centuries, become a busy trading port and hub of political, economic and royal power, and by the late twentieth century, Bangkok was a sprawling mega city that had earned itself the title of 'the most primate city on earth' (Baker and Phongpaichit 2005: 199).

The story of Thailand's development since the middle of the twentieth century has also been marked by the often under-recognized growth of socioeconomic inequality (Phongpaichit and Baker 1998) and related disparities in housing. For those who already had a strong foothold and were thus able to stay at, or reach, the top, luxury housing estates provided both shelter and a means of displaying one's position of material advantage. For those at the bottom of the socioeconomic ladder, slums provided one of the most important housing delivery systems and continue to do so to this day (Viratkapan and Perera 2006). Indeed, the story of socioeconomic inequality can be seen in the microcosm of the battles for inner-city land in Bangkok, between the wealthier classes on the one hand, and the urban poor on the other.

This study took place in one of thousands of slum communities in the city which, along with the growing number of slums located in the suburbs and in Bangkok's neighbouring provinces, house over a million people.

The 1950s

The first officially recognized slums in Thailand emerged in Bangkok in the 1950s.[3] In 1954, the Thai government announced the Land Ownership Act, which required people to register the land they were living on and declare ownership of it. Many were unaware of this process and what it required of them, or did not understand its implications, and did not take part in registration procedures. Land that was not registered immediately became the property of the government, inhabitants became illegal trespassers and were evicted, and the land was sold at very low prices to private investors who built factories on it. Those who worked, or came looking for work, in the factories erected makeshift accommodation nearby, and gradually, as existing factories expanded and new ones sprang up, these informal clusters of improvised housing grew and were labelled 'slums'. Informal settlements around Bangkok port expanded particularly rapidly, as sea-based trading activity increased. Many families migrated from the Isan region in the north-east of Thailand, which has long held the stigma of the most impoverished part of the country.

In the late 1950s, under US planning guidance, the city of Bangkok was restructured, and this entailed turning canals into roads and selling even more land to private investors. These processes meant that some slum communities were demolished and their residents evicted, since they were located either next to canals (sources of water for inhabitants) or on other prime estate. Evicted families settled on vacant land and moved to alternative slum communities, which continued to grow.

The 1960s

In the 1960s, luxury estates sprang up throughout the city to house those who were benefitting most from the country's rapid economic growth, and the creation of these enclaves entailed even more slum demolition and evictions. Also, with the erection of these estates, the price of nearby land, housing and rent rocketed, and pushed those without sufficient money onto still vacant land in other parts of the city. By 1968, around fifty slums had been identified in Bangkok. During this decade, the city authorities created the Slum Improvement Office, which saw slums as eyesores and obstacles to modernization, and responded to them by demolishing the dwellings, evicting the residents and selling the land to private investors. Once again, many families resettled in other remaining slums, while others began new settlements on unoccupied land.

The 1970s

In the 1970s, there was a proliferation of housing estates for the middle classes in Bangkok, which again meant that the slum dwellers living on this newly desirable land were evicted to make way for slum clearances, and were priced out of local housing and rental markets. During this decade, the Thai government set up several slum committees to find a more agreeable solution to Bangkok's 'slum problem' than clearances and evictions. This entailed initiation of a resettlement scheme, which saw slum dwellers relocated to housing projects on the outskirts of the city, where work opportunities were few and social networks patchy at best. In 1973, the Thai government, with World Bank funding, set up the National Housing Authority (NHA) to build new low-cost housing for the poor. However, over time the NHA's much-needed subsidies from central government were reduced until financial support stopped altogether, meaning that severe limits were placed on the capacity of the NHA to deliver on its mandate. In 1977, the Thai government developed a new policy towards slum communities. Known as the National Slum Upgrading Programme, this was intended as an alternative to previous demolition/eviction and relocation approaches, focusing instead on improving slums, for example by providing physical infrastructure such as concrete pathways, drainage systems and water supplies.

The 1980s

In the 1980s, as Thailand reached the height of its economic boom, property development in the inner city and even further increases in land prices meant more slum clearances and evictions, despite the stated intentions of the national upgrading programme. During this period, housing conditions for the urban poor in Bangkok deteriorated. The 1980s also saw further restructuring of the city, this time under German planning guidance, which focused on the creation of raised expressways to ease severe traffic congestion problems. This meant yet more evictions for slum dwellers, as the land that some were living on was cleared to make way for these transport links. Remaining slums expanded to accommodate evictees, and yet more new settlements sprang up to house others. By 1985, almost one thousand slum settlements had been identified in Bangkok.

Also during the 1980s, civil society activism grew throughout Thailand, including in the area of urban poverty and housing, and there was increasing resistance on the part of NGOs, slum residents and left-wing scholars to the investors and developers wanting to make more profitable use of Bangkok's increasingly valuable land. However, civil society activities were fragmented and struggled to cope with the scope of slum dwellers' needs for assistance.

The 1990s

Throughout the 1990s, the Bangkok Metropolitan Authority (BMA) worked with the NHA to deliver low-cost housing in the city, and both operated with a mandate to assist the housing needs of low-income communities. In 1992, the Thai government also set up the Urban Community Development Office with the stated intention of finding a sustainable solution to urban poverty and the 'slum problem'. In 2003, the Thai government, through the NHA and other partner organizations (specifically the Community Organizations Development Institute, or CODI) launched a nationwide, two-pronged approach designed to respond to the housing needs of the urban poor. The first of these was the *Baan Ua Arhtorn* programme, which sought to design and build low-cost flats at subsidized rates, and the other was the *Baan Mankrong* programme, which focused on upgrading existing slum settlements. Despite these seemingly positive policies, at the time of fieldwork there were over two hundred slum settlements throughout Thailand earmarked for relocation (Viratkapan and Perera 2006), and two slum communities in which I conducted this study were in the process of being demolished. Furthermore, the physical infrastructure in many communities remained woefully inadequate. For most families, housing insecurity was a persistent feature of life, as were the shortcomings of the physical environment – water and electricity supplies were often intermittent where present, and sewage and rubbish collection systems were not always reliable.

In sum, since the middle of the twentieth century, official responses to slum communities have shifted from eviction to relocation and finally to new, low-cost housing provision and upgrading, although the success of these remains questionable. Thus, the participants in this research have been afforded a place in the city but theirs is a highly ambiguous one, marked by poverty, tenure insecurity, substandard housing and inadequate infrastructure, as well as by widespread experiences of prejudice and stigma.

Khlong Toey Slum

The research for this study took place in Khlong Toey slum, which has provided low-cost housing for millions of people on low incomes since the early twentieth century. It is the largest and most notorious slum in Bangkok. There are around twenty-two distinct communities, although this figure is not fixed as the threat of demolition is ever-present.

Settlement in what is now the central cluster of Khlong Toey slum communities began in the late 1930s, when around two hundred families were hired to build Bangkok port and its warehouses. Construction was suspended during the war years but regained momentum afterwards, and from the late 1950s expanded rapidly as the Thai government pursued its industrial development strategy with vigour. As industrial activity around the port increased, the need for manual labourers grew. Combinations of urban poverty and low education provided a local workforce, and drought and crop failure pushed rural agricultural workers away from their paddy fields in the north-east towards Bangkok port to earn a living (Duang Prateep Foundation 2003).

Port workers built houses on a small area of vacant swamp land close to the dockyards, and over time this grew into the largest concentration of poor people in the country. Throughout the 1960s and 1970s, the number of inhabitants continued to multiply as the port provided work, as industry boomed and factories sought labour, as the nearby Sukhumvit area and its businesses, shops and entertainment facilities grew and provided unskilled jobs, and as housing remained cheap, albeit insecure (Duang Prateep Foundation 2003).

The early 1970s saw an escalation of evictions and relocation schemes for inhabitants of Khlong Toey slum communities, mirroring the nationwide official response to the 'problem' of slums during that decade, and this pushed many families off the increasingly valuable land, out of the inner city and in many cases into suburban housing projects, away from social networks and viable sources of income. Many returned. Concomitantly, this period was marked by a growth in the political organization of Khlong Toey slum inhabitants and by protests against forced removal, spearheaded by a woman who grew up in the slum and is founder director of one of the major NGOs working there.

From the mid 1970s onwards, the NGO presence in Khlong Toey slum continued to grow, and this, combined with the government upgrading policy in 1977, meant that service provision and physical infrastructure in some areas improved: wooden walkways were replaced by concrete paths, running water and electricity were piped into houses, a rubbish collection service was created, and the informal slum school established in the late 1960s was officially recognized by the Bangkok Metropolitan Authority and became a state school providing education for many slum children. Still, rural migrants and the urban poor were drawn to Khlong Toey from the countryside and neighbouring areas, natural population growth added to the population density, and it swelled beyond capacity. Existing settlements spread and new communities developed within the district as the gradually improving infrastructure struggled to keep up with the demands of those who were living in them.

Throughout the 1980s and 1990s, new social problems emerged and intensified, and contributed to earning Khlong Toey slum its reputation as one of the most dangerous places in the city. Drug use, gang warfare, gambling and violence became integral features in the tapestry of slum life and popular representations of it. HIV-AIDS became a major issue with which NGOs were forced to contend. The institutionalization of children and young people into orphanages in the slum increased as individuals and families struggled to cope with the strains of urban poverty and the disappearance of available childcare, especially in the form of kin networks, and as NGOs provided growing numbers of spaces for them. Meanwhile, old social problems persisted. Lack of money, illegal tenure, forced eviction and house fires continued to form the backdrop of insecurity against which slum dwellers lived their lives, and these issues persisted throughout fieldwork.

The Khlong Toey slum communities are located between Sukhumvit Road to the north, which contains some of Bangkok's main business, shopping and entertainment spots, and the Chao Phraya river to the south, which houses Bangkok's first port. Several of the communities border each other and have formed a central cluster, and where one community begins and another ends is not always obvious even to longstanding residents, although allegiances to particular neighbourhoods and related identities were strongly felt. Other slum communities are more isolated from each other and from this central hub. Cutting through the middle of Khlong Toey district is a railway line, two elevated expressways and the main trunk road leading away from the port. Traffic and pollution problems are severe.

According to the Khlong Toey District Office, in 2005 there were around 17,322 houses spread throughout the slum communities, although it is unclear how 'house' has been defined. Estimates of the total slum population ranged from around 84,000 (Khlong Toey District Office 2005) to 135,000 (Duang Prateep Foundation 2003). Three of the slum communities – those in the central hub where NGO presence and activity was strongest – were on land owned by the Port Authority of Thailand, which was leased to the NHA and rented, via landlords, by residents. This lease agreement ran out in 2005, and inhabitants' tenure status on the land was uncertain and under negotiation at the time of fieldwork. One slum community was situated on land owned by a private company and inhabitants rented their dwellings legally, although even here housing security was not a given, as the increasing value of inner-city land made its sale for urban development a very attractive prospect. One slum community was on land owned by a private company and residents' tenure was illegal. Residents in all remaining slum communities were officially classified as illegal squatters on land owned by the Port Authority of Thailand (Khlong Toey District Office 2005). This study took place in six of Khlong Toey's slum communities, each at varying degrees of proximity to/isolation from the central hub, and spanning the range of tenure statuses.

Notes

1. In this context, meaning at least fifteen households per *rai* (a *rai* is a unit of land that is just over two hectares).
2. This brief overview of the relevant aspects of Theravada Buddhism draws on data collected with participants during fieldwork and on the work of L.K. Mills (1999).
3. The historical information here draws on three sources: Boonyabancha's (2002) article on community development and slum upgrading in Thailand; Viratkapan and Perera's (2006) article on slum relocation projects in Bangkok; and a chapter entitled 'The Beginning of Slums in Bangkok' in a Thai language book entitled *Bangkok Housing*, which I got translated into English. This book was in one of the NGO libraries at the time of fieldwork, but I was unable to confirm its full reference details as my translator was subsequently unable to locate it. It is referenced in this book under the author 'Anon-DPF'.

2

What Do We Know about Growing Up in the Slums of Bangkok?

There is very little written about children or young people living in urban poverty in Thailand, at least within academic circles in the English language, as an explicit focus of attention. There have been academic studies conducted in Thai slum communities, the most notable being Thorbeck's 1987 study *Voices from the City: Women of Bangkok*, which took place in the slum where I conducted fieldwork. However, none have focused specifically on young people and the issues of importance to them. There has also been other non-academic work describing the lives and struggles of Bangkok slum dwellers, the most notable being the 2005 work by Father Joseph Maier who has run NGOs in Thailand's slum communities for a number of decades. However – as is to be expected – while this work paints vivid portraits of everyday slum life, including of the lives of young people in the slum in which this study took place, it tends to stop short of analytical interpretation or engagement with theory.

Despite the relative lack of scholarly attention given to young slum dwellers in Bangkok, there is a body of literature concerned with 'youth in Thailand', either as a whole, or with a focus on particular groups therein. While this does not tend to consider young people's socio-economic positioning in any depth, it is useful to explore it to ascertain what implicit assumptions it holds about people like Som, Boo and their peers. Within the development industry, there is also a growing body of work concerned with 'youth and development', and again it is instructive to consider this in order to understand the way in which it conceptualizes young people in developing countries, and by implication the young people in this study. In addition, there has been a surge of attention given to 'global youth studies' in recent years within the social sciences, and it is useful to reflect on this body of work in order to discern the ways in which young people's everyday cultural practices, agency and interactions with structures are framed.

This chapter outlines these overlapping bodies of literature in turn,[1] highlighting the areas therein where I believe the findings from my study can add something of value, and highlighting the individual studies and bodies of literature that have been fundamental in shaping the way I have interpreted my data and the development of my conceptual framework.

Youth in Thailand

In the 1980s, a cross-disciplinary body of academic literature emerged, dealing specifically with youth in Thailand, and this has been gradually expanding over the past few decades. This began with Anderson and Anderson's ethnography (1986) of Thai Muslim adolescents and was followed by a handful of studies in the 1990s. By the end of the first decade of the millennium, around thirty articles, books and book chapters were dedicated to the study of Thai youth, and this continues to grow.

This small but expanding body of knowledge, and its echoes within the English language Thai media and government circles, is largely characterized by three trends. First, it is marked by a focus on the interrelated notions of risk and destruction. Connected to this, there is a tendency to focus on the topic of sexuality and to a lesser but notable extent drugs, and on various risk-related issues pertaining to these. Second, studies of Thai youth are characterized by the use of research that seeks to explore well-defined, predetermined areas of investigation and by a tendency to employ quantitative methodologies. Third, Thai youth studies tend to take insufficient account of people's socio-economic positioning. The result of these three tendencies is the production of a partial understanding of the lives of young people, and very little coverage of the everyday, lived experiences of people such as Boo and Som occupying positions of socio-economic disadvantage.

Risk, Destruction, Sex and Drugs

Studies of Thai youth focus overwhelmingly on the interrelated notions of risk and destruction. There is a broad trend in the conceptualization and representation of Thai youth as both *at risk* – from each other, from inadequate parenting and from 'Westernization' – and *a risk*, to themselves, to other people and to the broader moral, cultural and socio-economic orders. This focus on risk in turn gives rise to an association of Thai youth with destruction – actual or potential. Through the widespread focus on sexual risk behaviours, young people appear as a destructive force that not only threatens their own health and that of others, but ultimately destroys life itself. Through the emphasis on their vulnerability, for example to 'external' (Western) influences, particularly in the realm of sexual practice, young people become not only the perpetrators of destruction but themselves its key victims, their health and their moral integrity thrown into question, and their lives devastated. Some of the articles in this literature pay particular attention to risk among young women (e.g. Allen et al. 2003), while others focus on young men (e.g. Nelson et al. 2002). Some deal with the prevalence of certain risk behaviours or vulnerabilities (e.g. Sattah et al. 2002), while others focus on the contributing factors and destructive consequences of these (e.g. Cash et al. 1999). Whatever the particular focus, the notions of risk and destruction are prominent in discussions of young people in Thailand.

There are a few exceptions to this emphasis. In their paper presented to the International Population Conference in 2005, Malhotra et al. explicitly recognize that 'the same forces that are fuelling risk behaviours are also creating aspirations and ambitions for success and achievement among adolescents' (Malhotra et al. 2005: 2). In her 2004(a) study of the 'computerized generation', Thianthai attempts to gain an understanding of the everyday experience of computers among teenagers in Bangkok, and approaches this without reference to risk or destruction. And in their 1986 study of young Thai Muslims, Anderson and Anderson report on research into adolescents' conceptions of the self, sexuality and autonomy, and again the notions of risk and destruction are absent here.

However, these approaches are a far cry from the majority of studies dealing with sexuality among Thai youth, which focus overwhelmingly on the risks associated with sexual attitudes and practices and the resulting damage caused to selves and society. Here, several sub-topics emerge as key sites of investigation: risks associated with sexual behaviour and HIV-AIDS/STDs (e.g. Morrison 2004), risks connected with teenage pregnancy (e.g. Manopaiboon et al. 2003), early sexual intercourse and the associated risk of cervical cancer (e.g. Kanato and Saranrittichai 2006), condom use and the risks associated with its non-use (e.g. Thato et al. 2003), increases in and risks related to premarital sex between partners (e.g. Podhisita et al. 2004), sex education needs in light of risks faced and posed by young people's sexual practices (e.g. Vuttanont et al. 2006), sexual health service needs in light of risks connected to young people's sexual behaviour (e.g. Ford and Kittisuksathit 1996) and what is referred to as the 'gender double standard' in sexual relations and the particular risks faced by young Thai women due to this (e.g. Tangmunkongvorakul et al. 2005). In discussions of these sub-topics, references to the destructive consequences of the sexual risks that young people pose and face abound, with frequent mention of long-term physical and mental health problems, infections, physical trauma, death, morbidity, mortality, suicide and depression, to name a few. These in turn contribute to an overall sense that Thai youth are bent on both self-destruction and destroying the health and lives of others.

In addition to a focus on sexuality, some studies are concerned with drug use, and in particular with the risk factors leading to it (e.g. Sattah et al. 2002) and the increased risk it poses for contracting HIV-AIDS (e.g. see Nelson et al. 2002).

That a concerted literature on Thai youth has begun to emerge in the last few decades, and that this should emphasize risk and destruction with particular reference to sex and drugs, is, in a certain sense, unsurprising. Complex combinations of socio-economic, cultural, migratory and epidemiological processes brought about potentially harmful as well as positive changes in Thai society over the last quarter of the twentieth century, and young people are disproportionately affected by these, or at least experience them in specific ways (Thianthai 2004b; German et al. 2006; Ford and Kittisuksathit 1996). In addition, adolescence is commonly the life stage when people become sexually active. Also, the history of Western sociological enquiry is one of seeking to study and alleviate the problems associated with modernity, and more specifically with industrial capitalism (Carrier 1996), and this has arguably left its legacy on those writing about other societies that have experienced more recent modernization, such as Thailand. Tied to this, the history of youth research in the West, in particular in the United States, is one rooted in a model of deviance, a paradigm that appears to hold sway over many of the commentaries discussed here. Therefore, focusing on sexuality and risk in discussions of Thai youth is in certain ways to be expected. However, while it may be unsurprising that these studies are preoccupied with risk and destruction, they leave much unknown and unsaid about other aspects of the everyday lived experience of growing up in Thai society.

The majority of studies on Thai youth report on research that is relatively 'closed', that investigates predefined topics selected by researchers, even if the research was designed to elicit young people's experiences of and perspectives on particular issues. This could be a result of a certain cleaning up in the writing process, whereby authors claim to have been guided by particular research questions at the outset rather than acknowledging the iterative and sometimes retrospective nature of formulating research questions. However, in the majority of cases, this closed approach appears to dominate, certainly if reported methodologies are taken at face value.

Related to this, the majority of the studies concerned with Thai youth are quantitative in design and provide little by way of in-depth understandings of young people's own perspectives and experiences, or analyses of how these perspectives are located within wider moral, cultural and socio-economic frameworks and produced through wider sets of discourses. In a sense, the dominance of quantitative methodologies and resulting etic understandings, and certainly the predefining of research questions, is understandable and arguably important in light of the pressing health and social issues affecting Thai youth and the desire to produce targeted, representative knowledge aimed at making relevant policy recommendations, and given the related funding constraints on social research activity. However, it means that the questions asked of young people in the production of knowledge about them, and therefore the topics deemed worthy of attention in relation to their lives, are largely driven by external agendas, leaving young people's inner life-worlds to fall out of the picture altogether.

In addition, the majority of studies into Thai youth either make no mention of socio-economic positioning or point to it briefly or indirectly, for example through reference to agricultural background, work status or attendance at vocational school, all of which signify lower socio-economic status. Even where it is acknowledged, ensuing discussions are not sufficiently attuned to issues arising from the experience of occupying positions of socio-economic subordination. Only a minority refer explicitly to socio-economic status as a significant issue structuring the lives of young people. Where differences between 'lower' and 'upper'-class youth are identified, there is a tendency towards viewing those of lower socio-economic positioning as more prone to risk-taking behaviours, or there is no attempt to explore the experiences of impoverished youth in any detail.

The overall result of these tendencies is the construction of a partial picture of the lives of Thai youth, and a missing picture of those struggling to get by. Discussions of agency are notably absent, and although the predominant focus on risk and destruction might imply its (problematic) existence, on the whole there is very little attention given to its exercise or outcomes, intended or otherwise.

Standing in marked contrast to the majority of studies on Thai youth is the work of Mary Beth Mills, whose ethnographic fieldwork focuses on young women from rural Thailand working in low-wage, low-status jobs in the industrial sector in Bangkok. Through an analysis of selected cultural practices, Mills offers a rich and critical analysis of participants' interactions with some of the broader cultural, moral and socio-economic structures in which their lives are embedded. In this, attention is directed specifically towards the agency of marginalized young women. In particular, readers are invited to consider how the active construction of certain ('modern'/'good') identities can 'stretch, if only temporarily, the limits of … subordination' (Mills 1997: 54). Mills' mobilization of concepts such as hegemony, ideology, domination, marginalization and exploitation demonstrates the sensitivity of her research to the particular and significant constraints experienced by participants in light of their socio-economic positioning, while her focus on the construction of the self, on aspiration and on the continual selection between potential self-images points to the recognition of agency, albeit as exercised in highly constrained circumstances. Mills' frequent acknowledgements of the ambivalence, tensions, contradictions and nuances that attend participants' cultural practices reveal the sensitivity of her research to the complexities that exist at the interface of agency, culture and structures. In this, Mills provides a welcome departure from the majority of studies on Thai youth.

A further illuminating study is Montgomery's (2001) ethnography of child prostitution in a Thai slum. While this work focuses on children as opposed to youth, it is worth noting as it is one of the few studies that stands theoretically in contrast to the dominant literature on young people in Thailand. Through detailed analysis of participant narratives concerning who they are, what they do, and their experiences within the family and community, Montgomery provides an insight into the exercise of agency in a context of severe exploitation. While she concentrates on participants as active agents, for example with regard to their constructions of themselves in moral terms, and thereby offers a corrective to the media and NGO reports that more commonly emphasize their 'utter passivity' (2001: 69), she locates their narratives and experiences firmly within a context of interlocking structural oppressions – gendered cultural norms surrounding filial obligation, a labour market that provides inadequate remuneration for the families of poor children, and ultimately socio-economic inequality upheld by a free market and a neglectful state. In this context, agency entails negative and reproductive consequences, as evidenced in parents' pimping of their children and children's pimping of each other in the effort to get by.

While Montgomery and Mills have both provided insightful ethnographies of marginalized young people in Thailand, their approaches – in particular with reference to the exploration of agency as exercised by those in positions of socio-economic deprivation – are in a minority within the broader body of knowledge concerning Thai youth.

Youth and Development

Alongside the increasing academic attention given to youth in Thailand, the past few decades have witnessed a growing concern on the part of the Thai government and development institutions with issues around youth and development, manifested in the creation of a governmental framework to address this, and in the publication of several reports concerning the situation of young people and youth policy in the country. This concern with youth and development in the Thai context can be understood in part with reference to the multiple and complex transformations that have taken place in the country over the past few decades, which have affected youth disproportionately, and with reference to the increasing attention given to youth within the wider international development community.

As well as being strongly marked by the same emphasis on risk and destruction identified within the academic literature, here framed in terms of the threat that young people may pose to economic development and stability, the attention to youth and development within the Thai governmental and international development spheres is characterized by a further two tendencies. First there is a tendency to focus on youth as a productive resource and development as the creation of productive labour, and a related assumption that aspirations are – and should be – restricted to the realm of productive activity. Second, the attention to youth and development is marked by a contention that development is 'up to you(th)' (World Bank 2007: vii), that young people should be responsible for bringing about their own development and that this can be achieved as long as they make the 'right' choices and act accordingly. In addition, this emerging discourse is characterized by the use of macro-level data, which may provide useful information on certain national and global trends but offer nothing in the way of critical insight into the perceptions, practices and lived experiences of young people themselves.

The Thai governmental framework for addressing youth and development issues has, over the years, included the National Youth Office, the Office of Youth Promotion, the Commission of the Promotion and Development of Youth, the National Council for Child and Youth Development, the National Youth Commission and the National Youth Bureau (United Nations Economic and Social Commission for Asia and the Pacific [UNESCAP] 2000). The ministries dealing with employment and health, and especially education, have also paid significant attention to youth in their policies and planning activities. The history of each of these ministries, departments and offices, and their relationships with one another, is complicated in light of the numerous military coups and changes of government that have taken place in Thailand over the past few decades and the resulting restructuring of government institutions and responsibilities therein. However, it is notable that throughout the tumultuous recent history of the Thai political infrastructure, a dedicated framework for addressing youth, and in particular youth and development, has remained.

Youth as Productive Resource and 'Development' as the Creation of Productive Labour

From within its evolving institutional framework, the Thai government has issued several national youth policies, a long-term (twenty-year) plan referred to as the 'Prospective Policies and Planning for the Development of Youth (1982–2001)', and several five-year child and youth development plans that grew out of Thailand's National Economic and Social Development Plans. From 1994 onwards, Thailand's youth policies identified 'youth as an important human resource in society, which required development so that they could contribute to national development' (UNESCAP 2000: 9). This emphasis on youth as productive resource is also manifested in the discourse of Thai government officials. In his address to the first World Conference of Ministries Responsible for Youth, Prasit Damrongchai, Permanent Secretary in the Office of the Prime Minister, stated:

> ... in order to develop full potential of Thai youth to be competent in the labour market, special measures on learning process are developed to enable the students to have adequate knowledge and basic skills for employment. (Damrongchai 1998)

The Thai government's attention to issues around youth and development, and the focus therein on developing young people's productive labour in the service of the economy, is mirrored within the Thai-oriented texts of some of the dominant international development institutions operating in the country, as well as within those concerned with the global youth community.

In 2000, UNESCAP produced a report on the 'youth situation' in Thailand, a publication that grew out of the UNESCAP-initiated project 'Capacity-Building in HRD [Human Resource Development]: Policy-Making for Youth in Asia and the Pacific'. The introductory message to this report reads: 'Youth are key agents of socio-economic development and technological innovation' (UNESCAP 2000: vii). The document is divided into six chapters (Youth and Development, Youth Education, Youth Health, Youth Employment, Youth Participation and Future Directions for Youth Development), and the focus on young people as productive resource runs throughout. In the discussion of youth education, we are told that:

> Thailand's relatively weak human resources base was a major contributing factor to the economic crisis which began in 1997 … Educational curricula … require strengthening to ensure their relevance to the rapidly changing needs of the economy. (Ibid.: 27)

In the concluding chapter it is argued that:

> Greater coordination is needed between the education and employment sectors to ensure that graduates meet the demand for labour in an increasingly competitive international environment. (Ibid.: 116)

The focus on young people as productive resource can also be found in the World Bank's 2008 Thailand Social Monitor (TSM08). The stated aim of the TSM08 is to 'inform the development of a comprehensive youth development strategy in Thailand' (Benveniste 2008: 4). It has at its core three chapters, each of which deals with a 'key transition' in youth: 'growing up healthy', 'learning for work and life', and 'moving from school to work'. Each of these chapters reports on national statistics and discusses young people's vulnerabilities regarding a particular transition, and makes policy recommendations designed to expand opportunities, enhance capabilities and provide second chances therein. The focus on young people as productive resource runs throughout these core chapters, as well as the introductory and concluding ones. At the outset, in arguing the case for the relevance and 'urgency' of dealing with youth issues, the report states:

> the abundant young labor on which Thailand has relied for economic growth will soon be in shortage. To maintain its future growth and competitiveness, Thailand will need to place renewed emphasis on strengthening the capabilities of its young people and boosting productive opportunities for them. (World Bank 2008: viii)

In its discussion of growing up healthy, the rationale for attending to young people's health is spelled out: 'Influencing health habits and lifestyle formation during youth is critical for avoiding the loss of productive human capital' (ibid.: ix). Similarly, in its discussion of 'learning for work and life', the report stresses the importance of 'improving the quality and relevance of education to prepare youth to meet the demands of the labor market' (ibid.: x). In its discussion of 'moving from school to work', the report states that 'some youth drop out of school and start work too early, which can affect future productivity and income' (ibid.: xi). The message here is clear: it is in their capacity as productive resources that young people are valued, or of interest.

It is in the World Bank's 2007 World Development Report, *Development and the Next Generation* (WDR07) that the notion of youth as productive resource emerges with particular intensity. Despite some claims that the document represents a 'pioneering' journey into new territory for the World Bank (e.g. Lundberg 2006, cited in Moore 2006: 10), the text remains steadfastly rooted in conventional Bank ideology, and in this on the focus on human beings as 'capital' serving the needs of national and global economies.

Aimed at governments and policy makers in developing countries, the WDR07 was heralded as a 'landmark' report that takes the Bank into previously unchartered waters, such as the espousal of an analytical framework that claims to attend, for the first time, to the 'demand side' of the economic equation. With its unprecedented attention to young people and its claims to determine the 'youth friendliness' of policy climates, the report may represent a welcome consideration of a hitherto neglected category. The recurrent use of statistics, graphs, tables, charts, scatter diagrams, text and quotations from young people, as well as the deployment of buzzwords such as 'participation', 'agency' and 'well-being', may also make for an initially convincing, if somewhat impenetrable, read.

However, beneath the claims of novelty and the report's somewhat slippery evidence base, and indeed at the very heart of its 'youth friendly' analytical framework, the notion of youth as productive resource looms large, a notion that sits squarely within traditional World Bank ideology. The report is replete with references to the task of building human capital in youth and to the importance of this in generating economic growth. It marks out five areas of youth transition: education, work, health, family formation and citizenship. In the chapters dedicated to each of these, as well as in the surrounding chapters and in the underpinning conceptual framework, the emphasis lies squarely on turning global youth into productive labour. In the overview, we are told that 'labor is the main asset of the poor' and as such needs to be made more productive (World Bank 2007: 2). In the introductory chapter, the report states: 'If made well, decisions about [the five] transitions will develop, safeguard, and properly deploy human capital' (ibid.: 5). In the chapter outlining the report's analytical framework, it states: 'Human capital, once developed, needs to be used productively' (ibid.: 50). In turn, the report is clear that 'the human capital formed in youth – whether in skill levels, or health, or civic and societal engagement – is also an important determinant of long-term growth' (ibid.: 29).

The Bank's attention to youth itself may very well have been new, and the sheer amount of textual and numerical information provided may at first glance function to bolster the report's credibility. However, the way in which youth are constructed throughout the document does not represent the departure into unchartered waters that the report's authors and others claim it to be; young people are clearly presented and valued in their capacity as 'capital' serving the interests of national and global economies.

In the UK, the publication of *Development and the Next Generation* created a ripple of discursive activity within the development industry and the political establishment, as well as within the academic community,[2] seen for example in the organization of two discussion events hosted and attended by development institutions and senior civil servants.[3] Here, the echo of youth as productive resource resounded clearly: 'we have a brief window of opportunity to harness the talents of this youthful generation and inspire rapid economic growth' (Mitchell 2006: 2).

Aside from the moral questions surrounding the valuing of young people in the developing world – or anybody anywhere for that matter – as human capital inputs useful for economic growth, focusing on young people as productive resources allows only for a very partial understanding of their experiences as economic agents, let alone of their experiences in other interrelated realms of activity. It is true that within the youth and development discourse there is mention of other aspects of young people's incorporation into market structures, for example in the references to young people's consumption habits in the TSM08 (p. 4) and in the WDR07 (p. 33). However, discussion of this is both extremely brief and strongly rooted in the risk/destruction paradigm. Notable exceptions to this are found in the United Nation's 2005 *World Youth Report* (United Nations Division for Social Policy and Development 2005) and its 2011 *State of the World's Children* report (UNICEF 2011), wherein issues such as consumption practices, global youth culture, identity building, adolescent rights and mental health are discussed, making for a more nuanced and holistic approach to the complexities of young people's lives in contemporary development contexts. However, despite the relative sensitivity of these UN documents to the complexities of contemporary youthhood, it is the World Bank and related documents that form the dominant discourse.

While it may be unsurprising that the majority of youth and development documents emphasize the productive sphere, and important to attend to this, viewing young people largely in terms of productive activity is neither the only nor the most illuminating way in which to understand their lives. In fact, it is in the exploration of their practices in other spheres that important and interesting dimensions of experience can be brought to light.

Related to the focus on youth as productive resource, the Thai-oriented and international discourse on youth and development is marked by a conceptualization of development as the creation of productive labour. It has been noted, in relation to Thailand's Eighth National Economic and Social Development Plan, out of which the country's national youth policy evolved, that 'the plan stipulates human resources development as the goal for national development (UNESCAP 2000: 3). This notion is strongly echoed in the TSM08. For example, the opening paragraph of the executive summary of this report states:

> Ensuring that young people become healthy, educated and productive workers, citizens and parents needs to be regarded at the center of the country's development strategy. (World Bank 2008: viii)

Note here the order in which young people are conceptualized, an order that runs throughout the document and is reflected too in the WDR07: first as workers and only then as citizens or (future) parents. The notion of development as the creation of productive labour is also emphasized in the WDR07, although here the ultimate goal is economic growth and poverty reduction (usually in that order):

> ... poor countries ... need policies and institutions that broaden the opportunities for young people to develop their human capital and use it productively in work. Indeed, the overall skills of the labor force, built

> largely in childhood and youth, strongly affect the climate for investment in firms. (World Bank 2007: 5)

One of the implications of viewing development as the creation of productive labour is that legitimized goals and aspirations on the part of young people become confined to the realm of productive activity in the service of the economy, while other goals and ambitions are positioned outside the realm of development or dismissed altogether as a threat to it. Identity building is aligned with irrationality, risky behaviour and violence (World Bank 2007: 59), and commodity consumption is aligned with negative behaviours, frustration, disillusionment and illegal conduct (World Bank 2008: 4–5). For the participants in this study, the interrelated processes of commodity consumption and identity building are actually integral aspects of a better life, and it is in the analysis of young people's practices towards these goals that important dimensions of experience are revealed.

'It's Up to You(th)': Young People Developing Themselves

The notion that 'it's up to you(th)' to develop themselves forms a core component of the WDR07's analytical framework, and can be found within a discrete highlighted section at the end of the document as well as in the repeated references to 'choice' and 'decision-making' found throughout. It is a prominent notion despite the acknowledgement of the role of government policy and programming in bringing about development goals.

The second policy lens in the WDR07 focuses on enhancing young people's capabilities and is applied in each of the five transition areas. Young people, we are told, must become capable of making better education choices, finding work, practising healthy behaviour, preparing for parenthood and exercising citizenship for development to ensue. Through the mobilization of this policy lens, emphasis is placed firmly on young people determining development outcomes through the decisions they make and the actions they take. There are two fundamental assumptions at work here: first, that 'development' can be achieved through personal endeavour; and second, that as long as young people *choose* to learn, work, practise healthy behaviour, prepare for parenting and exercise citizenship and *act* in accordance with their decisions, then positive outcomes will follow.

The notion that 'it's up to you(th)' and the assumptions this entails are not limited to this second policy lens; indeed, as the Bank's president notes in the foreword to the report, the entire conceptual framework is built upon an understanding of youth as agents of their own development: 'The Report identifies three policy directions for helping youth develop themselves' (World Bank 2007: xi). In this sense, broadening opportunities and offering second chances – the other two policy lenses – are needed to assist youth in taking the process of development into their own hands.

The idea that young people should assume responsibility for their own development is particularly pronounced in the closing section of the document – the last thing to be read and therefore to leave a lasting impression on readers. This spotlight piece, entitled 'It's Up to You(th) – Taking Action for Development', addresses itself directly to an imagined readership of young people, and its opening paragraph reads as follows:

> … This spotlight addresses young people directly about how to develop their own capabilities so they can seize the opportunities provided to them, but especially, so they can create opportunities for themselves, for other young people, and for everyone. (World Bank 2007: 225)

The highlighted text box directly below this opening paragraph presents the motto of 'four young women from villages in Sri Lanka who are helping young people and all people in their villages overcome poverty'. The motto reads:

> People will decide their lives
> People will identify their problems
> People will lead to self-help
> People will share the fruits

And below this, young people in the developing world are told in no uncertain terms that they:

> … must seize the initiative and invest – by developing your own capacity, and taking action to make youth investments successful … No matter who you are, you can take action as young people to make life better for yourself.

This notion that 'it's up to you(th)' to make life better for themselves also resonates throughout the WDR07 in the recurring references to young people's decision-making, empowerment and participation in the development process. Again, the Bank's mobilization of such terms here does not signify a departure into radical waters, despite the use of ostensibly radical language. Rather, in the Bank's vision, young people are to make decisions that build their human capital so that they contribute to economic growth, and their participation is required to better serve the needs of the national and global economies.

Thus, what may be couched as a radical message is better understood as a reiteration of the emphasis on personal responsibility for development outcomes, which sits at the heart of the neoliberal agenda, and as a further burdening of those already struggling with the task of building better lives for themselves.

It is true that the WDR07 stresses the need for government policy and action across the five transition areas, and that in the youth and development discourse as a whole, the state is seen as central in the process of individual and national development. However, a close reading of the texts reveals something akin to what Moore, in his (1999) critique of the World Bank's 1997 World Development Report, calls a 'contradictory melange of anti-statism and managerialism' (Moore 1999: 61). Much of the government policy and action proposed in *Development and the Next Generation* transpires to be about handing the responsibility for development – not least the cost of it – to individuals. Suggested government policies in each of the transition areas, such as introducing user fees in schools and reducing the cost of dismissing workers, actually reflect a vision of the state as withdrawing to such a distance that young people are left to determine their own development outcomes. Echoes of this notion – that responsibility for development lies with young people themselves and that the role of policy and programming is to support this – can be found throughout the youth and development discourse.

The documents that comprise this discourse are united in their use of macro-level data and in their uncritical approaches to that data. Where the micro level is addressed, it is through the marginal presentation of quotes from young people, which appear disconnected from the research contexts in which they were produced and from the broader discursive frameworks within which young people's narratives emerge. That these documents deal with macro-level data concerning youth and development, such as statistics regarding educational attainment, employment levels and health behaviours, and are uncritical in their use of it, comes as little surprise – their stated purpose after all is to provide national or global situation analyses and policy recommendations, and this leaves little room for engaging with the complexities of the micro level. And these statistics are no doubt useful for those designing policies and programmes and allocating funding for their implementation. However, while such data may provide useful information on relevant national, regional and global trends concerning youth and development, they are partial. Very different insights can be produced through a micro-level, in-depth exploration of young people's lives and dreams, and by investigating what happens when they think, choose and act in the very ways sanctioned by the emerging youth and development discourse.

The issue of young people's agency is both absent and present in the youth and development literature. There is no detailed treatment of the unintended outcomes that can ensue when it is exercised within the parameters available to those in positions of socio-economic deprivation, and yet it is ubiquitous throughout the discourse. It is ever-present in the assumption of an unproblematic relationship between its exercise and ensuing, desirable outcomes.

Global Youth Studies

Over the past few decades, there has been growing, interdisciplinary academic interest in the lives of young people in the developing world, with a focus on gaining in-depth understandings of the ways in which young people themselves conduct, experience and narrate their lives. Certain scholars are directing their attention to the psychological, physical, cultural, social, educational, religious, political and economic aspects of young people's lives, as these intersect with each other and are played out against a backdrop of global, national and local transitions. This interest is especially pronounced within anthropology and human geography as well as encompassing work more readily located in other bodies of literature such as ethnographies of urban poverty and subaltern studies, although its early roots can perhaps be traced back to the 'new social studies of childhood' literature that emerged in the 1990s and focused on children and young people as competent social actors capable of exercising agency and imparting knowledge about their own lives. While it is now well recognized that the new social studies of childhood entailed limited treatment of children's agency – tending to emphasize and celebrate rather than question or examine it in any detail – this body of literature nonetheless put the issue of agency at the heart of social scientific scholarship on children and young people and paved the way for later, more nuanced approaches to the interconnections between agency, structures and cultural practice.

So, what do anthropology and human geography, as well as the relevant scholarship within other related fields, say about children and young people in the Global South, in particular about the issue of agency as it pertains to them? The following discussion takes these overlapping fields of enquiry in turn and offers a brief overview of the aspects therein that are most relevant to this study.

The New Anthropology of Youth

Prompted by 'modernity and globalization and the ambivalent engagement of youth in local contexts' (Bucholtz 2002: 525), the 'new anthropology of youth' can be understood as a growing collection of studies that have at their core the analysis of young people's creative cultural practices in diverse locations around the world. The shifting landscapes in which these small-scale studies are located are marked by large-scale social, economic and political transformations occurring to greater or lesser degrees of rapidity and profundity. A central concern in the studies is to evidence young people's active negotiations of the complex cultural terrain to which these transformations give rise. While a minority of the studies in this literature deal with relatively wealthy youth (e.g. Holden's 2006 study of 'adolechnics' in Japan), the majority explore the cultural practices of young people marginalized in some way or another, in particular on the basis of socio-economic status or ethnicity, and usually a combination of both.

The new anthropology of youth consciously distances itself from the vast majority of early anthropological research produced in the first half of the twentieth century, in which young people were mostly studied with a view to understanding the rites of passage practices in different cultures and thereby understanding the processes by which cultural norms are passed from one generation to the next. With the possible exception of Margaret Mead's seminal and controversial *Coming of Age in Samoa* in the late 1920s, in which she refuted the widespread claim that adolescence is a universally traumatic and stressful stage of life, young people's presence in early anthropological texts was of a somewhat silent nature; they appeared as objects of study and were investigated primarily for what they could reveal about the cultures in which they were located – thought to be bounded and homogenous – rather than for what they could reveal about people's inner life-worlds and experiences.

This focus owed much of its analytic heritage to the discipline of psychology and its pervasive narrative on adolescence as a period of heightened biological and psychological transition, understood as necessarily stressful (Griffin 2001; Bucholtz 2002). Approaching the issue of young people and culture from the point of view of transitions to adulthood and full cultural membership is critiqued within the new anthropology of youth on the basis that it tends to construct young people as incomplete and falsely posits a notion of completeness in adulthood, and that it obscures young people's cultural agency – in particular the informal ways in which they socialize themselves and each other as cultural practitioners (Bucholtz 2002; Wulff 1995; Caputo 1995). The new anthropology of youth rejects the tendency to focus on liminality, conceptualizes young people as cultural agents and explores their agentive cultural practices in diverse contexts across the globe.

The new anthropology of youth also distances itself from early sociological and cultural studies, wherein research on youth cultures did recognize young people as cultural agents but tended to focus on the exercise of agency to deviant or resistant ends. In the United States, the study of youth cultures began as an outgrowth of criminology and delinquency studies within sociology (Bucholtz 2002; Nayak 2003), and thus had a focus on deviance written into it from the outset. Within early criminological studies, it was commonplace to view deviance as a result of individual personality defects, and it was against this notion that researchers at the University of Chicago fought particularly vehemently. From the 1920s onwards, the Chicago scholars produced a plethora of urban ethnographies into the 'shadier recesses of polite society' (Nayak 2003: 14), and through these argued that juvenile delinquency should be understood as the product of social structures and physical environments in the inner city, not as the result of individual, defective, personality traits. This notion was retained in the work of later Chicago scholars, while eventually there was a proposed move away from the discourse of deviance altogether (ibid.).

It was in part against this academic focus on deviance, as well as against negative mass media portrayals of young people, that scholars at the Centre for Contemporary Cultural Studies at the University of Birmingham rallied in the 1970s. The Birmingham scholars sought to counter the prevailing image of youth cultures as deviant using mainly textual and semiotic analyses, although some ethnographic studies were conducted. The Birmingham School's theoretical perspective was based on Marxist and neo-Marxist understandings of class and class conflict and on a Gramscian understanding of hegemony (Wulff 1995; Nayak 2003; Nilan and Feixa 2006).[4] These theoretical approaches informed the school's depiction of a social system – characteristic of late industrial society – wherein dominant classes create and define hegemonic culture to enhance their positions of power and wherein subordinate classes resist this through the creation of 'sub' cultures. Thus, the Birmingham School researchers reconceptualized what had previously been understood in terms of deviance, as young people's resistance to class-based oppression through (sub) cultural practices. Here, eminent volumes such as *Resistance through Rituals* (Hall and Jefferson [1977] 2006) can be seen as emblematic of a broad concern to understand youth (sub)cultural practice as resistance to oppression.

Of particular interest is the work of the Birmingham scholar Paul Willis, and his 1977 ethnography of working-class 'lads' in a school setting, in which he utilizes cultural production theory to understand their 'condemnation' into working-class jobs. At the time Willis was writing, a good deal of sociological study was preoccupied with the question of why class inequalities persisted in society, and those writing within the field of education were particularly concerned with the ways in which the education system functioned to reproduce such inequality. While structural theories of reproduction posited that class inequalities persisted (i.e. working-class children only went on to get working-class jobs) because capitalist production required it to be so, some were dissatisfied with such structural determinism and the implied lack of agency, with the way in which 'agency become[s] merely a reflex of structural determination' (Willis 1977: 111). Those scholars, dissatisfied with structural theories, argued that the working classes are far from mere passive bearers and transmitters of ideology, that they are – and should be recognized as – active producers of meaning. However, they also wanted to be able to explain why, given that working-class people are active social agents, they seem to 'accept their unequal fates' (ibid.: 120).

Cultural production theory – originally developed by Bourdieu – was proposed as a means of providing such an explanation. It holds that the cultural practices of the working classes are likely to be directed towards opposing dominant – middle-class – culture, and that these cultural practices result in 'entrapping decisions in a sufficient number to grittingly meet the requirements of [capitalist] "structure" and so help to reproduce it' (Willis 1977: 128). Thus, according to cultural production theory, by *challenging* domination through producing oppositional cultures, working-class people find themselves *confirming* the very inequality that subordinates them: 'The very strength and success of this cultural production brings some profoundly reproductive consequences' (ibid.: 130).

In Willis's ethnographic study, he demonstrates how, through the encounter with the dominant – disciplinary and authoritative – culture at school, a group of working-class boys develop a counter-school culture wherein they engage in practices that ultimately serve to reduce their chances of doing anything other than 'meaningless' industrial work. What cultural production theory provided was, among other things, a means of exploring some of the unintended and contradictory outcomes of working-class youth cultural practice.

Willis's work, and that of the Birmingham School in general, has been the object of considerable critique; it has been claimed that it privileges class analysis over consideration of other forms of inequality such as those related to race, ethnicity and gender, that it constructs a misleading picture of young people's (sub)cultures as coherent, homogenous, bounded wholes, and that it portrays young people as necessarily resistant (Amit-Talai 1995; Wulff 1995; Miles 2000; Griffin 2001; Bucholtz 2002).

The new anthropology of youth attempts to distance itself from the association of youth culture with resistance and deviance, aiming to deal instead with 'the entirety of youth cultural practice' (Bucholtz 2002: 525) in a myriad of contexts and in particular with the multiple ways in which young people, as cultural practitioners, negotiate local and global spheres. In this, it has also – regrettably – distanced itself from those analytical tools developed within the Birmingham School that encourage us to think about the *outcomes* of cultural practice, or agency.

There are a number of key themes in this literature. One is young people's engagement with globalization, and here there is a wholesale negation, sometimes more and sometimes less explicit, of the homogenization (or Americanization) thesis. Scholars are at pains to show how young people are not passive recipients of global or American cultural products, services, styles and meanings, but are actively involved in selecting, manipulating and reconfiguring them, if not rejecting them altogether. This position is accompanied by the argument that the notion of *a* global youth culture should be replaced by concepts such as 'cultural bricolage' (e.g. Shahabi 2006) or 'multi'-culturalism' (Amit-Talai 1995). In this sense, the new anthropology of youth emphasizes the local meanings that young people give to collective cultural preferences and practices, deriving inspiration and information from global sources, but engaging reflexively and in multiple ways with youth-oriented products, 'choosing or rejecting, transforming or synthesising' them (Nilan and Feixa 2006: 8).

Another key theme is that of identity, and in particular young people's active constructions of identity through cultural practices. Here the notion of hybridity is particularly salient, with emphasis on celebrating young people's creative combining of available subject positions or identities into new, hybrid forms through the integration of cultural and linguistic practices and the adoption of historic, national, regional and local affiliations.

A further key theme in the new anthropology of youth is that of commodity consumption. In some cases, this is more of a background, if ever-present, issue, implied in studies of young people's sartorial and music-related practices. In other cases, it is an explicit topic of discussion and here one of the central undertakings is to reconceptualize what has hitherto been portrayed as a process in which young people are passive, and to understand them as exercising agency. In this way, young people are recast as not only passively purchasing the products aimed at them by the youth culture industry, but actively selecting and applying meaning to them, or even rejecting them altogether.

Underpinning each of these themes, indeed sitting at the heart of the new anthropology of youth, is the issue of young people's agency. In discussions of globalization, scholars emphasize young people's active appropriation of the products, styles and services of the global youth culture industry; in discussions of identity, authors emphasize young people's active constructions of hybrid identities; and in those studies that focus on consumer practices, they emphasize young people's active 'ordering of the landscape of consumption' (Nilan 2006: 101). The kinds of verbs used throughout this literature indicate a strong impetus to give credence to the exercise of cultural agency in youth; here, young people create, constitute, generate, assert, define, invent, select, choose, construct, order, produce, make, synthesize, resist, pursue, shape, manipulate, redefine, negotiate, renegotiate, appropriate and re-appropriate.

This emphasis on agency is a welcome change from earlier anthropological research, which tended to frame youth as passive recipients of enculturation. However, the studies that comprise this body of literature are on the whole united by a tendency to provide evidence for and celebrate the exercise of cultural agency in youth, and there is relatively little in the way of critical analyses of its *outcomes*. In particular, there is a relative lack of attention to the unintended, negative outcomes that can ensue from the exercise of agency in conditions of severe socio-economic constraint.

There are a few exceptions to this, although the extent to which scholars explore these unintended outcomes varies. In Niang's (2006) study of 'bboys' in Dakar, we learn of the way in which a minority of them are committed to social and cultural transformation through their involvement with local hip hop culture, which they see as a resistant and challenging force. Yet we also learn how the very act of aligning themselves with this cultural form alienates the masses, whose support the 'bboys' would need in order to bring about change, as the masses perceive hip hop as an American fashion that is being slavishly followed in their country. In Sansone's (1995) study of young men of Surinamese origin in Amsterdam, we learn of the way in which these young Creoles actively manipulate traditions and create new styles in the leisure-time arena and how they enjoy a certain status through this, yet how, in the process, they effectively exclude themselves from the spheres of education and work and potential advancement through these. In Liechty's (1995) study of middle-class youth in Kathmandu, we learn of the way in which the young middle classes claim local power through the cultural discourse of modernity, yet in doing so, they place themselves in a position of marginality and dependence in relation to development donors.

Despite these exceptions, much of the literature within the new anthropology of youth is concerned with seeking out and reporting on the agency of young people around the world, with more critical approaches less commonplace.

Geographies of Youth in the Global South

Within the field of human geography, there has also been increasing attention given to young people in the developing world, especially since the 1980s (Dyson 2008). Scholars in this subfield are providing deep insights, many of them underpinned by rich ethnographic fieldwork, into both the micro level of young people's everyday lives and the macro level of the structures with which those lives connect – social, cultural, historical, political and economic. In this, these scholars can be understood to be doing a number of things: broadening a rather narrow focus on youth cultural practice within the new anthropology of youth to take in other spheres of activity (work, education, political activity) and the spatial and temporal dimensions of young people's lives, and correcting a geographical bias within more traditional youth studies towards the West. They can also be understood to be taking the scholarship produced within the new social studies of childhood and expanding the intellectual project of recognizing, emphasizing and celebrating agency in youth and pushing this further, towards exploring its complex and contradictory outcomes, in particular as these unfold in the lives of young people in positions of profound transition and structural disadvantage.

The key topics of interest within this body of literature are the education, (un)employment, livelihood, cultural, leisure and political practices of young people growing up in the Global South, as these are experienced in conjunction with markers such as age, gender and class or caste. And it is within these geographical studies of youth in the developing world that the issue of agency is approached with particular sensitivity, with clear interest in the complexities that exist at the interface of agency, everyday cultural practice and structures. Much of the scholarship in this field places explicit emphasis on the ways in which young people exercise agency through their everyday practices, but is also attuned to the structures that constrain their endeavours and, further, to the nature of the interaction between these through cultural fields, and to the potential for agency to bring about reproductive or otherwise negative outcomes.

For example, Katz's seminal (2004) ethnography of young people in Sudan and New York illustrates myriad ways in which structures and structural change penetrate deep into the everyday lives and play of the young people she studies, and how they respond through either *resilient* behaviours, practices aimed at *reworking* circumstances or by *resisting* exploitative circumstances, but how in order to take genuinely progressive action they require resources and inputs that are not available to them. In her ethnography of young people's work in the Indian Himalayas, Dyson (2010) explores the ways in which girls' friendships function both to provide opportunities (for mutuality and learning) and to entrench dominant, gendered norms around work and behaviour, noting how agency can be both 'imaginative' and reproductive. In their research into youth entrepreneurship in north India, Young et al. (2017: 99) note how, while engaging in new forms of enterprise in the higher education market, young men ultimately reinforce patterns of inequality, 'reproducing and expanding the very [private education] system that produced them as underemployed young people'. In their (2012) study of educated, unemployed young men in India, Jeffrey and Young note how their participants actively pursue friendship and mischief-making and come together across social divides to protest against state (in)action, but how at the same time these alliances are fragile and gradually eroded. In her (2015) study of peripatetic religious students in Kano, Nigeria, Hoechner notes how young migrants actively carve out identities for themselves as 'searchers for sacred knowledge' (2015: 69), but how, while this may provide them with a sense of self-worth, it also means that they become scapegoats for the social ills of the neighbourhood, as the very identities they assume are increasingly understood and portrayed as backward, poor and criminal within the local dominant discourse. In his (2010) article on young, unemployed, educated men in India, Jeffrey examines the ways in which the participants in his longitudinal study respond to the 'timepass' (passing time) they experience, not by passively accepting their fate but by actively constructing self-conceptions and identities based on this feature of their lives, by forging connections and novel, 'intimate cultures' with others through it, and by initiating social movements with political purpose against it. Yet he also notes the negative, reproductive aspects of these forms of agency, as young men's active construction of a timepass culture 'rested on exclusionary ideas about class, caste and gender' (Jeffrey 2010: 475), amounting to only 'partial penetrations of dominant culture' (ibid.: 477).

Much of Jeffrey and Dyson's other work over the past decade or so has been similarly concerned with the issue of agency among youth in the Global South and its attendant complexities. For example, Jeffrey notes the existence of 'negative agency' (2012: 245) and the scholarly progress made since the emergence of the new social studies of childhood away from merely recognizing agency and towards exploring the ways in which agency encounters 'plural, intersecting structures of power', is limited in effectiveness where opportunities for upward mobility are scant, and is caught in a central paradox of neoliberalism whereby young people's agency is increasingly constrained on the one hand yet increasingly asserted – and required – on the other (ibid.: 246). Dyson (2008) notes the distinction between 'transgressive' and 'emancipatory' behaviour in the participants of her study, showing how transgressions – which entail the exercise of agency to apparently resistant ends – can both subvert and reproduce social norms by reinforcing notions of socially sanctioned behaviour.

Other scholars writing within different fields of enquiry have also produced work similar in theoretical approach to that outlined above. Philippe Bourgois (1995), writing within the field of ethnographies of urban poverty, applies Bourdieu's theory of cultural production to his analysis of crack dealers in East Harlem. His acclaimed study of street culture among young men of Puerto Rican descent has become one of the most pre-eminent ethnographic studies in contemporary times, and it is useful to contextualize this in order to fully grasp the nature of his theoretical project. In it, Bourgois writes in part against structural explanations for poverty, within which the poor are reduced to the status of passive props of an inequitable class system, and in part against the culture of poverty thesis and the way in which this (in its most widely understood form) explains the persistence of urban poverty with reference to the 'intergenerational transmission of destructive values and behaviours among individuals within families' (Bourgois 1995: 16). The culture of poverty thesis was first introduced by Oscar Lewis, his most expansive account of it residing in his publication *La Vida* (1968). The thesis holds that some people living in urban poverty remain poor because – through intrafamilial, intergenerational socialization – they develop certain behavioural and attitudinal traits, a certain culture, which both allows them to cope with deprivation and perpetuates it. While the culture of poverty thesis was intended by Lewis as a reaction *against* the prevailing attitude that poor people are poor by their own making, it has been widely (mis)interpreted as a theory that holds the poor accountable for 'their' poverty (Harvey and Reed 1996).[5] Within this interpretation, the urban poor are understood negatively and pathologically, their passivity and fatalism claimed as the ultimate causes of their predicament rather than as symptoms of broader structural inequalities.

Bourgois imports cultural production theory from its Bourdieun roots at the intersection of social, cultural and education studies and applies it to the study of street culture in the context of urban poverty. Here, it is through participants' active production of an oppositional street culture, the realm most readily available to them for exercising agency and gaining respect among their peers, that they unwittingly reproduce the very marginalization they oppose and inflict suffering on themselves, their families and communities. They engage in a range of tactics to avoid this marginalization, including ones that result in 'self-inflicted suffering' (Bourgois 1995: 17–18). The unintended – and contradictory – outcomes of agency, in particular as exercised by people in positions of socio-economic disadvantage, are clear, as we learn of the ways in which young men's attempts to gain respect in the limited ways and within the limited spheres open to them, lead them into a life of drugs, crime and violence and impinge on their peers, families and communities with devastating effects.

Lila Abu-Lughod (1990) also explores agency with a critical eye. Writing within the field of subaltern resistance studies, she applies Foucault's ideas concerning resistance as a diagnostic of power in her analysis of young women in Bedouin communities in Egypt. As part of her ethnography, Abu-Lughod examines the contemporary cultural practices of these young women, in particular the relatively new phenomenon of purchasing and wearing consumer commodities such as lingerie, moisturising creams, lipstick and nail polish. She notes how, through these cultural practices that resist the elders' way of life, young women inadvertently enmesh themselves in new systems of power, specifically in individualized, sexualized forms of femininity in the context of Egypt's increasing integration into the global economy. Abu-Lughod's study thereby points to the way in which young women perpetually move into 'fields of overlapping and intersecting forms of subjection' (1990: 52), or alternative webs of power, through their active engagement in commodity consumption.

Towards a Theoretical Framework

It is clear, then, that there is an increasing body of scholars whose work can be located within various fields – especially in geographies of youth in the Global South, ethnographies of urban poverty and subaltern studies, but also within the new anthropology of youth and

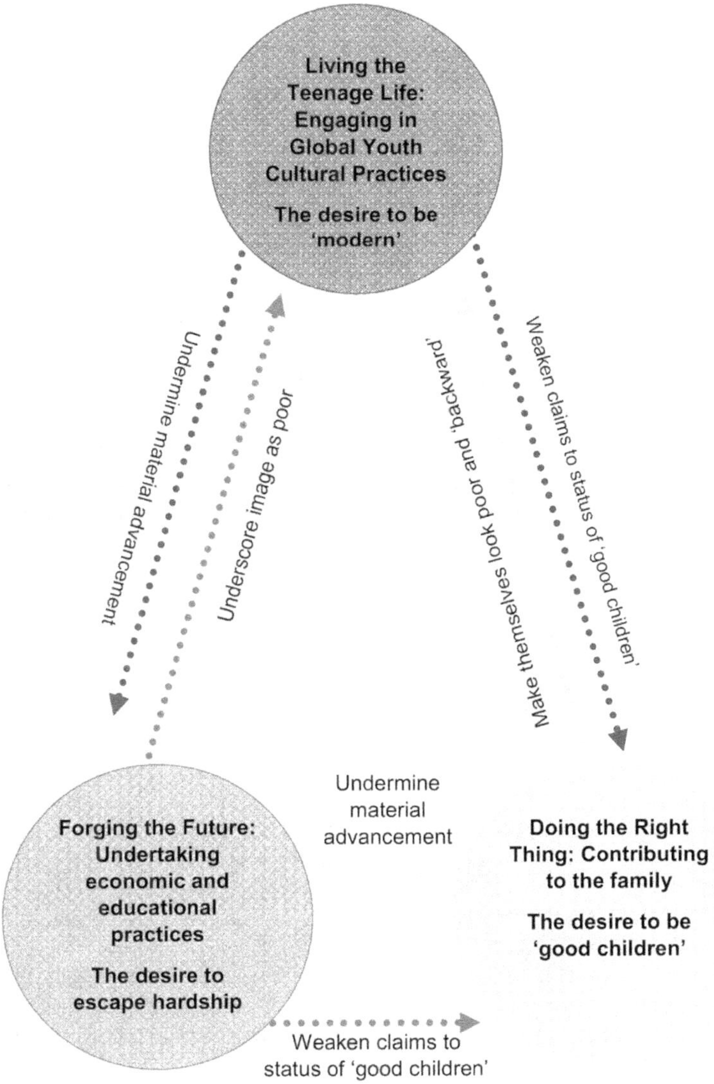

Figure 2.1. Diagram showing how action in each realm of practice can be precarious and have unintended consequences for other realms.

studies of youth in Thailand – who are theoretically oriented towards identifying not only the exercise of marginalized agency but also its complex and contradictory outcomes and the ways in which it interacts with multiple structures of power through given cultural practices. The theoretical concerns of my study are most closely aligned with this work.

The particular theoretical contribution I make is in the development of a conceptual framework that allows for the identification of multiple spheres of activity within which young people exercise agency, and the exploration of ways in which these might interconnect. Figure 2.1 illustrates this theoretical framework with reference to the empirical data I collected through fieldwork. Each circle represents a sphere of activity, a cultural field or realm within which young people exercise agency, and they are dotted to signify the way in which effective agency can be patchy. The dotted lines that connect each circle represent the unintended, negative effects of that agency on the other selected spheres of action. While the diagram is 'populated' with concepts from my research, it could be applied in other studies, with other – even additional – spheres of action and their spill-over effects replacing the ones that appear here. The empirical chapters in this book are dedicated to unpacking the particular ways in which activity in each sphere of action and its negative effects play out in the lives of young people growing up in the slums of Bangkok. First, though, I offer a personal and reflexive account of the process of fieldwork.

Notes

1. It should be noted that what are understood and presented here as discrete and bounded bodies of literature are, in reality, overlapping. I treat them as distinct in order to aid discussion and pull out the key, relevant issues and themes in each.
2. See for example Luttrell-Rowland (2007) and Kamat (2007).
3. The first event, held on 21 November 2006, was hosted by the Overseas Development Institute (ODI), the Chronic Poverty Research Centre (CPRC) and Peace Child International (PCI). Notes of this event are available from http://www.odi.org.uk/events/2006/11/21/362-meeting-report.pdf. The second event, held on 5 December 2006, was hosted by the All Party Parliamentary Group on International Development (APGOOD) and the ODI. Notes, presentations and sound files of this are available from http://www.odi.org.uk/events/apgood/index.
4. See Kaplan and Kelly (1994) for the argument that the work of the Birmingham School entailed a *mis*understanding of the Gramscian notion of hegemony.

5. This widespread interpretation is ironic given that the concept of culture was originally espoused in the social sciences as a means of getting away from reliance on biologically deterministic explanations of social phenomena (Perlman 1976), and given Lewis's own acknowledgement that the ultimate causes of poverty are to be found in capitalism's destructive dialectic and not in the inherent character of poor people.

3

FIELDWORK

This chapter offers a personal account of the processes of research design, fieldwork and analysis, and is divided into five main sections. In the first, I describe the process through which I came to conduct this study, and in the second I discuss the fieldwork I undertook with wealthy participants. The third section deals with the fieldwork in the slum and the fourth section discusses the process of analytical interpretation. It ends with a discussion of research ethics.

Research Journey

I never set out to live in Bangkok, much less become resident in its largest and most notorious slum. I first visited the city in March 2005, passing through for a week on my way to the north-east of Thailand to study the lives of children growing up in rural poverty, as part of a university project exploring well-being in developing countries.[1] During this initial trip, I took a taxi from Bangkok airport to my hotel in the business district, and I passed Khlong Toey slum, which, although I didn't know it at the time, would later become home for a while. If you have ever travelled by car in Bangkok during rush hour, you will know that there is time enough to see a lot of things, in some detail. Through the window of my air-conditioned taxi, I saw a black, stagnant river with rickety houses perched on broken stilts, almost falling into the water. There was a bridge linking the houses to the main road, which was made of wood and had planks missing. In between some of the houses there were narrow wooden walkways and children hanging up washing in an open-air living room. When the taxi turned into Sukhumvit Road, the first thing I saw was a Starbucks coffee shop. Followed by McDonalds, Kentucky Fried Chicken, Dunkin' Donuts, Häagen Dazs and Boots the Chemist. I lost count of the 7-11 convenience stores whose orange and green stripes, bleeping doors and uniformed counter clerks later became emblematic of the city. Then I noticed the street stalls lining the pavements alongside the multinational shop fronts, selling wooden souvenirs, counterfeit designer shoes, tee shirts and mobile phone accessories. There were young men pushing trolleys laden with food, somehow managing to dodge the swerving buses that overflowed with passengers, and old women carrying baskets suspended from long poles that balanced across their shoulders, almost bent double under the weight. Middle-aged women sold pineapples, watermelons and mangoes from glass cabinets on wheels, and children stood in the middle of the road selling jasmine garlands through car windows. The taxi drove through Siam Square and young people sat around in groups, chatting on their mobile phones, laughing and flirting, wearing Stussy baseball caps and carrying Louis Vuitton handbags.

For the next few months, I lived in the north-east of Thailand, in a rice-farming village with a woman whose husband lived and worked as a taxi driver in Bangkok, sending home welcome earnings and less welcome rumours of sexual promiscuity. I made friends with the mother in the house opposite, who had named her daughter Money in the hope that she would one day work in the capital and send her earnings home. An old man told me of his concerns about his granddaughter who worked in a factory in Bangkok and had started wasting her money on all kinds of expensive, 'nonsense' beauty products. I listened to my neighbour's stories of childhood and to her accounts of today's young men and women in the village who were heading for the capital on the labour migration trail and bringing back all sorts of new and unwanted customs. I learned something of the position that Bangkok held in the popular imagination as a symbol of socio-economic advancement and moral degeneration.

I observed many things during my stay upcountry: the way the electrical storms flashed in the night sky like fluorescent strobe lights as they swept across the wide open landscape courtesy of a government cloud seeding project; the way the whole community pulled together to help an old woman in the village when a storm ripped the roof off her house and dumped it into the dried up riverbed; the way I was advised to avoid the house at the end of the lane because the middle-aged couple who lived there were HIV positive. But, captivating though these things were, I also learned that I was not well suited to rural fieldwork.

I returned to the UK to rethink my plans. I thought about Bangkok, about the children in the slum and the street vendors, and about the teenagers in Siam Square with their designer handbags, about all I had seen there in my short stay and all I had heard during my time in the village. I wondered what life might be like for young people at different ends of the socio-economic spectrum living in a context marked by profound change as well as continuity, what it might be like to grow up in a country that prides itself on the observance of tradition as well as the embracing of modernity, and how life might be different for young people of different ages living in the families that benefited most and least from Thailand's 'miraculous' development. I decided to return to Bangkok and conduct my study there.

Hammersley and Atkinson (1995: 54), in their outline of ethnographic methods, note how the 'problem of obtaining access to the data one needs looms large in ethnography'. However, in the years since Hammersley and Atkinson made this statement, the internet has become all but ubiquitous, simultaneously expanding the world of opportunity and shrinking access to it. I searched on Google and found two entry points for fieldwork: an NGO working with children in Khlong Toey slum where a member of staff was willing to meet me to discuss conducting fieldwork there; and a long stay guest house run as an informal cultural exchange in the home of a relatively wealthy Thai family. In the autumn of 2005, I returned to Bangkok, initially based with this family and visiting the slum, and later moving into the slum and focusing my efforts there.

Life in the Affluent Suburbs

Fieldnotes

'Bua,[2] Bua come. Bua are you up yet up yet? Bua, are you lazy today?'

Yes, Bua is feeling lazy today; she is still in bed, half asleep. It is just before 5 o'clock in the morning, Mae Yaiy [my host grandmother, a retired teacher and matriarch of the household] is calling me, and I think for a moment about pretending not to have heard her, but I have been pulling this trick for a week now and I think she has become wise to it. So I drag myself out of bed and into the garden, which is steeped in the scent of fresh jasmine and the grey stillness of dawn.

Mae Yaiy is wearing a long white dress and standing under the mango tree, rotating her arms slowly in opposite directions. As I approach, her grin becomes so wide that her eyes disappear and she chuckles into her chest – at last the lazy foreign house guest is out of bed at a reasonable time and can share in Mae Yaiy's secret of finding true happiness. She signals for me to follow her movements and for the next half hour we bend and stretch together, in preparation for the serious business of meditation that is to come. We walk slowly, barefoot, across the different shaped stones that have been laid in a wide circle and we rock back and forth on the old, worn coconut shells that are set into the soil, both designed to invigorate the pressure points on our feet. Mae Yaiy leads me to a low bamboo table and again indicates that I am to copy her. I close my eyes, inhale slowly through my nose and breathe out through my mouth. We sit like this for about thirty minutes, Mae Yaiy still and calm, me fidgeting around crossing and uncrossing my legs, shaking my feet to get rid of the pins and needles, peeking out every now and then to see what Mae Yaiy is doing and thinking about what I might eat for breakfast.

A cock crows next door, the Moalam music [traditional music from the Isan region of Thailand] from a distant radio floats over the garden wall and the smell of frying garlic mingles with the jasmine. Pots and pans begin to clatter, voices call out and a man walks down the street pushing a trolley full of brushes and brooms, tooting his horn as he goes. Mae Yaiy shoos me into the house to get washed and dressed – the monk will be here any moment to collect his alms. We sit and wait outside the front gate and when a bright orange robe sweeps around the corner Mae Yaiy calls to Pook, the housemaid, to bring the food out.

Pook brings out a bowl of sticky rice, a bag of salted fish curry, a can of Pepsi, a packet of Oreo biscuits and three small oranges, and when the monk approaches, Mae Yaiy summons her two grandchildren, Noi (a sixteen-year-old girl) and Moo (a thirteen-year-old boy), to come and give him the offerings and pay their respects. The monk stands with his head bowed and his bowl extended and when it is full he says a prayer for the family. This ritual takes place every morning and Mae Yaiy hopes that making merit in this way will help her grandchildren achieve a safe passage into the next life and that in the process they will play their part in keeping Thai culture alive. When the monk has gone and Mae Yaiy has given the signal that Noi and Moo are excused, they rush back inside to enjoy another few minutes on the computer before they leave for school, and Mae Yaiy laughs loudly when I ask if she has ever played one of their online games.

P Sup, my host father and middle-ranking civil servant, climbs into the minivan and starts the engine to get the air conditioning going. P Yoo, my host mother and account manager at a travel agency, Noi and Moo follow. Moo turns the minivan TV on and the advertising jingles provide the soundtrack for their journey into the city.

They leave together like this every day. P Sup drops Noi and Moo off at their respective schools, then drives P Yoo down the road to her office before heading on to his own. For them, it is important that the family goes together, that the children are escorted to school, that they travel as a unit; this way they keep their children close to them and accompany them – quite literally – on their journeys through life. When school finishes, everybody meets at P Yoo's office and the four of them travel home together. On the days that Noi has extra tuition after school, P Yoo, P Sup and Moo go out for dinner and pick her up when the class finishes; this way they still travel as a unit. If they go to the cinema in the evening, they go as a family. As they drive off, P Yoo tells me to make sure I am home for dinner – I am part of the family now and that means staying close and following their rules.

I leave the house shortly after the Surawits and am accompanied by the sound of birdsong as I walk down the lane to the bus stop. I hear the pounding of a pestle and mortar and for a few seconds everything seems to beat to the same rhythm. I pass the big spirit house outside one of the neighbours' homes and see the garlands of jasmine and bottles of Fanta that have been offered to the spirits that guard the property. The drinks are pink, green and orange and match the colours painted on the spirit house and the ribbons that have been wrapped around the tree beside it. The smell of incense mixes with the wood smoke that comes from an open fire in someone's front yard. I pass a man cooking at his food stall and the chilli that he is frying makes my eyes water. I sneeze and he laughs. At the front of the lane, a tuk-tuk driver who was dozing on the back seat of his vehicle is woken by the beeping of a reversing van, which is carrying two calves, a heap of straw and a pile of logs. I see my bus coming along the main road and run to jump on – they only seem to stop if they are stuck in traffic.

I get off the bus and everything is still. It is like a scene from a film – people who were walking along the pavement halt in their tracks, shop owners stand to attention in their doorways and a young girl balances the bike she was riding between her knees. Nobody speaks. The Thai national anthem blares out from a loudspeaker attached to a lamp post, as it does every day in the morning and early evening, and everybody stands with their arms straight, their hands placed neatly by their sides and their gazes fixed on the distant horizon.

After a couple of minutes, the anthem stops, the hustle and bustle of rush hour resumes and I continue the short walk to the sky train station where I meet Am, my interpreter. Together we make our way to P Bun's house, an old colleague of Am's who has agreed to be interviewed. We take a twenty-minute journey through the city's central business and shopping districts where the air-conditioned train weaves its way in and out of the skyscrapers and multi-storey shopping malls that have earned Bangkok its reputation as a global centre of hyper-consumerism. We get off the train and are greeted by LCD screens suspended from the ceiling of the station showing adverts on a loop for Nescafé Red Cup, Pond's whitening face cream and Dove whitening underarm deodorant.

We walk past Starbucks where a handful of people sit sipping caramel mochaccinos, and to a taxi stand where Am hails a cab that takes us to P Bun's neighbourhood. We arrive early, so Am asks the driver to drop us at the bottom of the road and we make the short journey on foot to P Bun's house – it would not be polite to turn up before the agreed time. The lane twists and turns and I follow Am as she zigzags across the road trying to stay in the shade of the high walls that shield the houses from view. An aeroplane soars overhead and its brilliant white trail slices through the still, cloudless sky. We arrive at P Bun's house and ring the bell, and the metal gates open automatically, revealing three large, shiny silver cars parked under an ornate wooden canopy.

The gates close behind us and P Bun comes out wearing an LA Gear tracksuit and a pair of Chanel sunglasses balanced on her head. Am and P Bun used to work for the same company and haven't seen each other for a long time, so for the first twenty minutes of our meeting we sit on the leather sofa in the air-conditioned living room sipping iced lime juice, while they exchange gifts and pleasantries and news of shared acquaintances. We slip seamlessly into the interview, in which P Bun talks about her childhood and youth in Bangkok with her parents and sister, about her experiences at university, about the time she spent in America in her early twenties, about meeting her husband – now a successful businessman who owns a chain of holiday resorts on the coast – and about her experiences of parenting. Soon her son and husband emerge from the computer room and join us, and P Bun asks the maid to get some lunch ready. We while away the next couple of hours eating and talking until Am senses that it's time to leave. On our way down the lane, I notice that some of the walls have broken glass set into the concrete on top, others have barbed wire that has been wound into coils and cemented in, and the rest have sharp metal spikes that point to the glare of the sun and to the call for protection that accompanies the material wealth they contain.

Researching in the Affluent Suburbs

My life in the affluent suburbs was comfortable, protected and ordered. I was woken up with breakfast in bed every morning by Pook, the 25-year-old housemaid from Myanmar who had left her four-year-old daughter back home in the care of her parents so that she could earn money and send it to them. Pook slept on the floor outside Mae Yaiy's room and worked from 4 a.m. until 9 p.m. every day except Sunday. During the day, I attended Thai language lessons, and as time went on I began conducting fieldwork with other wealthy families and with people living in Khlong Toey slum. I spent mealtimes with my host family, accompanied them on day trips and met some of their wider family and friends. I joined them on a short holiday, visited them at work and at school and was introduced to Am, a former colleague of my host mother's and aspiring interpreter.

Immaculately presented, in her early thirties, with a degree in English and Business Management, Am grew up in a western suburb of Bangkok with her mother, father and older brother. When I met her, she was working part time in the family business managing rental apartments, and described her main hobby simply as 'people'. She had a big extended family, a wide circle of friends and an enormous network of acquaintances. During our first meeting, which I had arranged with a view to ascertaining Am's proficiency in English and capacity to interpret, she said she had heard of the English phrase 'nosey poker' and indicated that it was an apt description of her natural tendency towards ascertaining the finer details of people's lives. In many ways, our introductory meeting stood as testimony to this – as we sat drinking tea and eating cake in a spotless, air-conditioned café on the bustling Khao San Road, every question I asked her seemed to invite at least five in return: What was my childhood like? Did my family miss me? Was I homesick? Did I have a boyfriend? She would fold her napkin carefully, dab at the corners of her mouth and wait patiently for me to answer. We sat for hours chatting during our first meeting, and by the end of it I realized that Am's skills – and the skills I required in her – stretched way beyond her capacity to interpret and lay more fundamentally in her inquisitiveness, in her ability to act as cultural broker and in her talents for building rapport and listening with interest.

Soon after we met, Am and I approached the two schools where my host family's children studied, with a view to conducting research in both. At Am's suggestion, we took along letters printed on headed paper from the university in the UK to which I was attached, letters of recommendation from Am's ex-employer and copies of my interview guide. We dressed in our most appropriate clothes and Am guided me through the labyrinth of unspoken rules – when to speak, when not to speak, which gesticulations to perform with the utmost care, which to avoid and how to carry my body in a way that imparted respect. We were interviewed by a number of school staff who asked lots of questions about my research, and eventually we gained access to a number of relatively wealthy children, and through them their parents.

Despite being government run, and therefore ostensibly free, both schools operated a two-tier system whereby one 'basic' curriculum was delivered in Thai at little cost, and another 'special' curriculum was delivered in English at some considerable cost. We were passed onto the coordinators of the English language curricula in each school and they agreed to host the research on the condition that we spoke with the children in English, so that they could practise talking with a native speaker.

From then on, and throughout my stay in Bangkok, we visited both schools regularly to talk with young people (fifty in total) about their lives – the way they spent their time, the people in their lives, the money and material things they had access to, and their hopes, dreams and concerns for the future. We interviewed boys and girls between thirteen and eighteen years of age, all of whom attended school and a significant number of extra classes at Bangkok's burgeoning tuition centres (these form a kind of parallel, private education system for families who can afford it, designed to give an academic edge to those in state schooling with their sights set on the country's top universities). Most of these young people lived in detached houses with their parents and siblings if they had them, none of them worked as they all received weekly spending money from their parents, and all of them were planning to go into higher education. Many had spent time in Europe, America or Australia.

We also interviewed most of our young participants' parents, as well as other adults in Am's social networks. We travelled extensively throughout the city – to the schools, universities, hospitals, government buildings and law offices where they worked, in jobs ranging from the middle management of a bank all the way up to the higher echelons of the Thai judicial system. We visited the tuition centres where their children studied outside school, the shopping malls and food courts where they spent their leisure time, and people's homes – asking them about their childhoods, their perceptions of what had changed since they were young and about their experiences of parenting. The adults we interviewed had all completed compulsory schooling and most were educated to degree level. Some held Master's degrees and/or PhDs, all earned sizeable incomes, most owned their own homes and many had significant savings and other assets.

Am was gifted in the art of conversation – she would giggle when others giggled and nod earnestly when the things people said demanded silence and sincerity. She had an amazing ability to cover all of the questions on a semi-structured interview guide in a way that made the discussion seem like a natural and obvious occurrence. She was from the same world as the people we met; her schooling, her family background and her career meant that there was a familiarity and recognition between her and our participants and enough common ground for her to navigate us successfully through our interactions. Occasionally we spoke entirely in Thai – Am leading and me participating as best I could – and sometimes we slipped between English and Thai, taking it in turns to ask questions and move things on when appropriate. Most of the time we talked in English, which our participants seemed to do with ease.

However, despite the access we were afforded to these young people and their families, over time I became more and more intimately involved in slum life, and after a few months I decided to shift my attention more fully towards the slum, which I had been visiting from the outset. Although focused on slum life from this point on, I continued fieldwork with wealthy families throughout my stay, and this proved invaluable. It provided something of a gauge with which to help make sense of slum dwellers' experiences, it allowed for insights into how people at different ends of the socio-economic spectrum perceived each other, and it provided some respite from what I experienced as a challenging research environment.

Life in the Slum

Fieldnotes

I'm on my way to the slum to meet P Ning, my contact at the NGO there. I get off the bus and the first thing I see is a man lying face down on the ground. He seems to be in his forties and the skin on his shins and feet resembles the texture of tree bark. One of his legs dangles over the curb and there is a pool of vomit next to his face. The sun is already beating hard and it is only 10 a.m. I wonder how long this man will lie here, what his fate will be. I look to the two women standing at the bus stop and one of them shakes her head briskly; a warning? Not to touch him? Not to look at him? I side-step around his head and cross the road.

Walking with my back to the river, I cross a railway line, and looking to either side I see houses backing on to it and children sitting on the tracks playing. A group of motorcycle taxi drivers look up from a board game and I smile as I meet their gaze. They stare back and I struggle to read their expressions. I walk on and pass an old woman who is sitting in the doorway of a derelict shop. She rocks backwards and forwards muttering to herself, and a long stream of brown liquid runs in the gutter under her bare feet. She picks something up from the ground and puts it in her mouth. The people at the food stall opposite avert their gazes. I walk on, past the community centre and past a food stall when I hear someone calling me: 'P Bua, P Bua have you eaten yet?' It is Tam; he is eating a bowl of noodle soup and invites me to join him. Tam is twenty-two years old and a recovering drug addict and now acts as a mentor for other young men who are trying to piece their lives back together having lost them for a while to the oblivion of substance abuse. Tam shows me his nails. They are long and each painted a different colour: 'Are they beautiful?' he asks. 'A little bit', I tell him. He strokes his hair: 'Do you like my hair, do I look good today?' he asks. 'A little bit', I reply. He places both hands on his tummy and asks if I think he is fat. 'A little bit', I say. He insists that he looks handsome today and laughs, but is stopped short by a woman who is shouting at a young boy.

The woman has a stick about a metre long and she starts whipping the boy with it across his torso. He tries to protest but this seems to enrage her further. I look to Tam (what should we do?) and he shakes his head and stares into his bowl. The boy tries to run away and the woman grabs him by the sleeve, but now cannot hit him properly with the stick because it is too long and she is too close to him. So she drops the stick and beats him about the head with her hands. The boy stops protesting and brings his arms to his head to shield himself from the blows. The fear in his eyes before they disappear behind his hands stays with me for the rest of the day, and the next day, and the one after that.

Tam gives me a lift to the NGO on his motorbike and I spend the rest of the day there, reading everything I can find in English, trying to look as if I am doing something useful and wondering what I might have done to help the boy. I leave at around 5 p.m. and before I head home I pay a visit to P Jok at her food stall. She makes me a drink that is bright orange and so sweet that any flavour it might have had is undetectable, brings it over to the table and then hurries off to serve the customers who have started dropping by on their way home. I sit for half an hour and watch the late afternoon unfold.

Mopeds carrying whole families chug past and children chase each other down the street laughing. A truck comes round the corner and about forty balaclavas bob up and down in the back. Construction workers. A girl pulls up on a bike wearing a red spaghetti strap top; the English text printed across the front says 'I might not be perfect but some parts are irresistible'. An old woman walks past wearing a sarong; her back is stooped and she is chewing *maag* – 'traditional Thai chewing gum' made from betel leaves, chewed and held in the mouth for long periods of time (it is most common in rural areas, particularly among older women, and stains the mouth and lips a deep red colour). A little boy approaches the food stall, picks up a hand-held electronic game that P Jok keeps by her chair and sits down opposite me to play. He looks up and smiles and reveals a mouth full of black teeth.

I make my way to the bus stop and wait for about fifteen minutes. The noise from the traffic is deafening. The fumes are unbearable and I try and breathe as little as possible. A man swaggers barefoot through five lanes of speeding traffic, holding his palm up to the oncoming cars. Horns blare and brakes screech. A street cleaner sweeps the rubbish from the gutter by the bus stop into her dustpan and urges the young girl trailing behind her to keep up. The girl has difficulty walking because she is only wearing one shoe. I look at the river that runs under the two flyovers and parallel to the road I am on. It is black, stagnant and putrid; decades of pollution make it look like an oil slick. Mosquitoes dance on the surface of the water and they look like raindrops. On the opposite riverbank there is a dead dog and a pink plastic chair with three legs laying upside down in the mud. Along the riverbank, and at points falling into the river, are the backs of people's houses. They are made of wooden slats with corrugated tin roofs and are supported by crooked poles. I wonder what happens to the houses and the people in them when the rainy season comes and the river rises. A section of metal on one of the houses catches the light from the early evening sun and turns to gold.

Researching in the Slum

I slipped gradually into life as a resident of Khlong Toey slum, although welcomed with open arms from the day I set foot inside. I began with a few sporadic visits to the NGO I had approached before setting out for Bangkok, during which I gained approval to do fieldwork, read what literature I could and tried to gain acceptance more widely among local residents. I was also introduced to Ganya, a young woman who had been born and brought up in the slum, had her education sponsored through the NGO, was fluent in English and interested in working as an interpreter.

Ganya described herself an atypical Thai woman: 'I'm not like other Thai girly girls. I am big, I have got curves and I am taller than most. I live in Khlong Toey, I love to dance to hip hop and I drink – this is not what a Thai girl is supposed to do'. Her command of English, formal and colloquial, as well as her general communication and interpersonal skills, were exceptional. Apart from spending time in the English language classrooms and lecture halls of one of Bangkok's newer universities where she was studying, she spent a significant amount of time meeting Western travellers in bars and nightclubs and believed that this, as well as her formal immersion in English and her Christian beliefs, afforded her the ability to look upon her own community and culture as a something of an outsider – with a sense of other norms and perspectives. Early on in fieldwork, Ganya said that she saw it as her newfound purpose in life to give a voice to the young people in her community, that it was her good *kamma* to have found me to take their stories and hers to a wider audience:

> You know, I think it is my duty to tell the world about the kids here in Khlong Toey. This is why I have a gift for languages. And I think I have met you so that we can do this together ... I can put their stories into English and you can tell them to people in your country.

Ganya descends from one of the original families to settle in Khlong Toey. At the beginning of fieldwork, she thought she was an only child, but by the end she had discovered that she had two younger half-sisters on her mother's side whom she had not met. Throughout my time in Bangkok, she lived with her father, who had taken custody of her following the breakup of his relationship with her mother, and they lived in a room in a large rental house in one of the upgraded slum communities.

Ganya understood from experience many of the issues and struggles that young people in the slum contended with. She grew up in a context of severe housing insecurity and moved frequently, leaving a trail of rental debt behind her. She had been homeless for a couple of years, sleeping intermittently on friends' floors and in a stock cupboard at a local church, went hungry, sometimes for protracted periods, and supported her father who had come and gone from her life. She did not know her mother or her mother's whereabouts, although towards the end of fieldwork they were reunited. When she was younger, she had dropped out of school to look after her paternal grandmother who was in ill health and who died after a protracted illness, leaving behind a web of intrafamilial disputes. Although there were differences and inequalities between Ganya and other slum participants, most notably in terms of education and related earning potential, many people still thought of her as one of them – an insider with shared experiences who could empathize with them and with whom they were willing to share their stories. She was well known in her neighbourhood; people would call out to her everywhere she went, stop to chat, ask questions and tell her anecdotes from their day. Sometimes it would take an age to walk down the street with her. She provided me with an implicit seal of approval and functioned as a bridge between me and other residents, although her insider status also precluded certain people from fieldwork. For example, one of my neighbours was having a casual relationship with Ganya's father and this was a source of some disquiet for Ganya; and her paternal extended family had fallen out with each other in the wake of her grandmother's passing, which prevented us from conducting research with them.

Shortly after I met her, Ganya told me she knew of some young people who were interested in finding out more about my research and possibly taking part, and that I could meet them at the community gym which took place in the early evenings in the front courtyard of the NGO and was run by P Sib, a community police officer known locally for his rapport with and compassion for the young people of Khlong Toey. After a successful first meeting with P Sib, we began attending the gym regularly and it became one of our main fieldwork sites. We also visited a local internet café frequently, and this too became another key site for the research. We set up two weekly English clubs, one in the playground of a community school on weekday evenings and another on Saturday mornings in an old train carriage that had been donated by the Belgian government and turned into a library. These clubs went some way towards legitimizing my presence in the slum; to continue there without a respected and clearly defined role would have been difficult.

For the next couple of months, Ganya and I fell into something of a routine, me bussing in from the other side of town and both of us attending the gym most days, running our English clubs twice a week, spending time at the internet café and hanging out at street food stalls, chatting with each other and the stall owners. Sometimes we had to work hard to dismantle the roles that were assigned to us; in the community where we set up one of the English clubs, the leader insisted that we report to her on arrival, announced us to the community on the loudspeaker system, referred to me with the exalted title *ajaan* ('professor') and took a register at the start of our sessions. But little by little, as we got to know young people, we began inviting them to take part in group discussions or research activities – social mapping, neighbourhood mapping, body mapping, neighbourhood walks, day reconstruction activities and ranking activities designed to elicit how they viewed and valued their material possessions. Through these I felt a certain validation; group-based activities are often promoted in research with young people on the basis that they can help minimize the effects of power imbalances between adult researchers and young participants (e.g. Thomas and O'Kane 1998). As an approach, they arguably become all the more important when the young people one studies are also relatively powerless in ways other than age. However, what tended to happen in these group encounters – as well as the teasing, flirting, singing, dancing, chatting, chasing, play fighting, withholding of information and ignoring of my research agenda altogether – was that the power imbalances between young people functioned to silence the voices of some group members. Sometimes these disparities were subjectively felt and sometimes more objectively obvious, and they were especially heightened around the issue of age. Age hierarchy was paramount, with the smallest of age differences ascertained at the outset of social interactions to establish seniority and related behavioural norms. Also, while these group activities were useful in providing insights into socially acceptable scripts, or those of the more dominant people within the group, there was no obvious place for discussion of more personal experiences and feelings.

So we started to invite young people for individual interviews. This was ostensibly problematic because there were two of us – adults – and usually only one child at a time, but they were taken by young people as opportunities to give expression to issues that did not readily surface in group sessions, and were often accompanied by a request to meet again. We would sit in the grounds of the NGO, in the playground of the community school which doubled as a sports ground and hangout for young people in the evenings and at weekends, on benches and at food stalls on the streets of the slum chatting – about how they spent their time, their relationships, their use of money and material things, the difficulties and sources of happiness and sadness in their lives, their life histories and their dreams for the future. Sometimes we would venture outside to the cafés and shopping malls that stood as constant reminders of the lives that our participants could not afford. Occasionally we were invited into young people's homes, and gradually we built up a group of key informants.

We initially intended to meet adult carers through the young people we were getting to know, but this proved difficult. In some cases, if a young person had disclosed issues that were sensitive, shameful or painful, or which highlighted tensions between them and their adult carers, they were reticent to open the door to their home lives. In other cases, our chosen adult carers were too busy or did not want to take part, and in a few cases, young people could not identify anybody who they considered to be caring for them. So we cast our net wide, inviting anyone with children to share their experiences – of caring for young people, of being children and teenagers themselves, and of the broader changes and continuities in growing up. We would go to people's homes and places of work and these were often the same and mostly in the slum. Sometimes our discussions were spread out over a number of sessions as people juggled talking with us as well as work and childcare and the heavy demands these entailed. I also interviewed staff and volunteers from some of the local NGOs, exploring the kinds of issues they faced in their work.

Moving into the Slum

After a few months, at the suggestion of a small group of young people with whom I had grown particularly close, I moved out of the material comfort of my wealthy homestay and into the slum. I rented a room in a shared house located in an upgraded area, on a busy road that accommodated several shipping businesses, minimarts, food stalls, churches, open air karaoke bars, motorcycle taxi stands and a large rubbish recycling centre. Behind the houses on this road was a shipping container yard, the docks and the Chao Phraya river. My house had three storeys and stood in a terraced row of around twenty others, most of which had shops or food stalls on the ground floor, many of which doubled as living quarters for those working in them. On the ground floor of my house, there was an electronic repair shop, a bathroom and a tiny backyard where inhabitants washed dishes, did laundry and made offerings to the spirit house. There were four rooms each on the first and second floors accommodating a mixture of couples, families and groups of friends, and another bathroom on the second floor. There seemed to be around thirty people staying in the house at any one time, although it was sometimes difficult to keep track of who were residents and who were guests.

My room was on the second floor and had a window at the far end that faced out onto the shipping yard, and to the left onto the corrugated tin roofs that undulated like a rusty patchwork quilt and turned a beautiful, deep rusty colour in the late afternoon sun. Every night at around 1 a.m. I would fall asleep to the groaning of metal cranes, and the floor would tremble as the shipping containers were unloaded onto the ground. On one side of the room, separated by a concrete wall with large chunks missing, was the bathroom, which I shared with around twelve other people. Every morning at 4 a.m. I would wake to the sound of one of my neighbours coughing and vomiting into the toilet as he prepared himself for his shift in the fish canning factory where he worked. He said he had been ill for over a month but needed to keep working to earn money to pay the rent for the room where he lived with his wife and their two young children, to buy food for them and to pay for school equipment.

Next to the bathroom was a room housing a group of four men in their mid twenties who worked as casual labourers at the port. Most evenings at around 9 p.m. they would turn on their karaoke machine and sing along to Thai pop songs for around two hours. On the other side of my room was Ide and Jem's room. Ide was a young woman from the north-east of Thailand whose parents had died a couple of years previously. She had moved into the slum with her boyfriend and was addicted to *ya baa* (methamphetamines), although she was in the process of trying to quit. About twenty minutes after I moved in, as I sat unpacking my clothes, Ide knocked on my door and beckoned me into her room. I followed and she sat down on the mattress and tied her upper arm with a strip of material that was baby yellow in colour with little teddy bears printed all over it. She tried to inject herself in the forearm and I grimaced as she fiddled about finding a suitable spot for the needle, a process that was complicated because much of her skin was scarred, scabby or congealed with old blood. I never did learn why Ide wanted me there with her, but I sat on the edge of her mattress as she prodded and poked, then told me to get out, shouting at me not to tell Jem as I left. But Jem found out about the drugs and I spent the early part of that evening, the first in my new room, listening to their shouting and to the sound of objects being thrown against the wall. After about an hour, their door banged open and Ide's belongings came flying out onto the landing, followed by Ide who stumbled around in front of my doorway and landed in a heap, asking if she could leave her things in my room. She disappeared for two days, and when she came back her lip was split and swollen, she had a black eye, and she told me she had slept in the alleyway outside a friend's house around the corner.

Living in the slum not only afforded me a glimpse into home life for my immediate neighbours; it allowed for insights into life – and death – for people living in other parts of the community and in other communities, as I now had more legitimate reasons for straying off the main roads, through the back alleys and into the narrow walkways where housing density was greater and the dramas of everyday life seemed to unfold with increased intensity. One afternoon, I accompanied a social worker on a visit to one of her clients, a woman in her mid forties, who flew into a rage and threw her thirteen-year-old daughter across their small, makeshift hut that was tucked under a bridge crossing the river, sending her crashing into the pots and pans that hung on the opposite wall, displaying a level of violence that I had not witnessed before. Walking home late one night with a friend – a French volunteer working for a local NGO – we passed a teenage girl sitting outside her house crying. My friend knew her, and when we stopped to ask what was happening, she told us about her mother who had been sent to prison for dealing drugs and how she was now responsible for looking after her three younger sisters and paying the rent – with no regular income. She became more and more agitated until a drunken man in the house opposite stood up from his doorstep, shouted at her and threw his bottle of beer in her direction, narrowly missing her head. Another afternoon, after I had dropped my clothes off to the laundry woman and was taking the scenic route back to my room, a group of children came hurtling around the corner of the narrow alleyway shouting, screaming and pulling at my arm to change direction. I carried on, my curiosity piqued. As I turned the corner, I passed an open front door and saw a body hanging from the ceiling, swinging gently to and fro. It belonged to a young man who had been addicted to methamphetamines and badly indebted to a local money lender, who apparently saw no prospect of freeing himself from the clutches of either.

Living in Khlong Toey slum not only gave me an insight into certain aspects of home life for inhabitants, it also gave me a glimpse of certain features of street life. Early one morning, as I sat eating breakfast at a food stall outside my house, I saw a boy of about eight being pushed off a wall by a friend, land face first on the metal bumper of a pickup truck, knock several teeth out and cut his top lip open. A man in his thirties picked the boy up, sat him on his motorbike and drove off down the road, hitting him repeatedly over the head and shouting that he was supposed be going to work, but that now he would have to take him to the doctor instead – presumably losing much-needed earnings in the process. A number of times, I saw twelve-year-old Jagalen sleeping in the alleyway outside her grandparents' house while they drank and fought inside. On a few occasions, I saw Ide walking down the street in the early hours of the morning, heavily made up, her eyes wide. 'Out on business' was her stock answer whenever I asked where she was going. Only after living there for some time did I learn of the ubiquity of glue sniffing, begging and gambling. What initially seemed striking in the apparently isolated visions of young men slumped in alleyways with their noses in small plastic bags and their eyes vacant, in the sight of barefooted men begging for leftovers at food stalls, and in the groups of women huddled inside doorways playing cards and passing money to and fro, became unexceptional and routine, if subtle and hidden from immediate view.

Of course, life in the homes and streets of Khlong Toey was not only marked by struggle and conflict, but by fun, laughter and tenderness. Once I moved in, a friend invited me to eat dinner with her and her father in their home, and we giggled as I watched them dressing up in each other's clothes and shoes, impersonating each other and laughing affectionately. After moving in, I would see sixteen-year-old En working alongside her mother in the evenings, sometimes until 1 a.m., at their food and karaoke stall, and I would watch them dancing and giggling together in the snatched moments of down time, as they prepared dinner and got ready for the next rush of customers. Returning to my room at the end of the day, I would sometimes see my neighbour Jem cradling Ide in his lap as she cried with anger and exhaustion and the physical and emotional demands of trying to come off drugs.

Moving into the slum marked an important shift from being a complete outsider to gaining some of the credentials associated with being a neighbour – albeit a very temporary one – not least experiencing daily life in what was felt by all to be a demanding and oppressive physical environment. Although I would never be an insider – my stay was always short term, for the purpose of research, and the option of leaving was always open to me – being present, day in day out, night after night, buying food from street vendors, getting my clothes and shoes mended by local seamstresses and cobblers, accompanying people as they worked, attending the community gym, hanging out in the evenings, frequenting the local internet shop and going to the local markets, shopping malls, bars and nightclubs with my new neighbours seemed to engender an increased trust and openness in people.

After I had been living in the slum for a few months, I met Note, a young man in his early twenties who had been born in Khlong Toey, sold at birth to a wealthy foster family from outside the slum but suffered a breakdown of family relationships. He had lived on the streets for a number of years, earning money by racing motorbikes on one of the main thoroughfares cutting through Bangkok, and had spent time in a centre for juvenile delinquents before being taken in as an orphan by one of the slum NGOs and supported in catching up with the education he had missed. As I sat in one of the local internet shops one afternoon writing emails home, Note came and sat next to me, introduced himself in perfect English, asked what I was doing there and on hearing my answer offered to help – he was on summer vacation from his studies, was staying and volunteering at the orphanage, had some spare time on his hands, knew plenty of people and could do with some extra cash. Note became another key informant, and meeting him opened the door to a life that had come to straddle the worlds of slum living on the one hand and extreme prosperity on the other, and beyond this to a new set of young people with links to the orphanage.

Through fieldwork with Note and Ganya, I learned about the backgrounds, everyday lives, hopes and dreams of around fifty young slum dwellers, whose lives reflected the internal diversity of Khlong Toey slum communities. They ranged from thirteen to twenty-two years of age and their education levels spanned incomplete primary schooling to completed upper secondary schooling, and for Ganya and Note, tertiary education. They were involved in a variety of jobs: cleaning, rubbish collection, street and market stall vending, preparing products such as fruit for sale by mobile street vendors, waitressing, labouring at the port, labouring at the market and labouring at cafés and restaurants. Some received money from adult carers to get them through the week, others were financially self-sufficient, and some supported the elders in their family. Their dwellings included houses made of wood and concrete, government-built flats, and huts made of wood, MDF, corrugated iron and tarpaulin. Young people lived in a range of (shifting) family structures – with both parents, with extended families, with single parents, with neighbours, with and without siblings and cousins, with adult siblings and in one case with a partner and young son. The adult carers we met included mothers, grandmothers, aunts, a great grandmother, neighbours and the occasional father, and among these adults education levels ranged from incomplete primary schooling to diploma level. Adult carers were also engaged in a range of income-generating activities: street vending, market stall vending, mending shoes, washing clothes, day labouring at the port, cleaning, waitressing, motorcycle taxi driving, day labouring at the market, recycling rubbish, factory work and construction work. Household incomes varied, but none came close to those of the wealthy families. A few households had savings about the equivalent of a month's earnings and most households had debts to local, informal money lenders – some so large that the borrowers could see no way of repaying and were considering absconding.

With the exception of three young people who spoke fluent English, our conversations with slum dwellers took place in Thai, with Ganya or Note leading and me taking an increasingly confident role as time went on and I became more familiar with official Thai, with the north-eastern dialect that had travelled with rural migrants into the verbal landscape of the slum, and with some of the slang that found common expression among young residents. We recorded our more formal interviews whenever permitted, Ganya and Note later producing translated transcriptions which I got back-translated. I wrote copious notes and kept a fieldwork diary to record the everyday observations and interactions that were becoming more frequent and more intimate as time went on.

Bourgois, in his ethnographic study of crack dealers in New York's East Harlem district, notes how, 'in order to collect "accurate data", ethnographers violate the canons of positivist research' and 'become intimately involved with the people we study' (1995: 13). There are also a number of potential obstacles to this intimacy. My age was one – older than young people but not a real adult according to the usual markers such as marriage, childbirth or recognizable work. My gender was another – female yet trying to understand life for boys and young men as well as girls and young women. My race (white) and educational status were also potential obstacles to intimacy, and my relative material wealth was noted – an explicit source of jealousy for some, a prospective source of money for others and a constant reminder of the injustice of a socio-economic system that privileges a few and punishes the majority. All of these were potential challenges to the interpersonal intimacy required of ethnographic fieldwork. But the slow budding of friendship worked to forestall the possible distance posed by these identity-related obstacles. And yet herein lay a problem. It was partly because of these friendships that I later found it so hard to pull back from the everyday concerns, preoccupations and struggles of individual people and see the patterns and theories that could apply to them as a group. And it is because of these friendships that I initially hesitated to analyse and represent people in ways that could be construed negatively.

Life Back Home

My fieldwork came to an end in the autumn of 2006. I gave away the few luxuries I had bought – a kettle, a fan, a reading lamp – packed up what remained and said my goodbyes. I returned to the UK, and although home and dry, found myself all at sea with the piles of inchoate data I had amassed – voice recordings, transcripts, journals, fieldwork notes and newspaper cuttings – and the pile grew as I stayed in touch with some participants via email, telephone and social media and a return visit to Bangkok in the summer of 2007.

Through extensive coding and analysing all of this data, the notion of *searching for a better life* emerged as a particularly prominent and encompassing issue, and within this, certain areas of everyday practice stood out: young people's engagement in global youth cultures (*living the teenage life*), their efforts to support their families (*doing the right thing*) and their endeavours to escape material hardship (*forging the future*). In this study, exploration of 'a better life' is restricted to those aspects that were most apparent during fieldwork, although it should be recognized as an even broader phenomenon.

I initially interpreted young people's attempts to build better lives as successful and I interpreted them as exerting a significant degree of control over their lives and identities and the circumstances in which they live. On reflection, there were three main reasons for this interpretation: first, a prior alignment with the not-so 'new' social studies of childhood, which is heavily geared towards seeking out and emphasizing young people's agency; second, my closeness to participants and their own understandings of themselves and their situations; and third, the high value placed on maintaining one's public image and not 'losing face' within Thai culture. On many occasions and in many ways, participants constructed themselves positively and as successful, or at least as hopeful of success.

However, as time elapsed after fieldwork, during which I became more immersed in the data and more distant from participants, it became clear that 'success' stories were often relatively short-lived, and that situations can and do change all too readily. I had '[got] so close to [my] subjects that [I] end[ed] up parroting their point of view without linking [it] to the broader system of material and symbolic relations that give it meaning and significance' (Wacquant 2002: 1,523). As the physical and emotional distance between myself and participants grew, I became increasingly aligned to other literatures, in particular those studies that revealed the contradictory and negative outcomes of everyday practice, and I began to see that the participants in my study might not be that different from those in other critical ethnographies, in their socio-economic positioning and in the related implications for the outcomes of agency.

A Note on Ethics

It is customary in studies about children and young people to include a section dedicated to the discussion of research ethics, said to warrant special attention on the basis that disparities in power between adult researchers and young participants are particularly heightened, for example making withdrawal difficult on the part of young people. There is an implicit understanding here of the way power operates in the context of social research – that it mirrors the structural positions occupied by privileged, adult researchers and underprivileged, juvenile participants. There is clearly truth in this, but it is a simplification. While I occupied a privileged position in relation to young people in terms of several axes of social difference, they would readily, and skilfully, turn research events to their own advantage – into the opportunity to flirt with someone they were attracted to, substituting their own activities for the ones I had planned, turning research activities into karaoke sessions, and sometimes using their participation in the research as a means of achieving something for themselves such as help in learning English. Or they would vote with their feet and not turn up at all.

These routine discussions of research ethics are often limited to explanations of how informed consent was sought, how anonymity and confidentiality were ensured and how harm was avoided. While clearly fundamental to conducting ethical research, in the course of ethnographic studies each of these can become increasingly complex. Over time, the boundaries between research and non-research time, between one's role as researcher, friend, neighbour, customer and service user can become more and more blurred. I probably did not inform every single person whose views have shaped this study that their narratives might be taken into consideration, and it is possible that even key informants momentarily forgot my research purposes in the course of everyday interaction, thereby problematizing the assumption of ongoing consent that is properly informed. Increasingly, there were instances when my role as researcher was not obvious – during leisure time when research was not my primary intended activity but when relevant issues surfaced. Mindful of this, I would try to remind people of my role as a researcher, for example commenting that I might write about particular issues or events as they happened. But on the whole, this was met with a peculiar look or an exasperated instruction to 'stop working and relax'.

Anonymity is complex. Changing people's names is a start, and I have done this with all participants in writing up this study. But often this is not enough, and researchers try to disguise other aspects of people's identities as well as the location in which the study has taken place. To this end, I have changed certain biographical details, making it harder for those who do not already know participants to identify them. But for those who do know participants, they may well be recognizable; to change someone's details so completely that they are not recognizable even to people who know them would be to risk crossing an admittedly blurry line towards altering the data that in turn shapes the story I tell. I have not altered the name or location of Khlong Toey slum, and I have made this decision with three main things in mind. First, I do not believe that naming the location will put participants, or others, at risk of harm. Second, the particular history and characteristics of Khlong Toey slum are pertinent to certain aspects of the story I tell, and these are discussed where relevant in the text. Third, the history and characteristics of the slum are important in a broader sense: this particular slum has enjoyed a certain degree of resident activism and significant NGO presence, and although the different communities that comprise it are heterogeneous, with different demographic and socio-economic profiles, these arguably make life for the young people living there *better* than life in other slums. The history of activism and NGO presence also arguably make the chances of success in trying to build a better life all the greater. In short, the participants in this study were the more fortunate slum dwellers, whose communities are relatively well served and who have had a voice in debates over the 'slum problem' in Thailand. For other young people in other slum communities in Bangkok, and in Thailand's other cities, life and the chances of improving it will no doubt be even harder.

Confidentiality was also at times something of a misnomer, especially in the slum where the notion of privacy seemed at odds with local norms governing social interaction. Group activities, individual interviews and everyday conversations would often become public events with audiences, as strangers and people known to us stopped by to see what was going on, listen in and sometimes join the discussion.

Avoiding harm in ethnographic research with children and young people is especially complicated. Morrow and Richards (1996) argue that adult researchers have an ethical obligation to protect young people at risk from harm, but it is by no means clear what this entails in practice (Montgomery 2007). Even avoiding physical harm is not always straightforward – should I have tried to stop Ide injecting herself with methamphetamines? How? If I had known that she was on a drug rehabilitation programme and was being supported by key workers run by a local NGO, and if I had been quicker to process what was happening, perhaps I could have gone to find somebody to help, but at the time I had no idea of the context surrounding the incident. Was I right to pay Note for the work he did, guessing that he might spend it getting drunk and riding a motorbike through the streets of Bangkok? If I had refused to pay him, would that not have been exploitative? How would I have felt if my funders had refused to pay me on the basis that I was putting myself in harm's way by the very act of living in Khlong Toey slum?

The complications around avoiding harm become magnified in research that deals with the range of emotional, psychological and social experiences, that evokes painful emotions and memories that cause distress. In a more formal interview, we can give people the option to pause or terminate discussions or not answer particular questions altogether, although even here a certain harm has arguably already been inflicted in the very sparking of a particular memory or setting in train of a troubling thought process. But in ethnographic research, we are there all the time, trying to understand everyday life as it takes its natural course. In a context where life is pressured and hard and where violence is part of the everyday fabric – albeit widely seen as wrong – doing research in a way that avoids harm would entail missing a crucial part of the story.

Discussions of ethics in studies of children and young people are often found tucked away in a discrete section at the end of a discussion of data collection methods, as if ethics are only applicable 'in the field' and are amenable to being neatly packaged up and considered in isolation from the broader processes of research design, reading, analysis and writing. Although this is understandable – such discussions have to go somewhere – it is perhaps misleading.

My initial decision to research with young people at different ends of the socio-economic spectrum, and later to focus on those in slum communities, speaks of a concern about socio-economic inequality and a desire to speak out against it somehow, and in this sense this study has been an 'ethical' undertaking from the outset. This is in line with the urban ethnographies that have emerged from the more radical corners of academia in the United States over the past few decades and especially with the more recent move towards 'public anthropology' and 'public sociology', which attempt to extend research knowledge beyond the academy, make it accessible to wider audiences and use it to support progressive social change. These movements are underpinned by a concern with injustice and an aspiration to use anthropological and sociological knowledge in order to address it (for example, see the Center for a Public Anthropology[3]).

Moreover, ethical considerations are inseparable from the processes of analysing, interpreting and representing people's experiences in a way that strikes an appropriate balance between analysis and awareness of structural inequalities on the one hand, and compassion and respect for those whose stories we tell on the other. As someone entrusted with the power to define and represent others in a position of structural disadvantage, I have done my best to make sure that the story that follows does justice to some of the prevailing issues and problems of its time and to the people whose lives it tries to capture.

Notes

1. Wellbeing Research in Developing Countries (http://www.welldev.org.uk).
2. This was the Thai name my host family gave me. It means Lotus and is a common name given to foundlings in hospital before they are properly named.
3. http://www.publicanthropology.org/.

Part II

4

Living the Teenage Life

This chapter discusses what was referred to among research participants in the slum as *cheewit wairoon*, or 'the teenage life'.[1] It opens with fieldnotes that describe a typical Friday evening in the lives of a group of young men and a group of young women, before offering some preliminary notes concerning the scope of discussion in the chapter and an outline of the key elements selected for investigation. It then explores some of the prominent meanings that young people attached to the practices outlined, the outcomes of those practices and some of their unintended side effects. It also points to the salient elements of the context in which participants are located and to the paradoxes that characterize their endeavours to live the teenage life – the contradictory ways in which their practices are at once widely condemned yet required of them by the consumer market. Discussion then turns briefly to the experiences of wealthy participants and points to some of the similarities and differences in living the teenage life according to socio-economic status. The chapter ends by reiterating the adverse outcomes of agency in living the teenage life, highlighted in the selected elements of the theoretical framework.

Fieldnotes

It is 6 p.m. on Friday night and Arun, Jim, Som and Em, or Bodyfit as they call themselves collectively, arrive at the community gym. The gym opens between 5 p.m. and 8 p.m. six days a week, and Bodyfit are among the twenty or so young people who attend regularly. They arrive together, as they usually do, saunter through the gates and find somewhere to warm up. Every so often they arrive with different hair; a new cut or style or a different colour. Today they have died their hair blond. Sometimes they arrive with a new gadget which they take turns to use and show to the captive audience of younger teenage girls who await their arrival and tease them mercilessly. Today, Arun has an MP3 player and sings loudly, in English, to a song he does not understand. Once Bodyfit have paid their respects to their elders at the gym, responded to comments about their hair and claimed a space in which to warm up, they begin the serious business of working out.

They take off their tops, feigning embarrassment when one of the girls calls out flirtatiously for someone to pass her a pair of sunglasses, start with a short warm up of stretches, bends and twists before collecting a set of rusty weights from a broken filing cabinet that serves as a store cupboard. Each day of the week they work on a different part of the body, and today they concentrate on their arms. As the evening wears on, the weights get heavier, the space taken up by the boys increases, and the noises that accompany their physical exertion get louder. They make frequent trips to the toilet inside the NGO, where they lean over the sinks to inspect their faces in the mirrors, pouting, fixing their hair, flexing their muscles and practising different body building poses. Halfway through the evening, P Sib, the gym's founder and instructor, brings out a full-length mirror and props it up against some railings. Bodyfit, along with the other boys and young men, set about covering themselves in body oil and take it in turns to pose in front of the mirror, seeing how long they can hold different positions, touching and complimenting each other, enquiring into the length of time it takes to develop certain muscles and looking beyond their own reflections to see who is watching them. P Sib passes around a few body building magazines and the boys pore over them and argue about which body is better and which they would have for themselves given the choice. The gym session ends, as it always does, with an arm wrestling competition and emphatic declarations of the evening's winner, which is usually Arun. At the end of the session, after a few last glances in the mirror, the Bodyfit boys help to pack away, pay their respects, sling their tops over their shoulders and swagger off, shoulders hunched, to Arun's house where they eat and get ready for their appearance at the internet shop.

They arrive at the internet shop at around 10 p.m. and stay, as usual, until around 1 a.m. when it closes, except for Jim who leaves to work for Arun's mother at midnight. The internet shop has a floor space of about twenty square metres, twenty-seven computers and countless stools and chairs, and is usually packed with young people. On most evenings there is a queue for computers, but Bodyfit rarely have to wait; they are friends with the owner's nephew who manages the shop, and always get at least two computers between them, close to the air conditioning, with web cams. Since the gym session, the boys have washed, styled their hair, applied body spray and dressed in baggy jeans, flip flops and sports tee shirts which they have modified by cutting a deep V at the neck to expose their chests, and cutting off the sleeves so that their recently sculpted biceps are on full display. They wear chunky silver chains around their necks, belts that sit loosely on their hips, and sunglasses, although it is dark outside and dimly lit inside.

Their arrival is met with teasing comments from some of the regular girls in the shop: 'who will you marry tonight?', 'you never told me you were a superstar', 'ooooh you're so high so', which in turn inspire flirtatious replies or the same feigned embarrassment shown at the gym, and always smiles that seem to speak of a contentment derived from being noticed. The boys go to their computers, order bottled fizzy drinks and begin setting themselves up for the evening's activities, uploading their favourite online games, playing hip hop music, adjusting the settings on the web cam to ensure the most flattering exposure, and opening the online networking programmes they use to meet and keep in touch with other young people. These preparatory activities are conducted with frequent glances to the other customers and towards the entrance to the shop, a way I suspect of keeping an eye out for anyone who warrants impressing.

Each of the Bodyfit members has a special online name, which they often use in their everyday interactions with each other, and always at the internet shop. These are English names and chosen on the basis of either 'sounding good', belonging to Western pop stars, reflecting the experience of unrequited love or indicating care and pride in physical appearance.

Bodyfit are masters of online multitasking. While new rounds of their favourite online game are uploading, the three of them who use myspace[2] check their accounts, update their profiles, upload new photos of themselves (usually flexing their muscles in body building poses) and send messages to other online networkers. Two members of Bodyfit use MSN Messenger, an online instant chat service that also allows users to build a profile and display photos, and additionally to invite other users to watch them via a web cam. They spend a good deal of time grooming themselves before they activate the web cams, fiddling with their hair, smoothing their eyebrows and arranging their tops to reveal their muscles. An informal and light-hearted competition exists between Bodyfit's three online networkers over the number, gender and nationality of their online 'friends'; the more the better, the more girls the better and the more girls from rich south-east Asian countries the better. Best of all a *farang* girl; when Arun made MSN contact with a white, English girl he met at a pub during her trip around the world, the entire clientele at the internet shop was informed and invited to look at her via the web cam. Tonight she is not online and at midnight I leave a rather dejected-looking Arun and make my way to Ganya's place.

Ganya has invited me to her room and then out to a club with her and two friends, and as I approach the building where we live, I hear giggles and tinny hip hop music coming from her open window. I let myself in and walk down the hallway, past piles of rubbish and broken machinery and the spirit house that sits in the old tree in the yard. I go up the stairs, past the graffiti of guns and hearts on the wall, onto the landing where someone has hung their washing over a bamboo pole to dry, and into Ganya's room where she, An and Su are getting ready. They have been to P Ning's beauty kiosk and had their hair curled, their nails painted and their eyebrows shaped and are now getting dressed and made up for the night. There is a low plastic table crammed with body creams, perfumes, lipsticks, blushers, eyeshadows, eyeliners, mascaras and boxes of earrings, and it grows increasingly chaotic as Ganya applies and reapplies makeup to everyone. When she is satisfied, she turns to her clothes rail and begins to assemble outfits for the three of them. Within half an hour, they are all standing in front of the cracked, full-length mirror giggling and clapping in admiration at their miniskirts, hot pants, spaghetti strap tops and high heeled shoes. Ganya puts the finishing touches to her ensemble – a huge pair of hoop earrings and some lip gloss 'to add a little mmmm', declares that she looks 'bling bling *leaow*' (bling bling now), and wonders aloud whether we will meet any rich, handsome men tonight.

We leave the house and head to the main road to hail a taxi. As we wait, Ganya gives An and Su some tips on how to walk. She struts a few paces down the street, pushing her bottom emphatically from side to side, then turns and waits for them to do the same. Amidst much giggling, they do, while Ganya issues instructions to stick their chests out, push their shoulders back, hold their heads high and be brave. In the taxi, Ganya gets a phone call from another friend whom she has planned to meet at the club, and although her friend is Thai, they hold their conversation in English, which An and Su admire and envy openly.

When we arrive at the club, we find a table and hover around it, shouting staccato sentences to each other and struggling to hear above the music. After a few drinks, Ganya shows An and Su how to dance, performing a routine that she devised through observing online hip hop videos at the internet shop and practising in front of the mirror in her room. She bends her knees and gyrates her hips, holds her arms above her head then runs her hands down her torso and up again, leaning forward to pout every now and then. An and Su try to imitate her but fall, laughing, against the table after a few seconds, and instead watch as Ganya edges her way closer to a group of young European men standing around a table in front of ours. When one of her favourite songs comes on ('Drop It Like It's Hot' by American rapper Snoop Dogg), Ganya beckons for An and Su to join her, and they look on as she reaches forward on every repetition of 'hot' and pinches each of the young men's bottoms in turn. Some of the young men react by returning the gesture. At 4 a.m., after several more drinks and numerous trips to the toilet to reapply makeup, marvel at the other clubbers' outfits and lament the relative shabbiness of their own, Ganya suggests we go home as she is teaching at 9 a.m. In the taxi, An and Su are keen to know what the men's bottoms felt like, and Ganya tells them that they will have to find out for themselves next time. They agree.

Young slum dwellers often prefaced or concluded their narratives and statements concerning the kinds of practices outlined above with phrases such as 'this is the life of teenagers' or 'this is the teenage life' (*cheewit wairoon*). Adult carers also made sense of certain practices common among young people with reference to *the teenage life*, often claiming that they never lived this life because it did not exist for them when they were younger.

The teenage life encompasses many facets, too numerous to capture here, including certain linguistic practices such as the use of slang, and particular types of relationship such as *gik* relations (casual alliances based on sexual attraction). Here I focus on a selected few – *tam hoon dee* (making a good body), *seu kong* (buying 'stuff'/commodity consumption) and *bai tiaow* (going out) – because they were particularly visible during fieldwork and particular sources of controversy in local and national discourses.

Tam hoon dee refers to the time and effort that young people put into fashioning their bodies and can be separated out into several constituent elements: grooming practices (the styling of hair, the manicure of nails, the application of body creams and fragrances, the use of makeup), sculpting practices (body building and working out, aimed at the production of particular body shapes and the accentuation of certain body parts), dressing the body in ways that indicate participation in current fashions (especially hip hop-inspired styles), adorning the body with jewellery and accessories (belts, sunglasses, bags) and moving the body in certain ways (walking with a swagger or a wiggle of the hips).

Seu kong refers to the purchase and use of commodities – especially branded ones – such as mobile phones, MP3 players, digital cameras, clothes, shoes, accessories, jewellery and internet time. This consumption does not necessarily entail having the actual money with which to sustain the purchase and use of these things, as indebtedness, borrowing and theft were not uncommon among young people, as was going without basic necessities in order to finance such consumption.

Bai tiaow refers specifically to locating oneself outside the home, unaccompanied by adults, in the streets, cafés and bars of the slum, and outside slum neighbourhoods in shopping malls, cinemas, karaoke booths, bowling alleys and cafés, and for older young people in the pubs, bars and nightclubs of Bangkok.

The boundaries between what I have separated out as discrete sets of practices were in reality blurred, but I treat them as distinct to aid analysis. The boundaries between everyday life for all in the slum and the teenage life were also porous – many of the practices characteristic of the teenage life were common to people of all ages, and it was often the *ways* in which practices were undertaken, the amount of time, money and effort put into them, the importance attached to them and the assumed intentions behind them rather than the practices themselves that defined them as peculiar to young people. Related to this, some of the adult carers were quite close in age to some of the young people, and some were likely to have aspired to the 'teenage life' themselves when they were younger, despite a common insistence to the contrary. The 'facts' of the matter are incidental; I draw on adult carer narratives not as windows into a past reality but for what they show of the ways in which contemporary young slum dwellers were perceived and defined by their immediate elders.

The meanings attached to the practices of the teenage life were also multiple and varied. Here I focus on a few in some detail to enable an in-depth analysis, and I attach particular meanings to particular practices. This is another analytical device; in reality, the meanings are probably applicable to a range of practices but I separate them out for the purposes of clarity.

So, what meanings do young slum dwellers attach to the different elements of the teenage life?

Looking *High So*

Young people commonly described their body work and consumption practices in terms of being *high so*, or *bling bling*, both of which are intended to denote wealth. Without the material resources that would actually substantiate their claims to wealth, trying to *look* the part took on a particular significance. Bodyfit, Ganya and her friends spent considerable amounts of time, money and effort that Friday night – and on many other occasions – in an attempt to create images of wealth, and pointed to the satisfaction they derived from being recognized by other slum dwellers in this way. Other young people were similarly keen to construct such images of themselves: as 22-year-old Sim commented, 'People they judge other people from their looks. If you don't dress very *bling bling* they won't see you. It's like that'.

On one occasion, an elderly staff member of a slum-based NGO said that he could not always tell young slum dwellers apart from others 'outside', such was the extent of their efforts to make themselves look *high so*. He said, 'They dress nicely and they have good shoes and mobile phones. You might never know they are poor people from the slum'. In a post-fieldwork email to Note, I commented that young participants seemed particularly preoccupied with looking *high so*, and he replied with the following:

> People judge and classify people by how wealthy they are. This may seem like superficial but it really matters in Thailand, especially when it comes to how people treat you. Unfortunately people in slum Khlong Toey are look down on as inferior by society. So people in slum Khlong Toey want to look good, like wealthy since society has such a negative perspective to them. People in slum Khlong Toey DREAM!! they dream BIG!! They want people in society to accept them and if society cannot so they will try and climb up until that point. (Note, email, April 2007)

Young people's attempts to create *high so* images were born in part of an awareness of their material status as *kon jon* (poor people), *kon chan dtam* (people of the low level) or *dek slum* (slum children), derived from living in Khlong Toey slum, and a desire to be free from the stigma these identities carried. During a life history interview, Sim reflected on her initial realization that society is comprised of those who 'have' and those who do not, and of the way in which this is reflected in how people dress:

> I started seeing the social things when I was about fifteen. I started to see how the society works. I was growing up and becoming a teenager and I could see the things around me, I could see the social. You have to understand it is different in the slum from outside. I can say the way people dress is different, my friends outside they are rich, they have very, very nice clothes, brand names shirts, expensive things you know, and when they're out they dress like princesses and it's very normal for them. It's like the look, you can tell the difference … Sometimes I got very upset that 'why? How come they have and I don't have?' I just kept asking, kept asking myself.

Other young people, particularly those who attended school outside slum communities,[3] recounted experiences of disputes with peers at school in which they were ostracized from friendship groups on the basis of being *kon chan dtam* or *dek slum*. The following excerpt is taken from a conversation with a young woman named Am:

> Well there was a big, serious fight with my friends at school … Mint was supposed to visit me and Fah but her boyfriend told her 'don't go because that place is shit, there is shit everywhere and the people there are low'. How could he say that? It really hurt me. Mint and the other girls in the group took his side, they didn't come and now she says that the people here are *kon chan dtam* … I know that some parents at the school want their kids to stay away from us because they are afraid of *dek slum*.

Am and the other young slum dwellers in this research tried hard to distance themselves from the low-level status imposed upon them in light of the poverty they experienced, and in this they relied heavily on their physical bodies, in this sense their main assets, adorning them as best they could with consumer commodities in an attempt to present themselves as high status and therefore socially acceptable.

However, escaping their low socio-economic status in this way was, in a sense, an elusive dream. They could only operate at the superficial level of appearances, and while the 'surface level' is enormously important in Thai social relations (as indicated for example in Van Esterik's [2000] book *Materializing Thailand*), having the material means with which to substantiate surface-level claims to high status is equally, if not more, significant.

In any case, young people's hard-won appearances did not really make the grade beyond the borders of the slum. Despite their best efforts to create *high so* images for themselves, participants continued to be identified by outsiders (and often to identify themselves) as *kon chan dtam*. While their carefully crafted appearances may have worked on other slum dwellers in terms of creating the illusion of wealth – especially on older generations, younger children and those experiencing extreme hardship – this illusion faded away all too easily when transposed outside of the slum environment. Trainers that were the envy of others at the community gym became tatty and defunct when they paced the floors of the city's glitzy shopping malls. Mobile phones, MP3 players and digital cameras that produced a queue of admirers and would-be borrowers at the internet shop became clunky and out of date alongside the latest models brandished across the enormous advertising billboards that towered above the expressways leading into the slum. *Bling* outfits that created intense excitement within the confines of the slum quickly became a source of discomfort next to the latest fashions paraded at the city's trendy nightclubs. Just as Mills notes in her study of migrant workers in Bangkok, the consumption patterns of people constrained by low incomes can provide 'only a weak approximation of up to date urban living' – there was always something better, something newer in the context of 'hypermodernity and intense commercialisation', and the ability to take proper command of the city's range of modern artefacts was 'partial at best' (Mills 1997: 47).

In addition to operating at the superficial level of appearances and not really achieving the desired images within the broader context, by trying to create the illusion of wealth, young slum dwellers unwittingly contributed to a perception of themselves as self-centred, materialistic teenagers. This perception applied in particular to young women. Ganya's father often despaired openly at the expense entailed in her evenings out, sometimes kicking her shoes around the room and calculating how many plates of rice he could have bought for the cost of one pair. Others were similarly unimpressed with the drain on financial resources and the self-interest assumed to define young people's actions. As the mother of one fifteen-year-old girl noted:

> My daughter has to have what others have, the good mobile phone, the clothes that are in fashion. In the past I wanted the things other people had but it wasn't important, I could be patient [*jai yen*, or cool heart] and just have the wish in my mind. It was just a wish, not something necessary. But now my daughter is so impatient [*jai rorn*, or hot heart]. She has to have these things. I tell her that we don't have money so it's hard to get these things, but she is not interested in my explanation. She thinks only of herself.

Commentary on the self-centredness and materialism of young men was relatively absent, but where it did exist was often more lighthearted, due in part to lower expectations of their orientation towards, and contributions to, the family (discussed more fully in the following chapter). When I interviewed the mother of a fifteen-year-old young man who had that day spent five hundred baht (the equivalent of her weekly income) getting his hair dyed blonde, she laughed heartily as she watched her son dancing on the other side of the street with his group of friends, all of whom had the same hairstyle, and declared, 'It's crazy, spending money on such hair. It's very expensive. Why doesn't he give that money to me? Ha ha ha'.

In Thailand there is a pervasive discourse that assumes a causal connection between material wealth and high moral status, riches being taken by some as physical evidence of accrued merit (*boon*). As noted in the Introduction, the accrual of merit is one of the fundamental principles within Theravada Buddhism and is achieved through the performance of good deeds, or 'wholesome actions' (L.K. Mills 1999: 73). As Montgomery remarks, also from research conducted in a Thai slum, 'Money is a symbolic assertion of merit because it is assumed that without merit there would be no ability to get money' (2001: 110). Conversations with participants revealed echoes of this sentiment: in discussions about the King of Thailand, people often stated that he is rich because he must have been very meritorious in previous life cycles. However, for young people in the slums, the *high so* image was only that – an image, one that was unsupported by material wealth and understood by adult carers to be sought at the expense of moral obligations to the family and related practical activities, particularly for young women. Without sufficient money to substantiate the appearance of material wealth and support their families to the degree expected of them, young slum dwellers – especially girls – were often cast as self-centred and their moral status thereby diminished.

The narrative of the self-centred, materialistic teenager was prevalent among adult carers in the slum, and this narrative existed within a complex and contradictory context in which self-interest, in particular in the forms of consumerism and materialism, were both publicly condemned and widely condoned. The following excerpt is taken from an article published in *The Nation*, Thailand's most popular English language newspaper:

> Today's youth tend to be superficial, self-indulgent and dependent on others … a privy councillor said yesterday. Phichit Kulavanich said he was worried that children were … becoming more and more materialistic. ('Councillor Slams Immoral Generation' 2005)

A few months later, in response to what was perceived and increasingly portrayed in the media as a morally questionable descent into materialism, the Thai Ministry of Culture proposed a nationwide project entitled 'Meet a Monk in a Quiet Corner', which entailed plans to place monks in shopping malls, aimed at steering people – and young people in particular – away from 'self-interested activities' such as shopping, and towards consideration of religious values. The Thai Minister for Social Development was quoted in an online article posted on the Australian Broadcasting Corporation website as saying: 'We could campaign for religion in places where teenagers gather' ('Monks to Rent Mall Space in Thailand' 2005).

This proposed 'Meet a Monk' scheme can be located within a broader national discourse known as Sufficiency Economy. This was formulated by the King of Thailand in the wake of the 1997 economic crisis, later codified within Thailand's 2007 Human Development Report (THDR07), and was the guiding philosophy of the country's Tenth National Economic and Social Development Plan (in place at the time of fieldwork). Sufficiency Economy thinking promotes a range of values, including integrity, honesty, perseverance, toleration [*sic*], and wisdom. However, it places specific emphasis on *moderation* and *responsible consumption*, and is applicable at the individual as well as household, community and national levels (United Nations Development Programme [UNDP] 2007: iii). Underpinning Sufficiency Economy thinking are the principles of Theravada Buddhism, explicitly cited in the THDR07 as the philosophical foundations of the Sufficiency Economy approach, although the report does note that these principles are 'not exclusive to any religion or culture as the logic is built around simple concepts of man [*sic*] and the world' (ibid.: 31). Of particular relevance here is Buddhism's orientation towards the renunciation of worldly goods, or material things, and ultimately of the self; of that 'troublesome and illusory "I"' (L.K. Mills 1999: 85).

It was in the context of the discourses sketched out here that the adult carer narrative of the self-centred teenager was produced and circulated, and through these discourses that young people were cast as failing themselves, their families, their culture and ultimately their country. Of course, this construction of young people is by no means specific to Thailand or its Buddhist orientation, although the form the construction takes varies in tone and texture from one context to another. Indeed, it seems to have become something of a *sine qua non* of modern societies, a reflection of the way in which global economic transformations are producing similar patterns in young people's lives, albeit in ways that are experienced and manifested locally.

At the same time as being widely condemned in young people (as well as in parents), lifestyles of materialism and consumerism are heavily endorsed and widely sought after in the contemporary Thai context. The media and advertising industries in Thailand grew enormously over the last few decades of the twentieth century, increasingly promoting goods and services associated with conspicuous consumption, as Thailand moved away from its agrarian roots and towards 'a new "middle class" lifestyle based on the growth of consumer capitalism' (Ockey 1999: 241). As Mills notes in her piece on modernity and marginality in contemporary Thailand, the country enjoys highly sophisticated modes of popular cultural production, notably television (and increasingly the internet), where conspicuous consumption is widely celebrated and where ubiquitous images of 'modern Thailand' and the luxury, convenience and status associated with them are promoted as highly desirable (M.B. Mills 1999: 34).

Khlong Toey slum is located in the heart of the inner city, a stone's throw from Bangkok's prestigious business and shopping districts and within easy reach of all of the city's main transport links, where the advertising of consumer goods, services and lifestyles is prolific. Bodyfit, Ganya, An, Su and their peers either had televisions at home or access to them at friends' and neighbours' houses, and all had potential access to the internet at local internet shops, where the promotion of 'up to date living' was extensive. In this context, young people – irrespective of their material means – were required to be 'responsible consumers', to renounce worldly goods and to replace consumption with religion, and yet the very logic of the economic system in which they were located requires their consumption, is dependent upon it.

Looking Sexy

Young slum dwellers also spoke of their body work and consumption practices in terms of looking *sexy*, and in this sense clothes were particularly important, especially the hip hop-inspired fashion that enjoyed a considerable following in the slum during fieldwork. For young women, this entailed wearing ostentatious jewellery, sleeveless tops, miniskirts, high-heeled shoes and heavy makeup (though not all of the time – the concept of *galatesa*, or 'time and place' was a strong orienting principle even for those widely accused of inappropriate presentations of the self). For young men, looking sexy entailed wearing baggy, low cut jeans, tee shirts that had been modified by cutting the fabric at the sleeves and neck, chunky neck chains, sunglasses, caps and trainers. For some 'metrosexual' young men, it also entailed wearing makeup. For the regulars at the gym, being sexy also entailed wearing as little as possible, at least during designated workout times.

Young people frequently cited items of clothing among their favourite material objects, and referred to the importance of being *sexy* in their explanations of why these things were important to them. '*Oooh sexy*' was a common way of praising a friend or acquaintance, just as '*mai sexy*' (not sexy) was a way of indicating that someone (usually me) had not made enough effort to make themselves sexually appealing.

Young people also attempted to emphasize their sexuality through forms of movement and embodiment. For young women, this included wiggling their hips from side to side as they walked, standing with their chests and bottoms sticking out and pouting their lips, while for young men it included walking with a swagger, their shoulders hunched forward and arms swinging in front of them from side to side. The physical body and forms of embodiment took centre stage in the tactics used by young slum dwellers to construct themselves in particular ways. However, as young people, and especially young women, attempted to make themselves look *sexy* through wearing certain items of clothing and habituating their bodies in certain ways, they fuelled perceptions of themselves as *sexually deviant*. The following excerpt is taken from the mother of two teenage girls, and is typical in its denunciation of young women's clothing:

> When my mother raised me she did it in the old-fashioned way, the same style as people in King Rama V period [laughing]. But now Western culture has come. Nowadays the clothes they wear, they are so small, like wearing underwear. It's changed so much, so quickly … We always wore *patung*[4] when I was young and I still wear it now. My mother wore *patung* too. But look at the way they dress today, such tiny clothes, spaghetti tops and short skirts. I can't accept this. They are very *bor bor* [pornographic].

Van Esterik discusses the privileging of the body as a site of meaning in Thai society, and notes that the 'body's appearance is critically important in interaction' because it is taken to reflect people's inner states (2000: 282). In the process of striving to construct themselves as *sexy* and acceptable in terms of the global youth culture industry through their sartorial and embodied practices, young women challenged expectations of female sexual modesty, thereby lending support to the notion that their inner states were marked by sexual indecency, that they were behaving immorally and posing a threat to the wider moral order.

The adult carer narrative on young women's sexual indecency, in particular relating to their sartorial practices, can be located within a broader national discourse that reached an annual peak during Songkran[5] for a number of years prior to fieldwork. At the time of the 2003 Songkran celebrations, the Thai government's Ministry of Culture attempted to establish a prohibition on young women wearing spaghetti strap tops:

> The Culture Ministry will ban spaghetti strap tank tops and hot pants in the upcoming Songkran celebrations – despite protests from young women. 'Wear a simple sarong', Culture Minister Uraiwan Thienthong said yesterday. Uraiwan will seek cooperation from major agencies to enforce the ban in all areas popular for Songkran water fights. 'Revealing clothes may induce sexual harassment', she added. ('Ministry Bans Tank Tops for Songkran' 2003)

Since 2003, in the run up to each year's Songkran celebrations, spaghetti strap tops and the young women who wear them have been routinely condemned by public officials within the Ministry of Culture, a condemnation underpinned by the Thai cultural norm – echoed in various local manifestations throughout the world – of female sexual modesty. In Thailand, young women are expected to be *riaproy*, which is variously translated as 'neat', 'orderly', 'polite' and 'modest' and carries overtones of sexual reserve. While in theory the concept of *riaproy* is age and gender neutral, during fieldwork it was used almost exclusively – and widely – in relation to young women, with reference to posture and movement as well as clothing. Being *riaproy* entailed a significant degree of bodily containment – a bowed head and limited movement of the hips and limbs, and clothes that conceal the body. Thaweesit, in her study of Thai women's gendered and sexual subjectivities, refers to 'a set of ideological discourses concerning being a "good" woman … that one should be virtuous, nurturing and monogamous', and she notes how 'Thai society emphasizes women's faithfulness and endurance in married life' (2004: 207). Similarly, Vuttanont et al., in their study of Thai teenagers' attitudes towards sex, note that in Thai society, 'girls are required to be docile, submissive, modest, and disinterested in sex until marriage' (2006: 2,069).

This cultural moral norm and the related repudiation of female sexuality exist in a context where the economy persistently promotes, and benefits from, the sexualization of young women, and increasingly men. At its most subtle, this sexualization can be identified in the provocative images of women found in advertisements for a vast array of consumer products. At its starkest and most pernicious, the benefit of women's sexualization to the economy can be seen in the (un)official sanctioning of prostitution. Thailand, and Bangkok in particular, is commonly referred to as the sex capital of the world, and its economy depends, to a significant degree, on women's bodies being sold in exchange for money. Montgomery notes:

> In an extraordinary and widely quoted statement by the Deputy Prime Minister of Thailand in November 1980, the existence of the sex industry was justified and acknowledged as the main tourist attraction. (2001: 99)

She goes on to cite a work by Ennew, which quotes the Deputy Prime Minister:

> I ask all governors to consider the natural scenery in your provinces, with some forms of entertainment that some of you might consider disgusting and shameful because they are forms of sexual entertainment that attract tourists ... we must do this because we have to consider the jobs that will be created. (1986, cited in Montgomery 2001: 99)

Although this statement was made in 1980, and while prostitution has not since seen such explicit official backing, it remains prolific in Thailand and especially in Bangkok, as does sex tourism and the local demand that helps to sustain it and the revenue that accrues. As Ganya, An, Su and their female contemporaries living in slum communities struggle to negotiate global and local sexualized notions of what it means to be young women, and as the moral panic and condemnation surrounding their sexuality quickens, the economy simultaneously demands their sexualization for revenue. They are damned if they do and damned if they don't.

Going *Inter*

Young people also spoke of their body work and consumption practices in terms of being *kon inter* (international people). To truly *go inter* (go international) – to have direct experience of rich, Western and south-east Asian countries – carried enormous symbolic value for the young people in this research. However, for the vast majority of them, this was a distant pipe dream. They could only imagine visiting or living in the places that they understood as the 'international' realm, so they aspired to align themselves with it in whichever ways they could. The very few who had travelled abroad were extremely proud of the achievement, held in high regard by peers and openly envied by the many who had not had such experiences. When 22-year-old Mim won a trip to Singapore to participate in an international computer gaming competition, he proudly declared at his celebration dinner, 'Now I *go inter*'. One of the guests at the dinner, 22-year-old Dome, told me later that evening that he was jealous of Mim because in his eyes Mim was *kon inter jing* – 'a true international person'. Dome also confided that he was jealous of others who hung out with English-speaking foreigners and spoke good English, indicating the presence of a hierarchy of experiences through which one could claim a more or less genuine international experience. When I spoke with Dome some time after this dinner, I asked whether he thought he would ever become *kon inter* like his friends. He replied that he would not, but that he was 'a little bit *inter*' because he spent a lot of time on the internet listening to American and Japanese pop songs.

For the majority of young slum dwellers, truly *going inter* – travelling to or living in rich countries – was not an option. For a few, the identity of *kon inter* was claimed through speaking English or having 'international' partners, and these practices carried a definite kudos in the slum. For older young women, particularly those who spoke English, befriending Western travellers – however fleetingly – also positioned them within the international realm, albeit on the periphery. Although in-person relationships (as opposed to those conducted online) tended to be relatively short-lived and limited to the time that Western travellers were in Bangkok, their symbolic value was high. Those who had received educational sponsorship from a slum-based NGO were also afforded a connection with the international realm through their correspondence with foreign sponsors. However, during fieldwork, I got no sense that these relationships functioned in the same way in terms of claims of *going inter* as the relationships forged by young people with young Western travellers. Most young slum dwellers, as in Dome's case, attempted to construct themselves as *kon inter* through online activities, through watching television programmes and listening to popular music from the West, Japan and Korea, through trying to follow Western and Japanese fashions, and for some – like Bodyfit, Ganya, An and Su – by emanating the embodied practices associated with hip hop culture.

For the young people in this study, attempting to identify as *kon inter* was in part a means of distancing themselves from the parochialism thought to be characteristic of slum life, including by many slum residents themselves. Older slum dwellers often referred to themselves as having 'no knowledge of the world', and many would laugh at what they called their ignorance of what lay beyond the geographical borders of the slum communities in which they lived and worked. Some referred to themselves using the offensive adjective *ban nork*, variously translated as 'uncivilized' and 'uneducated'. This self-deprecation mirrored a wider perception of slum residents as lacking in knowledge of the global sphere, knowledge that counts in contemporary times.

Statements such as the following, by the wealthy mother of a teenage girl, were characteristic in their positioning of 'Khlong Toey parents' as lacking knowledge of the wider world:

> I think the life is very hard for parents in slum Khlong Toey, they can't teach their children like we do because they don't have the same knowledge. At breakfast I can read *The Nation* with my daughter and teach her what is going on in the world, improve her in English at the same time. But in Khlong Toey I think no, these parents don't have the knowledge like this.

By attempting to construct themselves as *kon inter* by virtue of their body work and consumption practices, young people in the slum hoped to counter the perception that they had little or no knowledge of the wider world, to be free from the stigma of parochialism associated with slum living. The aspiration here was definitely *not* to forego their Thai identity; they were fiercely proud of being Thai – not least on account of not having been colonized – and often emphasized their Thai identity in other contexts. Rather, they aspired to add an international dimension to their self-images, which they could draw on as it suited them.

However, for most young slum dwellers, being truly international was an elusive dream. They could only enter the international realm in virtual, or proxy ways, and they continued to be constructed by outsiders, and in some cases to construct themselves, as parochial. Furthermore, in their attempts to construct themselves as *kon inter*, young people contributed to a widespread perception that they were turning their backs on Thai culture. The following excerpt is taken from a conversation with the mother of a seventeen-year-old girl and a fifteen-year-old boy, talking about some of the changes she had observed since she was young:

> PM Teenagers around here are very far away from Thai culture nowadays, they are not Thai people any more.
>
> SM What are they?
>
> PM They are *kon mai dee* [bad people], from *Pratet mai dee* [Badland].

The narrative of young people turning their backs on Thai culture found ample expression among adult carers in the slum, with Western culture (*watanatam farang*) usually held to account for enticing teenagers away from what were seen as their rightful cultural roots. In light of this, young people were commonly referred to – negatively – as *farang ki nok* (fake, inferior Westerners) whose spurious Western ways brought suffering in their wake. In response to my question concerning differences and similarities in the lives of young people now and when he was young, one father of a young woman in her twenties stated that 'Thai kids, when they see something new from the West, they have to have that thing … It drives them and their parents to suffer, to argue and get into debt'. Many other adult carers were similar in their antipathy towards what they perceived and experienced as Western imperialism and young people's concomitant abandonment of Thai culture in favour of the trappings of Western lifestyles. Interestingly, this perception was not mirrored by the adult carers of wealthy young people, who instead made it a priority to accompany their children into the international sphere, particularly through international travel, education and language acquisition. They recognized that this was necessary if their children were to be successful in life.

The perception of youth abandoning their cultural heritage can be located within a broader discourse concerning the deleterious effects of globalization on 'Thai culture' and 'Thai values', which in turn speaks of a profound anxiety concerning the moral order and the role of young people in threatening this. Throughout fieldwork, the newspaper *The Nation* was replete with headlines such as 'Morality losing ground',[6] 'Councillor slams "immoral generation"'[7] and 'Thais increasingly dissolute',[8] and these were followed by articles about how young people 'have not been steeped in traditional Thai values',[9] and about how the 'values, attitudes and behaviour of many Thai teens [are] in crisis because of excessive western influences'.[10] These narratives were widely echoed in various Thai language newspapers.

By attempting to *go inter* and claiming identities as *kon inter* in the ways available to them, the young people in this research unwittingly fed into the perception that they were abandoning their cultural heritage and thereby leading the country into a moral abyss. And yet young slum dwellers' attempts to construct themselves as *kon inter* and the moral panic associated with this exist in a context where government policy, promoted by multilateral financial institutions, prizes the Thai economy ever-further open to international trade and opens its doors ever-wider to international capital, where macroeconomic policy has 'incorporated Thailand … firmly within a global economy' (Baker and Phongpaichit 2005: 199), and where the labour of the urban poor has been used to facilitate this incorporation. Indeed, this openness to the global sphere has been a defining feature of Thai domestic and foreign policy since the reigns of King Mongkut and his successor King Chulalongkorn in the nineteenth century. In this sense, Thailand, or at least the Thai economy, represents the epitome of *going inter* writ large. Such a process is legitimated, indeed required, at the level of national and international macroeconomic policy, has been one of the key features of the country's economic transformation and remains one of the defining characteristics of its present economic orientation. And yet when Bodyfit, Ganya, An, Su and their peers in the slum attempted to align themselves with the international sphere in the ways available to them, they were readily condemned.

Being Modern

Young people spoke of their body work and consumption practices in terms of being 'modern' (*samai mai*) or 'developed' (*pattana leaow*) and in many ways this can be understood to encompass attempts to look *high so, sexy* and *international*. The following excerpt from a discussion with fifteen-year-old Naen on the subject of her mobile phone indicates something of the function of this object in constructing the self as a modern, 'developed' subject:

> The world has changed, we shouldn't sink back down to the world of nothing. Everyone in the world has mobile phones now and it's good to keep up. In the past, in my mum's time, they didn't have mobile phones because in the past Thailand wasn't developed. But we are developed now. We live in the modern world.

Mobile phones were prevalent among young people in the slum, and while not all shared Naen's ability to reflect on the broader socio-economic context of their possession, they clearly understood that mobile phones functioned to signify their participation in the modern world, that they were *the* critical contemporary accessory, a highly condensed symbol of status, popularity and modern identity – as useful for their symbolic, instrumental function as for intrinsic purposes. The following excerpt is taken from a discussion with fifteen-year-old Perapon, on the topic of the material objects most important to him:

> P The mobile phone is most important. Without the mobile phone I am not quite the same as others.
>
> SM Which others?
>
> P Everyone. Everyone has mobile phones nowadays.

The phrases *bat joo ban* (nowadays) and *samai mai* (the modern era) were prominent in participants' discussions, for young people in explanations of why certain things were important to them, and for elders in their narratives of despair at what they spoke of as negative qualities in the young generation. So strong was the desire to identify as modern that young people went to considerable lengths to do so. Experiences of theft were not uncommon during fieldwork, with expensive items such as digital cameras, mobile phones and MP3 players going missing, with friends or siblings being suspected of taking them, and with cycles of confrontation, denial and acrimony ensuing. Committing oneself to debt to friends and family or through hire purchase schemes, spending large proportions of one's income, saving considerable amounts of money for desired items and going without basic necessities were common practices in the drive to be modern. One young person, Gop, reported working every day throughout the summer holidays as a waiter in order to save ten thousand baht – almost three times his mother's monthly income – to buy the latest model of a mobile phone. The members of Bodyfit would sometimes go without dinner or pick at the lunch leftovers in the NGO canteen so that they had enough money to spend at the internet café later in the evening. At one time or another, Ganya, An and Su had all fallen behind with their rent contributions, but always made sure they had enough money to go clubbing.

For young slum dwellers, the eagerness to construct themselves as *kon samai mai* (modern people) was particularly significant as they were children or grandchildren of rural farming families whose poverty once pushed them off the paddy fields in the rural north-east of Thailand and into low-status manual labour in Bangkok's then burgeoning industrial sector, and whose 'old fashioned lives' (*cheewit samai gorn*), or elements of it, had followed them deep into the inner city and continued to inform the logic of everyday slum life. Comparisons of slum living with village life abounded throughout fieldwork, with older generations frequently referring to their slum communities as 'villages' and to themselves as rural, old fashioned people, pointing to how they ate rice every day, listened to *look toong* and *moalam* (Thai country music), dressed in *patung*, chewed *maag* and were uneducated. Young people understood that because of this connection between slum and rural 'old fashioned' life, they were seen by many as inferior. When I asked seventeen-year-old Bodyfit member Arun – an aspiring singer – if he had a favourite song at the time, he replied:

> Right now I like a song called *Jiem Doa* [to feel that you are not good enough for somebody]. It describes my situation. I like a girl but I am not good enough for her. Sometimes if I see her I sing a song for her, one that I made up. 'I am not that good, I'm from a poor family, my family is from the countryside. But I really hope that you accept me. I will try and change for you'.

Approaches towards rural people in Thailand are complex and contradictory. In a certain sense they are idealized and romanticized, celebrated in the popular imagination as the traditional, hardworking, rice-yielding 'backbone of the country', representing the vestiges of a happy and idyllic past, imagined though this may be (Montgomery 2001: 131). However, negative representations of rural people prevail, in particular of those from the Isan region where many of the participants' families originated. They were impersonated as clumsy buffoons in popular television shows, and were derided – and derided themselves – for being 'old fashioned' and 'as stupid as the buffaloes'. Young participants in the slum were well aware of their rural heritage and its association with backwardness and 'old fashioned ways', and of how this functioned to cast them as inferior, and they worked hard to distance themselves from the disrepute this brought.

For many adult carers in the slum, the modern era entailed two paths – the 'right' one and the 'wrong' one. According to them, the young people in their charge and in their neighbourhoods were taking the wrong path. The right path entailed supporting one's family and making use of the positive opportunities offered by the 'new civilization' to obtain a good education in order to get a well-paid, high-status job. The wrong path entailed, among other things, an orientation towards self-interest, manifested in particular through unsustainable practices of conspicuous consumption, increasing sexual depravity and the abandonment of Thai culture and values, all of which signalled a lack of consideration for the family and a threat to the wider moral order. Although young slum dwellers were also strongly oriented towards the 'right path' as defined by adult carers – wanting to support their families, get educated, find decent jobs and improve their material standards of living – this was often downplayed or conveniently forgotten altogether, leaving the narrative of the 'bad teenager' to circulate unfettered and dominate local discourse.

Displaying the Self

As well as spending considerable time, money and effort on body work and consumption practices, young slum dwellers were also powerfully oriented towards *bai tiaow* (going out), and of this they spoke often in terms of being seen. Evenings out were marked not only by a deep concern for appearances but by a strong impetus to display these to others and attract positive recognition in return. Arun verbalized this succinctly one evening at the gym: he was looking despondent, and when Ganya and I asked him what was wrong, he replied that he was feeling low because no one was taking any notice of him. He went on to say, 'All I want is for people to notice me'. He said he was disappointed because his efforts to look good were having 'no results', and when I asked him what a result might be, he said, 'People would notice me, appreciate my style'. He spoke of how much he was looking forward to the upcoming Strong Man competition, which was to be held in an exhibition centre on the outskirts of Bangkok, because there he imagined he would find a captive audience for the display of his carefully crafted biceps. He proceeded to describe in detail what he thought he might wear, and to show us photographs he had taken on his mobile phone, of himself posing in different outfits, asking us which one we thought would look best. On another occasion, Arun and the other Bodyfit members asked Ganya and me if they could accompany us to an English class we were teaching, and despite their professed desire to learn, they managed to turn the lesson into a fashion show, parading up and down the classroom in their hip hop outfits, adding one accessory after another until they were wearing about three each, nipping out to the toilets every now and then to spruce themselves up.

For other young participants in this research, displaying the images they put so much effort into creating was also of utmost importance. When they were out, their branded mobile phones, MP3 players and digital cameras – owned, given, borrowed or stolen – were on display, regardless of whether they were using them and often regardless of whether or not they actually worked. Fleeting comments and detailed discussions of these and other products, especially branded clothing, formed significant features in the verbal landscape of their social interaction, and they clearly delighted in any positive attention given to the appearances they forged. The few who spoke English made a deliberate point of doing so – loudly and emphatically – when they were out, with fleeting glances around to see who might be listening. Carefully crafted postures and well-practised movements were given ample expression on the streets and in the cafés and bars of the slum and outside, and explicit displays of affection among peers were common, with young people often seen holding hands, linking arms and play fighting in public places. All of these practices spoke of a keen desire to be seen and appreciated by other young people.

Going out was also a means of trying to augment the modern image one had worked so hard to fashion. When I went out to a new nightclub, bar or restaurant with friends from the slum, and when we visited the newly opened Siam Paragon (a five-storey shopping mall replete with designer shops and bedecked with courtyard fountains, twinkling lights and hundreds of square metres of immaculate glass walls), they would speak of their excitement at being somewhere so *high so* and how it made them feel *piset* (special), as if being in these places meant that they might soak up some of the high status associated with them.

However, displaying and attempting to augment one's image made for a very precarious balancing act. Young people from the slum easily assumed an inferior status once they traversed its geographical boundaries, as seventeen-year-old Som discovered when he attended the wedding of an ex-girlfriend, with whom he had broken up because – in his eyes – he was not rich enough:

> An and her new boyfriend got married a couple of months ago and I went to the wedding. It was in the Dusit Thani hotel. But I only stayed for an hour because everyone was wearing suits and ties and I was only wearing a tee shirt. I like that tee shirt, it looks *bling bling* to me, but they all had suits on. I don't have a suit. I tried to look smart but I am not like them. They looked down on me.

After recounting this experience, Som went on to say, self-mockingly, that he was 'just a *dek slum*', and when I asked what he meant, he replied, 'Well, maybe we're not supposed to go to those *high so* places'. At this point, Ganya interjected to say that she went to *high so* places and that she thought anyone should be able to if they wanted to, no matter where they were from or how much money they had. To this, Som replied that Ganya was different, she had a high education and spoke English and had friends like me. Som's experience and the way in which he decoded it reveals something of his internalization of the social hierarchy and his sense of his own place within it, blaming himself for contravening the rules of that hierarchy when his self-styled modern image did not make the grade.

In their attempts to negotiate the minefield of status construction and display their images as modern youth, producing their bodies for consumption by others, young people in the slum – and in particular young women – fuelled a perception that they were transgressing the cultural norm of passivity, promoted in Thai society as an 'ultimate virtue' (Montgomery 2001: 111). Narratives such as the following, by the mother of a teenage girl, were common:

> Today teenagers like to show off. In my time it was not like this, it was forbidden, we had to keep ourselves quiet and private, not show our feelings, but teenagers today they don't do this. They show off everything, they think this is normal, but I am from the old days so I think it's not good. If you ask me they are too arrogant.

Linked to the perception that by displaying themselves so explicitly young people were demonstrating an unprecedented arrogance, many adult carers interpreted young people's practices of display as a symbol of disrespect to elders, which in turn was taken as an affront to the system of seniority – one of the most fundamental organizing principles of Thai society. In her interview, a mother of three young women commented:

> In the past we really respected adults, we used to hide ourselves from them, try not to bother them. When we had to walk past an adult we bent our backs and apologized, made ourselves lower than them. I remember I used to be scared of adults, I wanted to disappear if I saw them! Now teenagers are not afraid like this, they don't try and hide themselves like we did. They want to show themselves, show themselves to everyone. Nowadays they are so arrogant. For me this is not respectful, they don't respect the adults any more. It seems like the adults are supposed to respect them nowadays.

Commentary criticizing the public display of the self tended to be aimed at young women. These practices of display were derided by adult carers for reflecting a shift away from hiding the self or adjusting it to seniors and towards brandishing the self, and for thereby challenging age-related norms of personhood. And yet this display is precisely what is required of young people in a socio-economic context that increasingly promotes, and is increasingly dependent upon, *conspicuous* consumption.

Addiction to Friends

Young people also spoke of going out as a way of spending time with friends, and for young women in particular this was coupled with attempts to free themselves from experiences of servitude and violence at home within the family. The following excerpt is taken from a conversation with 22-year-old Sim:

> At home there were too many people and too many problems. And my aunty wanted me to be like a servant in the house, 'Why don't you clean, wash the dishes, sweep the floor? Do the housework', like that. She hit me when I didn't do the things she wanted. So you know I started hanging out with my close friend, she took me away from the problems at home. This was when I was about fifteen. We went out all the time, hanging out together. We enjoyed hanging out together more than being at home.

For Sim and the others who echoed her desire to escape negative experiences at home, friendships were seen in part as a sanctuary, although they also functioned in much more complex ways. Young people spoke of the different worlds created and inhabited by them and their friends as opposed to the world of parents, which was often experienced in part as oppressive. Going out was one of the major ways in which young people found refuge in their friendships.

However, by spending so much time with friends, young people contributed to a narrative concerning a new and dangerous addiction. From early on in fieldwork, the phrase *dit puan* (to be addicted to friends) arose as a stock feature in adult carer interviews and everyday conversations about young people. This can be understood as a way of signalling disapproval of the latter's (and in particular young women's) practical and emotional attachment to selected peers and assumed concomitant neglect of the family and duties towards it. The following quote is taken from an interview with the mother of four young women:

> Kids today don't see the importance of family occasions like we did in the past. Mother's Day is supposed to be when children spend time with their mother and pay respect but now when we have public holidays all they do is go out with their friends ... The value of these public holidays has changed. In my day it was a time to spend with your family but nowadays children see it as time to hang out with their friends. They should call it Friend's Day. They are too addicted to their friends.

What was portrayed by adult carers in relatively simple terms as a new and problematic process whereby young people were forsaking their duty to the family in favour of friends and fun, was experienced by young people in much more ambivalent ways. On the one hand, young slum dwellers saw their friends as sources of support in both material and emotional terms, turning to them for money, food, shelter, comfort, advice and a non-judgemental ear, and as crucial elements in the audience for one's carefully constructed image. On the other hand, friends often made precarious and fragile support mechanisms; they too were poor, had unstable home lives and were equally caught up in the struggle to compete for social status. The following excerpt is taken from a conversation with seventeen-year-old Jim, one of the members of Bodyfit:

> Now I'm going to talk about Som. Actually, there is something I don't like about his way. He acts differently when there are girls around. I know it's natural for boys to pose when girls are around. I do that, too. But Som always poses by burning his friends, especially me, in front of girls. Once we met a group of girls and he hit me on the head and told them that I'm stupid. He called me a buffalo in front of them. Maybe I am not as clever as him. Maybe I won't be as successful as him ... still I think he should respect me.

In a context where status, image and appearance were highly valued, and where slum dwellers were alternately pitied and derided, young people struggled fiercely to carve out positive identities in part by competing with their friends for recognition. While adult carers bemoaned and simplified young people's alignment with their friends and through it constructed young people as bad, this alignment is increasingly useful to the consumer market, as the latter extends its reach into this sphere of young people's lives, including and perhaps intensifying its competitive aspects: profit-seeking marketers now pursue and gain 'unprecedented access to children's social worlds through widespread "peer to peer" (i.e. child to child) marketing' techniques (Schor 2008: 486).

In addition to weakening their moral status, the young slum dwellers in this research also undermined their own material advancement through their engagement in the teenage life. Time and money spent with friends, hanging out, fashioning the right bodies and consuming the right products was time and money detracted from studying and saving. The following is a particularly potent example of this, but serves nonetheless to illustrate a commonly felt tension between the present-day orientation towards the teenage life and future material advancement.

Ning was seventeen years old when I met her, and lived with her two younger brothers and her aunt and uncle in a small wooden hut in one of Khlong Toey's more peripheral communities. Her parents lived nearby but worked such long hours – her mother as a casual labourer and her father as a taxi driver – that they had to leave their children in the care of relatives. Ning dropped out of school when she was fifteen because the family was experiencing such financial difficulties that they could not afford the costs of her education. For a couple of years after leaving school, Ning helped out on her aunt's food stall and while doing this met a member of staff who worked at a slum-based NGO. As their acquaintance grew, this man came to recognize Ning's linguistic abilities and persuaded her to apply for a scholarship to complete her upper secondary education with a view to applying for an assisted place on an International Baccalaureate scheme abroad. Ning's application was successful and when I met her she was studying for her upper secondary exams and enrolled on an intensive English course at the NGO to prepare for studying abroad. Conversations with her revealed something of the struggle to manage the tension between living the teenage life and future material advancement:

> It's hard for me to manage my time. I love to have fun and hang around with my friends, it's so hard for me to put everything in the schedule and I always mess up. I want to study, I want to be good at English so I can go to study abroad but nowadays I always seem to spend time with my friends. I don't know why, because I know when I'm with them I'm not studying. Right now, I am so stressed because I cannot catch up with all the learning. I know this isn't good, I feel like I should manage my time better, spend more time studying. Actually, I feel very torn about what I should do. When my friends call me, when I know they are hanging out together I just want to be with them. We usually go out, hang around together, just hang around in the shopping mall, eating together, buying things, this and that. But I know that studying is more important so that I can go abroad and get a good job and have a good life when I am older.

Through continued post-fieldwork correspondence via a mutual friend, I learned that leading up to her exams Ning became more and more involved with her group of friends and less oriented towards her studies. She did not turn up to one of her English exams, and although she was allowed to sit it later on, she did not do very well. Despite this, the NGO appealed on her behalf and she was offered a place at an international college abroad. However, on her return trip to Bangkok during a college vacation, Ning became pregnant and dropped out of school again. While Ning's story is specific in its detail, it illustrates well the way in which young participants, through the lure of the teenage life, can undermine their own chances of improving their material standards of living.

While the practices of the teenage life and the meanings that young people attached to them speak of a sense of agency among young slum dwellers, they gave rise to a strong sense of disorder among adult carers. Among the more poetically inclined, metaphors abounded in the attempt to capture this feeling, with evocations of a 'tragic gap' having emerged between young people and older generations in the wake of the 'new civilization', the disappearance of 'borders' that once kept young people, and especially young women, close to their families, and the uncomfortable coexistence of 'different worlds' or 'different eras'. The father of one young woman spoke of the difficulty he had following his daughter in the 'new world':

> The world is spinning every day and I see my daughter has jumped on it. I stand still while it goes past and leaves me behind. The young people move with the new world and the parents stand still watching it spin … It's hard for me to follow her in the new world. The new generation is in the new world. It is hard for the parents.

Among wealthy parents, I observed nothing like the sense of generational disjuncture or lack of control expressed by adult carers in the slum. On the contrary, while anxiety about their children's vulnerability in contemporary times was considerable, so too was the control they were able to exert over their children and their experience of the world their children inhabited. Wealthy parents were able to escort their children almost everywhere, except into the classroom, and if this was not possible, older siblings or domestic servants did. They chose and monitored their children's after school, online, weekend and holiday activities carefully. To a degree, they controlled their children's choice of friends by selecting schools or curricula therein attended by children from similar backgrounds, and they voiced their concerns at the highest level of the school if they perceived their children were being led astray by peers. Perceived risks were dealt with by wealthy parents through this exertion of control, control that only money could buy. This did not go uncontested by their children, for example through arguments over the degree to which they were given freedom to travel on their own, but nonetheless seemed to be all encompassing and bound parents and their children closely together in particular ways.

Related to this, while wealthy young people were also objects of the wider pejorative discourses concerning Thailand's moral decay – as indeed were parents – and while their market saturation was evident in their consumption and related practices, thus aligning them in certain ways to their poorer counterparts, for them, being teenagers did not invite the same degree of moral questioning from elders. Their immediate elders were themselves living *high so*, international, modern lives and did not require their children's assistance in the ways that adult carers in the slum did. Wealthy young people's practices were underpinned by the financial resources necessary to make being modern subjects a material reality and not just a matter of shaky appearances. For wealthy young people, education – during the school day, after school and at weekends – was by far the dominant practice in their lives and one that was widely legitimated.

The Adverse Outcomes of Agency

Living the teenage life and all that this entailed in terms of actively constructing modern identities through body work, commodity consumption and display was a central feature of young slum dwellers' aspirations – something they were positively geared towards and which took up a considerable amount of their time, effort and resources. It formed a fundamental orienting principle in their everyday life-worlds. In this sense, the exercise of agency in this sphere of activity emerged with force.

However, it also entailed adverse outcomes. Even when young slum dwellers exercised agency in constructing themselves as modern subjects, the dream remained somewhat elusive. They entered the game on such disadvantaged terms that they had little choice but to operate at the level of appearances, without the material resources necessary to substantiate their identity claims. Once those carefully constructed appearances were transported outside the slum, they were, and could only ever be, pale approximations of the real thing. Furthermore, the exercise of agency in living the teenage life impacted negatively on young people's endeavours within other realms of everyday practice – in their attempts to do the right thing by their families and to improve their material circumstances. These processes are illustrated in highlighted elements of the theoretical framework diagram (Figure 4.1).

In attempting to enhance their socio-economic status in the ways most readily available to them, exercising agency within a cultural field at their disposal, young slum dwellers not only failed to make the grade, they inadvertently weakened their moral status and thereby unwittingly reinforced their subordinate subject positions within other spheres of action. By attempting to elevate their status through practices of unsustainable consumption, and distance themselves from the image of poverty associated with slum living, they unwittingly reinforced their positioning as self-centred, materialistic teenagers. By augmenting and expressing their sexuality, they inadvertently shored up their positioning as sexually deviant. By attempting to identify as international subjects and refuting the parochialism associated with slum life, they unwittingly lent support to others' constructions of them as cultural defectors. By trying to construct themselves as modern youth in the only ways available to them, and resisting the backwardness associated with slum life, young slum dwellers were cast as knowingly walking the wrong path offered by the modern era. By displaying their modern selves and thereby challenging the interconnected, more traditional norms of passivity and seniority, they further contributed to their positioning as arrogant and disrespectful of seniority. By identifying with friends – and for many young women rejecting negative experiences at home – young people once again contributed to the doubt cast on their moral status, as their alignment with friends was taken to signify an abandonment of the family, irrespective of other practices to the contrary.

Young people's engagement in the teenage life also functioned to undermine their efforts towards future material advancement: resources directed towards enabling participation in 'modern' youth lifestyles were resources unavailable for studying or saving.

Participants were widely condemned by virtue of their attempted engagement in these practices, and yet this engagement

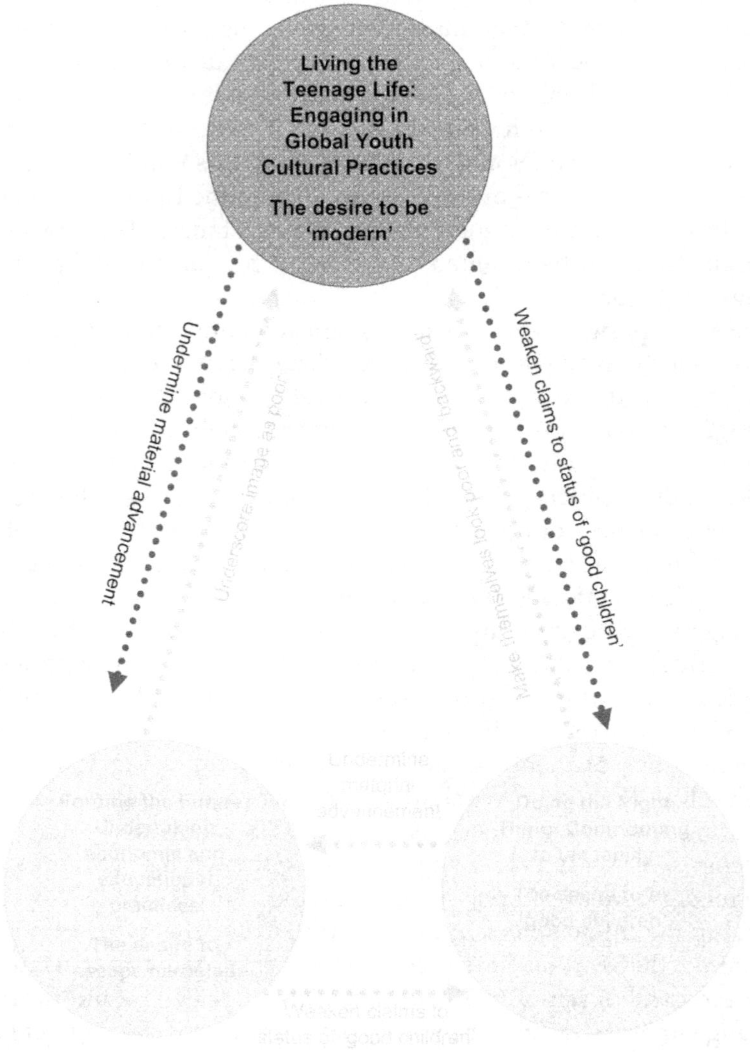

Figure 4.1. Diagram showing that global youth cultural practices can be tenuous and have unintended, negative outcomes.

was demanded of them by market forces, was 'eminently desirable' throughout Thailand (M.B. Mills 1999: 34), and was a relatively uncontroversial reality for those with money. In this, marginalized youth living in urban poverty can be seen as fall guys for the tensions that arise from the national pursuit of consumer capitalism and the nation's incorporation into the global economy.

Notes

1. As noted in Chapter 1, while the English term 'teenager' refers to thirteen- to nineteen-year-olds, participants in this research use it with reference to those between the ages of around fifteen and twenty-two.
2. The fieldwork for this study was conducted before Facebook became so ubiquitous.
3. The community school in the central hub of Khlong Toey slum communities teaches up to lower secondary level, and those continuing education beyond this stage travel outside their immediate neighbourhoods to other schools. Also, some of the slum communities are located nearer to other schools than the one in the central hub.
4. A long, tube-shaped cloth skirt.
5. Thai New Year, which spans three days in April and is widely celebrated (largely by young people) through street parties and public water fights.
6. *The Nation*, 30 June 2005.
7. *The Nation*, 20 August 2005.
8. *The Nation*, 31 August 2005.
9. *The Nation*, 20 August 2005.
10. *The Nation*, 26 September 2004.

5

Doing the Right Thing

This chapter discusses the contributions that young slum dwellers make to their families. It begins with fieldwork notes that detail a day in the life of several young people, focusing on the various forms of assistance they provide for their families. Following these fieldnotes is an outline of the categories within which their practices can be understood and the key patterns associated with them. Discussion then turns to young people's understandings of and feelings about the contributions they make to their families, and points to certain consequences and side effects of their endeavours. It then explores the tension that exists between attempting to contribute to the family and live the teenage life and investigates the ways in which young people approach this tension, pointing to further unintended outcomes. The chapter ends with a recap of the adverse outcomes of agency in contributing to the family, represented by the highlighted elements of the theoretical framework.

Fieldnotes

It is 4 a.m. and seventeen-year-old Jib gets up to begin her household chores.[1] She sweeps the floor of the small wooden house where she lives with her parents, washes the dishes from the previous night's dinner under the communal tap, and fetches breakfast for herself and her parents from one of the nearby early morning food stalls. After eating breakfast, her parents leave for work – her mother to clean offices and the rooms in a rental apartment block, her father to deliver a consignment from the port to the north of Thailand. Jib gets dressed and cleans the breakfast dishes before she begins the washing, which she does by hand in a plastic bucket in the alleyway outside her house. She hangs the washing out to dry and at 7 a.m. leaves for school. Both of Jib's parents work between twelve and fourteen hours a day, and Jib has full responsibility for the household chores.

Half a mile away in another community, thirteen-year-old Gop gets up to help her grandmother run her coffee stall, which is open every morning between 4.30 a.m. and 7.30 a.m. She sets up a few tables and chairs outside the two-roomed concrete house where she lives with her grandmother, mother and two brothers, takes customers' orders and collects their payments. The coffee stall is currently the main income-generating activity within Gop's household. Her grandfather, who used to live with them and earned money as a labourer in Khlong Toey market, died last year. Her father, who went to the Middle East as a construction worker when Gop was eleven, stopped sending money home a few months ago. Gop's mother is in poor health and only opens her food stall two days a week. She also has gambling debts. Gop's older brother does not work and is also indebted – to a friend from whom he stole a motorbike, raced it and crashed it without insurance. All of this means that Gop's contribution to the household economy is indispensable. After Gop has helped to pack away at the end of the morning's shift, she leaves for school.

At 8 a.m., seventeen-year-old Jim travels back from Nana, one of Bangkok's main go-go bar districts, to the community where he lives, temporarily, at a friend's house. He has been running his friend's mother's makeup stall since midnight and now makes his way back to her house on the bus. He picks up breakfast for himself and his friend's father on the way, and after they have eaten, Jim sets about sweeping floors, washing dishes and taking the household's dirty laundry to a neighbour who will wash it. When Jim returns, he gets out the homework he has been set this week by his teacher at the community school where he has enrolled to study for his lower secondary qualifications. He studies for about half an hour, then falls asleep.

Meanwhile, fifteen-year-old Jeeb leaves his house and makes his way to a friend's uncle's house, where he will spend the next few hours preparing fruit for mobile street vendors to sell. He earns around one thousand baht per week doing this work and these days gives half of it to his grandmother, with whom he lives along with his uncle and his uncle's second wife. Until recently, Jeeb's father lived with them as well but a few months ago he and Jeeb's uncle had a fight and his father left and now lives with one of his girlfriends nearby. Jeeb has worked since he left school at the age of twelve, earning money selling sweets and snacks around the community, recycling rubbish, fetching, carrying and delivering things for neighbourhood businesses, labouring at the port and labouring at a garden centre. Since his father left, Jeeb's financial assistance has increased as his father no longer contributes to the household income and his grandmother is struggling to repay debts and cover the cost of ongoing household expenses.

At lunchtime, 22-year-old Dome arrives at his uncle's house for his shift preparing fruit. Dome also earns around one thousand baht per week doing this work and gives some of the money to his older sister, whom he considers to have been his main carer since he was two. Dome left school when he was eleven and since then has worked doing a host of informal jobs around the community, much like Jeeb, and has always given a proportion of his earnings to his older sister.

It is mid afternoon, and thirteen-year-old Dtae comes home from school, collects the toy lottery tickets that he plans to sell and heads off for the local market, where he works until 8 p.m. His income is not stable; he earns between one hundred and two hundred and fifty baht a week, but he always gives one hundred baht to his mother each week. Dtae's mother used to save this money but now uses it for everyday household expenses along with the money she earns from her mobile food stall, since Dtae's father, previously a labourer at the port, broke his leg while inebriated and cannot work for the time being.

As market trading gets into full swing, the community gym opens and 22-year-old Ganya helps the volunteer instructors set out the weightlifting equipment. She warms up and begins working out but stops when she sees her father standing at the gate gesturing to her. She collects her purse from the keep safe cupboard, goes to her father and when he asks her for money to buy his dinner, she gives him fifty baht. She returns to her workout but leaves early, at 7 p.m., because today payment is due on the room she rents for herself and her father, and she has to catch the landlord to give him the money before he leaves.

Opposite the house where Ganya and her father live, fifteen-year-old Bew stands at a water-dispensing machine with Loi, her five-year-old informally adopted brother. Loi stands on tiptoes to feed one-baht coins into the slot, and they fill up several bottles and carry them home to the three-room concrete house where they live with Bew's parents and older brother. Loi used to sleep in the street outside Bew's house, after his father was sent to prison for drug dealing, his mother was unable to care for him due to her drug addiction, and no one else in his large, extended family could take him in. After three months, Bew's parents agreed to take Loi in, but they work long hours running their food stall downtown and it is Bew who looks after him. On the way home, Bew stops to buy dinner for herself and Loi and eats with him on a sheet of plastic on the floor in the living area of the house. When they have finished, she washes him, helps him change into his pyjamas and puts him to bed in the room they share with Bew's mother. Bew then sits down to do her homework but gets up frequently to reassure Loi, who cries out in his sleep.

As Bew comforts Loi, thirteen-year-old Bort is helping his stepfather into bed. He has already washed him down in the communal bathroom at the end of the alleyway where they live in a two-room wooden shack with Bort's mother, maternal grandparents, two brothers, uncle and three cousins. He has changed his stepfather's clothes and tried to make him eat something without success, and now switches on the fan to keep the mosquitoes away from his stepfather as he sleeps. Bort sets about clearing up the mess made when his father came home drunk that afternoon and fought with his mother. He sweeps up the pieces of broken bottle, rearranges the clothes rack and reassembles the pile of newspapers that sits waiting to be taken to the recycling centre in exchange for cash. Bort then goes out to look for his mother and check she is ok, and finds her at a neighbour's house in the middle of a gambling session.

As Bort heads home, fifteen-year-old Naen sets out to join her mother and father at their street café on the main road. Naen has been at school all day, after which she attended the community gym for an hour, did her deejaying slot at the community radio station, ate dinner at her aunt's food stall, and went home to relax for a while before starting work. As soon as she arrives at her parents' street café, she washes up a pile of plates and in order to reach the tables that need cleaning, she sidesteps a swaying middle-aged couple singing karaoke in front of the television. She restocks the condiments, does the next load of washing up and takes orders while her father has a break. At around midnight, Naen takes off her apron, has something to eat, then walks home to the flats where she lives with her parents, who will join her in a couple of hours when they have closed up for the night.

It is now the early hours of the morning and thirteen-year-old Deuy gets up to help her great-aunt go to the toilet, which is located in the corner of the room where they sleep, cordoned off with blankets attached to wooden poles. Deuy's great-aunt was recently run over and broke her leg so cannot walk easily. Deuy waits for her to finish, then escorts her back to the thin foam mattress where she sleeps, alongside Deuy, Deuy's brother, uncle and two younger cousins. Four-year-old

Boom, Deuy's youngest cousin, wakes up and also needs to go to the toilet, and Deuy gets up to escort him too. Deuy has lived here for a year, ever since her mother and aunt were sent to prison for drug dealing and illegal possession of firearms and her father disappeared, and since then she has become the main carer for her great-aunt and cousins. Neither Deuy nor her cousins go to school and Deuy spends her days looking after the little ones, fetching food, washing clothes and running errands for her great-aunt, and collecting rubbish for recycling. She does all of this with a feeling of satisfaction – she is fulfilling her duty to the family. Her one regret is that she would like to join the other children in the community in attending school, but thinks that she is probably too far behind now to catch up with them.

Contributing to the Family

Young slum dwellers were strongly oriented towards contributing to their families, despite local and national discourses that often suggested otherwise, and despite not always experiencing family circumstances that made this a straightforward undertaking. Forms of contribution were many and varied, and here I focus on a selected few that were particularly pronounced during fieldwork: financial provision (direct and indirect), care work and domestic work.

Financial contributions varied between young people and for individual young people over time. For some – like Dtae – direct financial assistance was a regular feature of everyday family life, while others – like Jeeb – gave money to their families at times of crisis or acute material hardship. In some cases, direct financial assistance was proactively offered by young people, while in other cases it was given in response to demands by adult carers, and sometimes adult carers would take money from young people's savings without asking. There were several factors governing whether or not, and the extent to which, young people made direct financial contributions to their families – the circumstances and related demands of their family, and their age and gender. The greater the financial difficulty experienced by the family, the greater the contributions made by young people; the older the young person, the greater their contribution tended to be; and young women's contributions tended to be of higher financial value and more regular, while young men's tended to be lower in financial value, although perhaps higher in emotional value, and more ad hoc.

A number of young people also made indirect financial contributions to their families by helping them with their work. This was sometimes regular and sometimes made only at times of crisis or acute family hardship, sometimes an everyday affair and sometimes only for one or two days a week. As with direct financial assistance, the main factors governing whether or not, and the extent to which, young people helped their adult carers with their work were the financial and health-related circumstances of the family, and gender, age and the related issue of whether or not the young people had their own jobs already. The greater the financial difficulty and the greater the health problems of adult family members, the more likely young people were to become involved in helping them with their work, if they did not work outside the home already. The majority of those who helped their adult carers with their work were girls in their mid-teenage years.

As well as contributing financially, young slum dwellers also helped their families by providing elements of the care work needed for elders and younger children. This form of contribution was highly gendered. For boys, caring for elders was ad hoc and consisted mainly of looking after fathers or stepfathers in ill health, which was often related to alcoholism, and of protecting – or trying to protect – their mothers when their fathers became violent. For the girls, caring for elders was an ongoing, daily undertaking and consisted of assistance with daily ablutions, performing grooming activities, fetching food and medicine, assistance with travel and providing emotional support.

Many young people were also involved in caring for resident younger 'siblings'; blood siblings, half- and step-siblings, informally adopted siblings, cousins and young children living on the streets. Again, this form of contribution was highly gendered, with the vast majority of it falling to girls – of all ages. This kind of care work entailed washing, dressing and feeding younger siblings, dropping them off and collecting them from school or nursery, helping them with homework and providing activities or watching over them while they played with friends. In this sense, it was an undertaking of considerable responsibility.

Domestic labour was the other form of family assistance common among young slum dwellers, and once again was gendered, being – and being seen as – largely the job of girls and young women. This domestic labour consisted mainly of cleaning and tidying the home, washing dishes, washing clothes or taking and collecting them from neighbourhood laundry services, filling water bottles and fetching food. Young women tended to perform these duties daily for between one and four hours, whereas young men tended to undertake them much more sporadically and for shorter amounts of time.

Making Merit

Young people spoke of the contributions they made to their families and households as a means of making merit (*tam boon*) and repaying the debt of gratitude they owed their parents and carers (*boonkun*), as the following excerpts indicate:

> Sim I give [my mum] money because I think that she's getting old, yes, and I just want to pay her back for everything she did for me. I give her money about twice a month.
>
> SM What did she do for you?
>
> Sim She gave me the life. In Thai culture we believe that the kid should show their gratitude to the parents because they give you the life, yes … For children in my culture it is important to show the gratitude. So we help our parents in every way we can. (Sim, 22-year-old young woman)

> I want to obey dad and make him proud. I will try and make him so proud of me. It's good to help our parents … this way we can make them proud and show our gratitude. (Bort, thirteen-year-old boy)

These excerpts are illustrative of the way in which other young people – including those in this chapter's opening vignette – framed their contributions. From them it appears that such practices of filial support were the result of conscious, strategic choices whereby young people decided to repay the debt of gratitude they owed to their parents. However, this filial debt and related obligations are part of a longstanding cultural norm that has been a basic organizing principle of Thai social relations for centuries and as such is written into a young person's life from birth. It is so deeply ingrained in the cultural fabric of the context in which young participants were located that it would be extremely difficult for them to operate outside of its logic. Mulder observes that in Thai society, children are taught that:

> Your mother loves you more than anybody else. She has given birth to you; you have eaten from her breast … She has been feeding you and caring for you. She knows what is best for you. You should return her love, be thankful to her, respect her, yet in all your life you will never be able to repay her for the overflowing goodness she has done for you …

> Never, never forget to return the goodness that she has given to you; be grateful and fulfil your filial obligation. (1990: 64)

In this sense, contributing to one's family, fulfilling obligations and repaying the debt of gratitude are undertaken because this is what is required of young people within the structure of Thai norms and expectations, according to a dominant local cultural script. Indeed, references to Thai culture and expectations therein were common in young people's narratives, indicating a heightened awareness of the moral cultural parameters in which they operated and of the way in which cultural norms shape daily life. Thus, young people could be understood as knowingly upholding one of the most powerful structures in Thai society, one that is both enabling and constraining of everyday practice and related identities. However, young people framed their contributions in terms of *choice*, thus emphasizing their own sense of agency and the creative ways they draw on a longstanding cultural norm in constructing themselves as moral agents.

During a group activity concerning young people's use of time, I asked participants to list all of the activities they had done the day before and then categorize those activities in their own terms and rank them in order of importance. The young people placed their practices of contribution in a category they labelled 'things we have to do', ranked them as the most important of their daily activities and emphasized their own decision-making in their undertaking:

> Nam These are things we have to do such as housework, helping our parents work and looking after the younger ones.
>
> SM Why have you ranked them as the most important?
>
> Nam Well, we must do them for our parents. But I choose to do them too, no one forces me. How I spend my time is up to me. (Nam, fifteen-year-old girl)

The other participants in this group activity, and other young people in their interviews and everyday conversations, echoed Nam's insistence on having no one force them to do anything, including performing their filial duties, and being the directors of their daily lives. This emphasis on choice allows for the presentation of the self as in control and, importantly, through *choosing* to perform one's filial duties, functions to construct the self in a particular way, in moral terms. Presenting oneself as *choosing* to repay the debt of gratitude through contributing to the family was a means of constructing oneself as a *dek dee* (good child).

Being a Good Child

> For mum I try to be a good son. This is very important. We help [our parents] at work and we follow what they tell us, not make them wait when they have asked us to do something. I want to make mum feel proud of me, like if I could get a job that pays a lot of money I could give it to mum.
>
> —Jim, seventeen year old young man

References linking their multiple contributions to the notion of being a good child were widespread in young people's narratives and can be understood as attempts to demonstrate moral worth. Among those who did not have parents to whom a debt of gratitude could be paid (because their parents had passed away, sold them at birth or entrusted them to the care of others), a certain resentment was evident. Twenty-two-year-old Note lamented the fact that he had never known his 'real' parents, in particular his mother. While he craved the nurture and sense of belonging that he imagined would characterize their relationship, Note also longed for the opportunity that parents afford children to make merit and thereby prosper in the moral realm in this and subsequent incarnations. When I asked Note what had been some of the most difficult things about his life, he replied with the following:

> The point is I have no family. That's the big point. I see other people and they have families and I can see when they have a problem they help each other. But I don't have that, I am alone. That's the thing, I don't have anybody for me to think about. If you say to me that Ganya is jealous that I have [a sponsor], well she has her dad, right? Me, I don't have this. No one to share the problems … no one to show *boonkun*.

After returning from fieldwork, I continued correspondence with Note, and helped him with the English grammar in some of his assignments. The following excerpt is taken from a piece of creative writing that he sent me to check before submitting it for assessment as part of his English course, and illustrates the importance of having an identifiable mother figure to whom one's filial gratitude can be shown:

> This is my story. I have never seen my parents or any relatives before and I do not know if I have any. I have no idea how I came to exist in the world. When I go to bed I dream I see a white cloud drift around me. I can smell flowers and I can walk on the air. It is a very beautiful atmosphere and suddenly I hear a sweet voice call my name. An Angel says to me 'I will give you one Super Power but not for you to keep, you must give it to someone else'. I say 'I want you to give the Super Power

> to someone who I have never seen before in my life' (I start to cry). I pray every day that she could come to my bedside, hug me, stroke my hair gently, kiss me and say good night … My angel, please give this Super Power to her. Make her happy and healthy, make her smile and make every day her day. Tell her that I am always waiting to help her and serve her in everything, to show her I am so grateful to her. Please give the Super Power to my lovely mum.

The desire to be, and be seen as, good children through contributing to the family was strong. However, the achievement was somewhat elusive. The combination of low income and high levels of indebtedness, alongside the lack of adequate social security and the hidden costs of schooling, made family requirements for money high. And yet, by definition, young people were ill placed to provide the money required: they were either at school and so could only work a limited number of hours in casual, low-paid jobs, or had dropped out of school at an early age and therefore had low earning power. None of them had the resources with which to contribute to their families to the extent that their families required.

Enhancing moral status was of vital importance to young slum dwellers, something they were strongly oriented towards succeeding in and a fundamental component of a good life as they saw it. As well as attempting to take part in the dominant culture of global consumer capitalism, marginalized youth struggled actively to define themselves in accordance with the moral conventions dominant in local culture, to participate in the latter and be accepted on its grounds. In this we see the struggle experienced by young people living in urban poverty in a context of profound socio-economic transition to negotiate two sets of cultural moral parameters, without the resources really necessary for success in either realm.

Furthermore, young slum dwellers' family contributions were overshadowed by the narrative of the *unhelpful teenager*, which circulated readily among adult carers in the slum and found wider resonances throughout the national Thai and English language press and the bemoaning therein of the immorality of today's youth. This narrative was closely connected with the discourses on young people's selfishness, materialism, cultural defection, arrogance, disrespect and addiction to friends, and became something of a standard feature in conversations with adult carers in the slum:

> Teenagers these days are lazy to help their parents. They spend all their time playing on the internet and hanging around. I had a hard life when I was young. I started working when I was thirteen, I worked in a battery factory and then I worked as a road digger making concrete roads

> and I gave all the money to my mum … Kids today don't work like this, they ask for money from their parents. Life is convenient for kids now, too convenient, they are too *sabai sabai* [comfortable/content/relaxed]. They don't work or help the family as we did in the past. (Mother of a fifteen-year-old daughter)

Commonly following references to 'lazy' youth were evocations of times past, when young people worked long hours in gruelling conditions with few, if any, opportunities to go to school. As well as being closely linked to the discourses concerning the 'teenage life', the narrative of the unhelpful teenager can be located in the collective parental experience of low income, high levels of indebtedness and the requirement to respond to the persistent demand to furnish young people with the trappings of consumer capitalism. The narrative is also best understood with reference to elements of Khlong Toey slum's collective history. Life would have been very different for many adult carers when they were growing up. There was no legal framework outlawing child labour as the Thai government only ratified the UN Convention on the Rights of the Child (UNCRC) in 1992 and the Labour Protection Act in 1998. Although education was officially compulsory, and had been since 1921, there were no official schools in the slum – the first school was formally recognized by the Bangkok Metropolitan Authority in 1976. There was also no national healthcare system at the time, as the universal health coverage scheme was only implemented in 2002. All of this meant that life as a young person for many of today's adults was largely defined by work and the pressing need for the incomes that children brought home to afford basic necessities and sustain life. By the time contemporary young people were growing up in Khlong Toey slum, the structures shaping everyday experiences in childhood and youth had changed significantly. The intervening years had seen the introduction of state schools into slum areas, the extension of universal compulsory education, first up to the age of twelve, then up to the age of fifteen, the official outlawing of child labour and the introduction of Thailand's first universal healthcare system. All of these developments, while widely appreciated and supported by slum dwellers, for both their inherent and symbolic value, placed considerable pressure on parents and other carers to support young people for longer, and a concomitant – involuntary – postponement of financial responsibility on the part of young people.

Adult carers' attitudes to the inadequate assistance from young people were not uniform; they varied significantly according to the gender of the young people in question. There were three main positions regarding the perceived lack of contribution made by young men: *happiness* that they did anything at all; *relief* that while they may not have been ideal sons in terms of contributing to the family, at least they were not engaged in illicit or harmful activities; and *resignation* to what was seen as an inevitable and unchangeable state of affairs. The following excerpt is taken from an interview with P Kat, the mother of two young men. When I asked if her sons did anything to help her, she replied:

PK When [the eldest son] gets paid 1,000 baht sometimes he gives me 100 baht. It's not very much.

SM How do you feel about that?

PK I'm happy. At least he gives me something. If he didn't give me any I would feel sad and ashamed. He is good to give me a little.

P Kat was a widow and lived with her two teenage sons and the two orphaned children of her third son who had died a year before I began fieldwork. When I met her, P Kat was in desperate need of money, to feed and clothe herself and her two grandchildren, to pay off the significant debts she owed to local money lenders and to restock her grocery shop which sat empty because she could not afford the products to fill it. The amounts of money that her eldest son gave her, and the fact that his contributions were not regular, meant that his assistance did not go far in alleviating the difficulties that P Kat experienced, and yet she expressed happiness that he gave her anything at all.

One of the striking features of P Kat's narrative is her emphasis on how she would feel *ashamed* if her son did not give her anything. Rather than emphasize the poverty she experienced, the cost and difficulty of raising her orphaned grandchildren, or how more money from her sons might have gone some way towards making ends meet, she spoke of the imagined shame that a small contribution from her eldest son averted. The high symbolic value of young people's contributions in terms of maintaining, diminishing or augmenting adult carer status and the related burden this places on young people cannot be underestimated.

Other adult carers expressed relief that while their sons did not help them as much as they might have liked, at least they were not involved in drugs, and resignation that a lack of assistance was to be expected from sons. The following excerpt is taken from an interview with Ba (aunty) Dum, the mother of three young men. I asked if her sons gave her money or helped out in other ways, and she replied:

BD [The youngest son] goes out and plays computer games all the time. If you ever need to find him he is in the internet shop. Nothing more than playing games. And driving around the neighbourhood on his motorbike. But it's very lucky for me that he isn't involved with drugs.

SM Would you like him to do more to help you?

BD He is a boy [laughing]. I think this is quite normal for boys, not just in my family but if you look around here it's the same for others.

While Ba Dum did not express the shame that P Kat imagined she would feel if her son did not give her anything, she emphasized the commonality of her experience, both in terms of her local neighbourhood and a wider gender stereotype. In this way, she forestalls the shame that accompanies having 'ungrateful', 'uncaring' or 'lazy' sons.

Daughters, on the other hand, were much more heavily criticized when they were perceived as not contributing enough. The following excerpt is taken from a conversation with P Noi, the mother of three young women:

> [My daughters] don't care too much about their mum, they hang out in the shopping mall with their friends ... They care only about themselves, about what they can buy and their group. They don't care so much for their family, they don't help their parents any more. This is the new era.

This quote is typical of the degree of negativity expressed when referring to the perceived insufficiency of young women's contributions. Here again, we can see an emphasis on the ubiquity of the experience, as P Noi contextualized her daughters' apparent ingratitude and lack of support with reference to a society-wide mood of the time.

Later in our discussion, P Noi went on to detail the amounts of money that her daughters contributed to the household income and how this had increased in the wake of their father's death a few months previously. The amounts were considerable; the two daughters who worked – as waitresses in go-go bars – each gave four thousand baht a month to their mother, which she used to buy groceries for her food stall and for the expenses incurred by her youngest daughter in attending school. And yet P Noi claimed that her daughters did not help her, as did other parents whose daughters contributed what seemed to me to be relatively substantial amounts.

Why was it that when P Kat, the mother of two young men, spoke of her son's ad hoc contributions of one hundred baht she was happy, yet when P Noi spoke of her daughters' regular joint contributions of eight thousand baht she claimed that this signified a lack of care about her? Expectations of young people in terms of the work they did in support of their families were highly gendered; the level of support expected from young women was high, that expected of young men was relatively low. Expectations of the kind of assistance provided were also gendered; the ultimate way in which a young Thai man is expected to provide for his family is spiritually, through entry into the monkhood – which can be for as little as two weeks – while the duty to provide materially falls largely to young women, and traditionally to the youngest daughter.

Although young slum dwellers attempted to construct themselves as 'good children' through contributing to their families, the dream of enhancing their moral status in this way often lay out of reach because they were by definition – by virtue of their age, socio-economic status and related earning power – poorly positioned to contribute to the extent that their families required, and related to this because the contributions they did make were often eclipsed by the gendered narrative of the unhelpful teenager. For young people in marginalized communities living in contexts of rapid socio-economic change, fulfilling one's side of the intergenerational bargain is a fraught endeavour, and for older generations living in urban poverty in transition economies, the struggle to come to terms with the shift in norms surrounding youth and parenting is no less challenging.

In addition to being ill placed to meet their families' pressing financial needs and having their contributions overshadowed by the narrative of the uncaring child, young slum dwellers' attempts to augment their moral status carried other, unintended outcomes. In the process of constructing themselves as good children in the particular ways available to them – by working in badly paid, low-status jobs to provide money for the family and by undertaking care work and domestic work for the family at home – young participants unwittingly reinforced their low socio-economic status, their positioning as *dek slum* (slum children).

One of the key ways in which outsiders understood young people in slum communities – as well as with reference to prostitution, drug abuse, alcoholism and violence – was by virtue of the work they did in contributing to their families, and for this they tended to be pitied. Throughout fieldwork, when wealthy parents, restaurant owners, conference and seminar delegates, local government officials and academics learned that I was researching in Khlong Toey slum, they expressed concern that the young people there were so poor they had to work to help their parents. In the popular imagination, providing assistance to the family was one of the defining features of poverty and disadvantage in contemporary youth.

Young people in wealthy families did not give money to their parents because their parents earned enough themselves. They were in positions to own their own houses and often other property, to take holidays abroad, to send their children to good state or private schools, to pay for extra tuition classes and to save for their children's university education. Young people in these families did not help their parents work because they did not need to, and in any case the work their parents did – as doctors, lawyers, lecturers, account managers, civil servants, business people – was not easily open to assistance from them. Wealthy young people were not carers for resident elders or younger siblings because their families could afford to pay for domestic labour and care workers. For wealthy young people, making merit, repaying *bunkun* and identifying themselves as good children in their teenage years was achieved primarily through studying, and for boys through temporary entry to the monkhood, and through the knowledge that studying – along with existing family wealth – would make them well placed to support their parents in their old age.

By attempting to identify and present themselves as 'good' sons and daughters and augment their moral standing in one of the main ways available to them, young slum dwellers unwittingly undermined their attempts to *live the teenage life* and reinforced their low socio-economic status: it was only young people in positions of socio-economic disadvantage who contributed to their families financially and were so integral to the performance of domestic and care work, and this was well understood across the socio-economic spectrum. In attempting to elevate their positions within the moral cultural realm, marginalized youth unwittingly entrenched their low positioning within the socio-economic sphere. They entered the game on such disadvantaged terms that they could only enhance their moral status in ways that further undermined their socio-economic standing and attempts to carve out identities as modern, global youth.

Young participants from slum communities were aware of the way their contributions reinforced others' perceptions of them as *kon chan dtam* (low-level people). After describing what she had done the previous day, including working at her grandmother's coffee stall in the morning and looking after her younger brother in the afternoon and evening, thirteen-year-old Gop commented:

> You may think that this is a *low so* life. Well, yes, I help my grandmother and my mum as much as I can. At least we are not like children in

> Myanmar or Laos, they have to work in the fields for twenty hours every day. Or they are housemaids for the rich people and they work twenty-four hours a day and hardly sleep. They are very backwards in Myanmar.

Gop's response to the identification of herself as a low-status person in light of the work she did for her family was powerful in its evocation of an imaginary, distant other whose greater contributions made for a lower socio-economic ranking than hers. In transposing the burden of low socio-economic status onto this imaginary other, she attempted to advance her own position in the hierarchy, at least in her own mind. It was no coincidence that Gop referred to young people in Laos or Myanmar; Thailand is renowned for its rapid and profound economic transformation from being one of the poorest countries in the world to being a middle-income, industrial powerhouse, and more recently a bastion of commodity consumption, while Laos and Myanmar continue to be placed well below Thailand in official development rankings. Young people in the slum saw theirs as a position of elevation relative to these poorer neighbouring countries, which they readily evoked and from which they readily distanced themselves, referring to the latter's lack of development and 'backwardness'. Young people in the slum were proud of what they saw as Thailand's superiority to Laos, Myanmar and Cambodia, although the irony that it was their parents or grandparents who provided the manual labour for the country's transformation, yet benefited least from it, seemed to be lost on them.

In addition to reinforcing their low socio-economic status, through their attempts to contribute to the family young slum dwellers also potentially undermined their future material advancement. Time and money spent assisting the family was time and money diverted from studying and saving. In its most severe form, this entailed young people being taken out of school in order to work for the family or provide full time care for young siblings or elderly relatives. In its more common shape, it entailed not completing the homework required to do well at school, being exhausted from various forms of work and falling asleep or 'switching off' during lessons, and not being able to afford the costs of schooling such as study materials and contributions for educational trips.

In sum, young slum dwellers were noticeably driven by the attempt to construct themselves as 'good children' through emphasizing choice in speaking of the contributions they made to their families; success in this moral realm was an important feature of everyday life and dreams. However, the desire to achieve high moral status in this way remained somewhat elusive. Family poverty and indebtedness and the related level of financial assistance required, alongside young people's low earning power, made young slum dwellers ill positioned to support their families to the degree needed, and the contributions that young people did make were easily overshadowed by the narrative of the uncaring teenager. Furthermore, in the process of attempting to improve their moral status, young slum dwellers inadvertently reinforced their inability to *live the teenage life*, although they worked hard to counter the negative connotations of supporting the family in part by invoking imaginary others who were worse off, thereby attempting to elevate their own status. Young people's attempts to support their families also potentially undermined their own future material advancement, diverting time and money away from studying or saving for the future.

In addition to all of this, young slum dwellers contended daily with the tensions that arose between trying to juggle their filial obligations on the one hand and trying to live the teenage life on the other – tensions that were approached in highly gendered ways and that resulted in an additional layer of contradictory outcomes, especially for young women.

Juggling

When young people attempted to support their families *and* live the teenage life, they became caught in a bind: on the one hand, they sought to be *dek samai mai* (modern kids) living lives defined by leisure, friends and fun, and on the other, they tried to be *dek dee* (good kids) and fulfil their duties to the family through work and financial remittances. While they attempted to deal with this on a practical level (for example by dividing their time between leisure activities and work), the tension was particularly striking with respect to the issue of identity and the identity work that young people engaged in.

Both young women and men experienced and acknowledged this tension, although they experienced it to different degrees and dealt with it in very different ways. In attempting to live the teenage life and fulfil their duties towards their families, young men tended to move in and out of different and sometimes contradictory identities, at times labelling themselves with reference to their leisure pursuits and at other times in terms of the work they did. The members of Bodyfit at times referred to themselves and each other using their online names or other generic, leisure-oriented designations such as *kon hip hop* (hip hop person), and at other times using the English phrase *work more*, a slogan used in a mobile phone advertising campaign at the time of fieldwork. However, while most young men expressed a wish to help their parents and be 'good sons', they tended to prioritize their lifestyles of leisure, resigning themselves to failing in their duty to support the family, and blaming themselves for being 'lazy' or 'useless' according to the contemporary cultural script of wayward youth. In response to my question concerning his feelings about how he spent his time, seventeen-year-old Arun said:

> My time is nonsense. It's so nonsense. I do other things instead of helping my mum work. I spend so much time doing this, and it doesn't please anyone except for me. It doesn't help my parents. I like to hang out with friends, play the guitar, go out, play *Counterstrike* on the computer. But these things aren't useful to my parents, they don't make any money. I know that I should spend my time in a better way.

When I asked Arun why he did not help his parents more, he said he did not know, and during a group discussion with the other Bodyfit members, they all took similar positions. They said they spent too much time hanging out, that they wanted to and should help their families more but did not, and were unable to explain why. These sentiments were echoed by other young men in their interviews and in everyday conversations, and there are several possible broader explanations as to why their material contributions were not more forthcoming, which point to familial, socio-economic, religious and cultural norms and expectations.

For some young men, families were absent; some had passed away, some were in prison and others had moved and were not in contact, meaning that it was not always clear to whom one's contributions should be made or to whom the debt of gratitude would be payable in this way. For those who had dropped, or been taken, out of school at a young age, the work options were limited to manual labour at the port or selling things on the street, both of which were badly paid, leaving boys with little to contribute. They were also of low socio-economic status and thereby in opposition to the deep-rooted desire to appear as *kon samai mai*, or modern people. For some, the pressure to construct themselves as modern seemed all-encompassing. Furthermore, one of the primary ways in which young Thai men can repay their filial debt of gratitude and make merit for their parents is by entering the monkhood, most commonly done on a temporary basis. It is likely that those of Buddhist faith would get ordained at some point in their young lives as a means of fulfilling their filial obligations. Ceremonies and parades through the streets of the slum marking initiation into the monkhood were common throughout fieldwork, and while young men felt a degree of pressure to provide material support to their families, they knew that their obligations could be fulfilled spiritually. The concomitant low expectations of young men on the part of adult carers no doubt worked to sanction their contributions being similarly low, as compared with young women. Furthermore, there is a tradition of matrilocalism in Thai culture whereby when a young couple marry, the man moves into the woman's family home. While contemporary living arrangements are in reality varied and encompass matrilocalism, patrilocalism and nuclear family setups, among others, it is possible that the notion of daughters being inextricably and permanently tied to the family and sons being loosely and temporarily affiliated persists, and that this has important ramifications for the support that young men provide, and are expected to provide, for their families.

While young women also took up different identities at different times in their attempts to juggle the teenage life and support their families, they tended to try and resolve the tension by constructing new, hybrid identities. During her interview, fifteen-year-old Naen said:

> It may seem like my duties are easy, but they are not. There's a lot to do and not enough time. I would like to have more time for myself, to hang out with my friends outside and see my boyfriend, not just spend time helping my parents. Well I do these things and it makes my parents mad. It seems that I can never please them with what I do. For them I don't help them enough.

When I asked Naen what she did when her parents 'got mad', she initially said that she stayed quiet because it was bad *kamma* to disagree with her parents. But staying quiet was not the only tactic she used. During a group discussion about young people's use of time, Naen replied to a question concerning what changes she would make, if any, to the time she spent at school by saying she would like to banish all of the teachers and have the pupils teach each other. When I asked her what she would like to learn about, she replied, 'I want someone to teach me how to be a really good *bitch*'. The following excerpt is taken from the discussion that followed this statement:

> SM A *bitch*?
>
> Naen Like a street girl but better, and a good one. Both at the same time … not like a *bitch* in America. Someone who is street but who can adjust it and still be a good kid.
>
> SM What's a good kid?

Naen Good kids help their parents and stay at home, they obey their parents all the time, they don't let their parents down. It's difficult to be a good kid and be a street girl at the same time. I don't know, I can't explain it properly.

SM I'm confused.

Ganya OK, first you have to understand Thai culture. It expects girls to be good, to stay at home, to do household chores and always help their parents, not to hang around with guys or be free to come and go. It expects them to stay close to home and focus on their family, help the family. This is a home girl. Then there's a street girl. The street girls when they leave school they stay with their group, they hang out in Khlong Toey, they stick with their street gang, they wear makeup and sexy clothes and flirt with guys, they take drugs and get pregnant. This is the life of street girls in Khlong Toey. The girls who contrast these two we call *bitches*. They don't stay at home, but it doesn't always mean they are bad ... It's not a street girl and it's not only a home girl, it's in between. These kids want to be street but they want to improve it, get educated, not to get into drugs or get pregnant or get AIDS. But they want their gang too, their style, their way of thinking and their freedom, their life outside the family, but they want to make their parents proud too. This is what we call a *bitch*.

Some young women attempted to manage the tension between the teenage life and contributing to their families by creating identities they forged from pre-existing stereotypes, and this kind of active construction of hybrid identities is often associated, in academic literature, with a celebration of young people's cultural agency. As Nilan and Feixa note in the introduction to their edited volume *Global Youth? Hybrid Identities, Plural Worlds*, 'the notion of hybridity ... involves, at least potentially, an "emancipatory" use of culture' (2006: 2).

However, while creating the hybrid identity *bitch* may signify an attempt on the part of certain young slum dwellers to actively negotiate the tension between two apparently contradictory spheres of action, in doing so they further reinforced perceptions of themselves as immoral and embroiled themselves in other pejorative discourses. In 2005, a Thai-American pop star, Tata Young, released a song entitled 'Sexy, Naughty, Bitchy', which soared to the top of the charts, was played on radio stations throughout the country and received a great deal of media attention. The lyrics of the chorus, repeated throughout the song, refer to the singer choosing her skirts to be 'a little too sexy', to having thoughts that are 'a bit naughty', and to playing 'a bit bitchy'. The last line of the chorus ends with the refrain 'sexy, naughty, bitchy me'. The verses of the song contain references to being the object of boys' fantasies, being the opposite of a stereotypical stay-at-home, innocent girl, and to rebelling against the idea of monogamy. The song and its artist sparked a good deal of controversy throughout Thailand. It was played repeatedly on the radio and television and was the object of much disquiet during fieldwork, and it prompted heavy criticism from the Thai culture ministry and members of the public, who phoned in to local radio stations in their droves to complain and tried to get the accompanying video banned from TV. Tata Young was accused of promoting immorality and posing a threat to Thai culture, wherein 'good' women are constructed as virtuous and obedient, with their virginity intact until marriage (Van Esterik 2000). While some rushed to Tata Young's defence, even suggesting that she represented a beacon of hope for the advancement of gender equality, the overall mood during the height of the controversy surrounding 'Sexy, Naughty, Bitchy' was one of contempt for her perceived sexual waywardness.

I do not know whether the young women in this study borrowed the term *bitch* from its use in Tata Young's song, but the meaning they gave to it was their own. They mobilized it in an attempt to manage the tension they experienced between seeking to live the teenage life on the one hand and support their families or fulfil their filial duties and be 'good' daughters on the other. It was chosen precisely as a means of signifying that they took their contributions to the family seriously, that their morality remained intact despite their engagement in the teenage life and all this unleashed in terms of perceptions as wayward and uncaring.

However, in selecting the label *bitch*, they fuelled others' perceptions of them as sexually wayward. This was compounded by the fact that one of the main ways in which young women from the slums are perceived by outsiders is, among other things, as prostitutes. Many of the conversations I had during fieldwork with non-slum dwellers exposed a pervasive misunderstanding that young women from the slums prostituted themselves as a matter of course, and for this they were pitied. Back at home in the UK, perceptions proved to be just as skewed and equally as offensive. I recall a conversation I had with a man who came to do some work on my house after I returned from fieldwork. We were discussing my research, and when he learned that I had lived in a slum in Bangkok, he said:

> I've got a mate who spends half the year in Bangkok, or is it Singapore? No, it's Bangkok. Yeah. He's a young lad. He works six months in

> England and then what he earns he can afford a very nice life over there. He says to me 'Kev, all I want is cheap food, cheap beer and cheap women'. And that's what he gets over there innit, I mean he can have a girl for a fiver a week. She's probably one of your mates in the slum ha ha ha ha.

While prostitution may be a reality for some, it is not true for all, and even where it is, the young women in question defined themselves with reference to things quite other than prostitution and went to considerable lengths to dissociate themselves from it, for example by constructing their relationships with men in romantic terms and downplaying the issue of economic exchange, or by emphasizing the needs and demands of their families and the priority that they gave to these. As Montgomery notes in her 2001 ethnography of child prostitution in Thailand, the impetus to distance oneself from prostitution and the stigma it carries is strong.

Regardless of the actuality of their circumstances, to be identified as prostitutes was extremely insulting for the young women in this research, who managed to get by and struggled to do well within a socio-economic system that marginalized them and within a set of moral cultural parameters that decried their sexual waywardness at the same time as relying on them for sexual entertainment, condoning men's virility and unofficially sanctioning male infidelity.[2] Many young people were aware of, and hurt by, this construction of slum women, and yet by adopting the identity of *bitch*, they unwittingly gave it credence – further fuelling the discourse that positioned them as sexually wayward.

Other identities constructed by young women in their attempts to manage the tension between living the teenage life and working for the family varied. Fifteen-year-old Nan spoke of the identity she had fashioned for herself:

> If you ask about me, I will tell you that I am a *Lock* girl. I like to hang out with my friends in *Lock* 1 in the [disused food stall] and chit chat. I used to be a runaway but now I live with my granny. I'm not like a home girl with granny but at least I am close by in case she needs me.

For Nan, a *Lock* girl straddled being a runaway and being a home girl. Like *bitch*, it was a product of pre-existing stereotypes self-consciously mobilized in an attempt to manage the difficulties experienced in living the teenage life and honouring their filial duties. However, also like the use of *bitch*, it had adverse, unintended consequences. 'Lock', followed by a number, is the name given to several slum communities in Khlong Toey. For Nan, identifying herself as a *Lock* girl was a way of signifying a closeness to home – relative to being a runaway – and the related duty towards her grandmother who was in poor health, and thereby attempting to enhance her moral status. However, in so doing, she reinforced others' perceptions of her as *kon chan dtam* (a low-level person).

Within the slum, the *Lock* communities were considered particularly 'low' or 'bad' places. They were notorious for housing drug addicts, thieves and violent gangs, and during fieldwork one of them was in the process of being demolished while others had been earmarked for clearance. Residents from other communities tried to avoid them when they could, and I was constantly advised not to walk through the *Locks* on my way to the bus stop outside. When I was first looking for a room to rent in the slum, I was warned by residents not to live in the *Lock* communities as they were 'bad' places and the people in them were dangerous.

The wealthy informants in this research were not aware of the slum's internal subdivision into separate communities, of the names given to them, or of the socio-economic and related moral hierarchies that operated between and within them, and so would not have grasped the complexity and subtlety that attended Nan's identification as a *Lock* girl. For them, the streets of the slum were outside, and on that basis alone they were seen as dangerous and inappropriate places to be. They were for passing through. While the streets were also perceived negatively by slum dwellers, for wealthy people they were particularly disreputable. Wealthy young people spent very little time outside: their houses tended to be air conditioned and were separated from the streets by doors, windows, security gates and fences. In the mornings they tended to travel to school by car, after school they attended extra classes in tuition centres, and in the evenings they tended to stay at home or pursue hobbies in other indoor spaces. For some wealthy Thais, young people in slum communities were defined in part by their existence on and alignment with the streets outside:

> The problem in Khlong Toey is with the environment, the kids there they don't know the good environment, so they soak up the bad one. You will see them hanging out in the streets, just sitting around. My son visited Khlong Toey once with his school because his school makes a donation to a foundation there. The kids there are poor, they don't go to school, they have no one to guide them. (Wealthy father of a teenage boy)

For this man – a consultant surgeon in one of Bangkok's top private hospitals – the streets were synonymous with immorality and poverty, states that he implied were linked and would be absorbed by young people if they spent too long in them. For others, the streets – in particular those of the inner city and especially those within slum communities – were synonymous with danger and dirt. For some people, being outside was associated with the darkening effects of the sun on the skin, and this in turn also signified low social status. In general, Thai people do not sunbathe; in fact, most Thai people I met avoided the sun whenever possible, and while this is undoubtedly connected to the discomfort that ensues from its heat, discussions with informants and friends, inside and outside the slum, revealed that it is also related to the fear that it would make their skin darker, and this in turn was associated with looking poor, dirty and backward. One morning after an English club session at the library train, I suggested a neighbourhood walk with a group of young women, and while they were reasonably happy to show me around the dark, covered maze of alleyways at the heart of their community, they would not spend more than a minute outside. When I asked why, thirteen-year-old Cream said that she did not want her skin to go black. At this, Deuy, another thirteen-year-old girl, retorted that it did not matter if it went black because where we were walking was like Sri Lanka anyway. They all laughed and when I asked what she meant, Deuy replied that the particular neighbourhood we were in 'stank like a toilet', that 'the people were beggars' and that the children of the community, including herself, did not go to school.

The *Locks* and the streets in general were viewed negatively by outsiders and slum dwellers alike, whether the emphasis was on poverty, other forms of low status, immorality or a mixture of all of these, and whether the association was direct or indirect – with reference to danger, dirt or skin colour. There was an assumption that those who identified with the *Locks* or the streets embodied that negativity, themselves becoming synonymous with it. In the process of constructing her identity as a *Lock* girl, although her purpose was to emphasize her morality, Nan aligned herself with one of the most disreputable places in the city, and in the eyes of outsiders came to be understood as poor and immoral into the bargain.

The particular choice of labels varied among young women, but the creation of hybrid identities such as *bitch* and *Lock* girl points to the considerable effort some went to in trying to deal with the tensions inherent in seeking to live the teenage life and fulfil their familial obligations, and to the way in which they forged identities with the very limited resources they had at their disposal. However, in constructing identities aimed at emphasizing attentiveness to the family and moral realms as well as to the teenage life, these young women unwittingly reinforced negative perceptions of themselves as 'low people', as immoral, or both.

The Adverse Outcomes of Agency

Enhancing their moral status was of vital importance to the young slum dwellers in this study, something they were strongly oriented towards succeeding in and a fundamental component of a better life as they saw it. They struggled actively to define themselves in accordance with certain moral conventions dominant in local culture, to participate in these and be accepted on their grounds. And they endeavoured – self-consciously – to manage the tensions between the latter and the teenage life, to participate in both sets of moral-cultural parameters.

However, the exercise of agency towards these ends is not the end of the story. Although young slum dwellers attempted to construct themselves as 'good children' through contributing to their families, the dream of enhancing their moral status was an elusive one because they were unable to contribute to the extent that their families required, and because the contributions they made were overshadowed by the gendered discourse of the unhelpful teenager.

Moreover, by attempting to identify and present themselves as 'good' sons and daughters and augment their moral standing in the main ways available to them, young slum dwellers unwittingly undermined their identities as modern, global subjects and reinforced their low socio-economic status. In this research, it was only young people in positions of socio-economic disadvantage who contributed to their families financially and were so integral to the performance of domestic and care work, and this was widely recognized. Here, young slum dwellers entered the game on such disadvantaged terms that they could only enhance their moral status in ways that entrenched their low socio-economic standing. Furthermore, in trying to manage the tension between living the teenage life and contributing to the family, young women reinforced both their low socio-economic *and* moral status; by selecting labels and hybrid identities for themselves that were intended to reflect their commitments to their families as well as to the teenage life, they signified to others immorality as well as poverty. And in their attempts to emphasize their moral worth – through contributing to the family and through creating identities designed to signify adherence to local cultural/moral norms – young slum dwellers undermined their future material advancement; the considerable time, effort and resources devoted to constructing themselves as *good children* were time, effort and resources not available for doing what was necessary for escaping material hardship in the longer term. These processes are highlighted in the relevant sections of the theoretical framework (Figure 5.1).

The way in which young slum dwellers presented their practices of contribution as a matter of *choice* speaks of a strong sense of agency; of

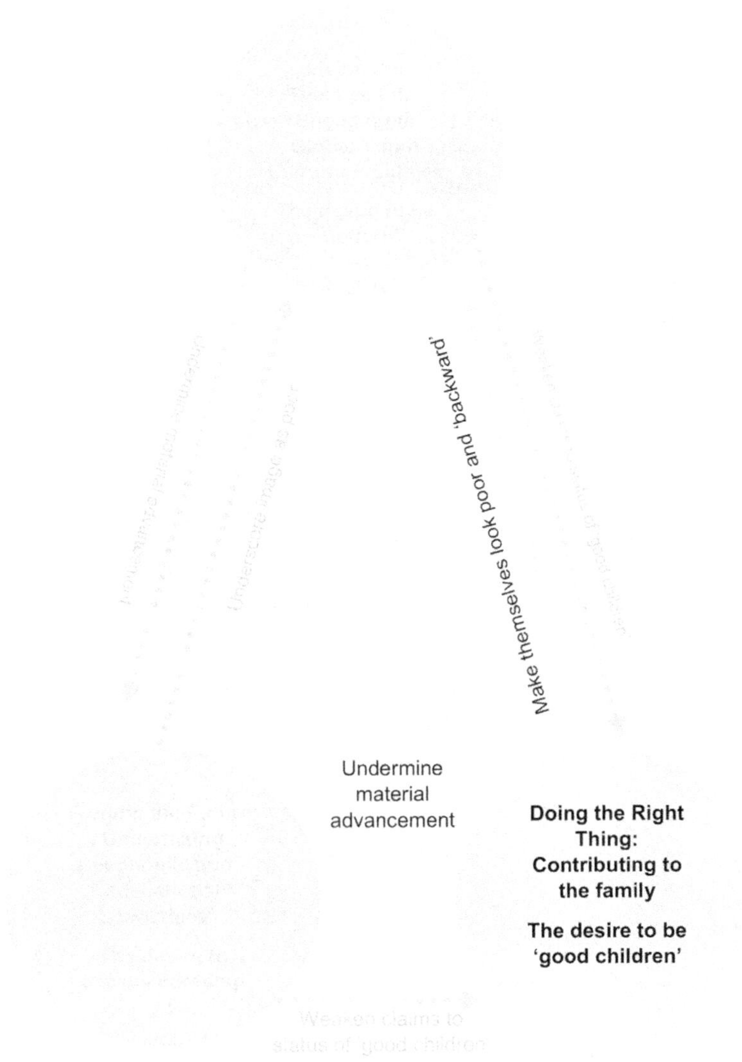

Figure 5.1. Diagram showing that contributions to the family can be inadequate and have unintended, negative outcomes.

a sense of the self as in control of its moral identity and as the director of daily life in the moral realm. This sense of agency is further emphasized in the self-conscious creation of hybrid identities, wherein young people select from the different scripts at their disposal in the configuration of new subjectivities intended to show their alignment with both global consumer culture and local cultural-moral norms. And yet young slum dwellers remain profoundly manoeuvred by a complex combination of local and global cultural, moral and socio-economic forces, and their exercise of agency within this sphere has negative outcomes that undermine other goals that are important to them. The very identities they choose for themselves reflect the gendered and generational cultural norms that determine which practices and ways of relating are and are not acceptable, as well as the socio-economic inequalities that give rise to their disadvantaged positioning and others' negative perceptions of them. This ironic sense of agency in the face of being profoundly manoeuvred points to one of the major tensions that arises in the construction of the self in modernity.

Notes

1. These fieldnotes detail a day in the life of several young people, focusing on the various forms of assistance they provide for their families. The fieldnotes are compiled from a mixture of interviews, everyday conversations and observations. I highlight forms of contribution that were common throughout fieldwork, and I present them in this way to show something of the breadth of support that young people give and the depth of their experiences in this sphere.
2. Despite the outlawing of the 'mia noi' (minor wife) phenomenon in Thailand, the practice of having several 'wives' was not uncommon in the slum.

6

Forging the Future

This chapter considers young people's attempts to forge better material futures for themselves. Again, it opens with fieldnotes, in which I present brief case studies of three young slum dwellers, focusing on their current living arrangements, their dreams for the future and the tactics they use to try and turn those dreams into reality. This is followed by a discussion of a 'better future', which offers a working definition of how the concept is utilized here, notes various limitations to the scope of its treatment in this chapter, and points to some of the prominent local and national discourses that inform it and in part explain the centrality of the concept in participants' narratives and practices. Discussion then explores the key practices involved in young people's attempts to build better material futures, noting the relevant patterns according to age, gender and socio-economic position. The next section highlights one of the overarching characteristics of young slum dwellers' attempts to get ahead, namely the way in which they seem ultimately responsible for forging their own futures, returning to the case studies used in the opening fieldwork notes to illustrate this. Discussion then turns to the prominent way in which participants speak about the future and the process of working towards it, identifying a resonance between the experiences and narratives of young people in their search for a better future, and the ideals promoted within certain elements of the context in which they are located, suggesting that it is by virtue of operating in accordance with these very ideals that young slum dwellers find the journey towards material advancement so arduous and the destination so hard to reach. The chapter closes with a recap of the negative outcomes of agency in the forging of material futures, shown in the selected elements of the theoretical framework.

Fieldnotes

Bee

When I first met her, Bee was thirteen years old and was living with her mother, her eleven-year-old half-sister and her adopted younger brother – the six-year-old son of her mother's cousin who came to live with Bee and her family after his father died of AIDS and his mother discovered she was HIV positive. Bee and her family lived in an upgraded area in a rented room in a two-storey, wooden *soi* (lane) house, an overcrowded dwelling with unreliable water and electricity supplies. Bee was studying at the local community school and her mother did numerous jobs, including cleaning offices, washing clothes for neighbours and casual labouring. Her half-sister had dropped out of school and did not work, and her adopted brother attended a local NGO-run nursery.

At the time of fieldwork, Bee was planning to continue her studies to the highest level she could. She dreamed of having a well-paid, secure job as an adult, either as a teacher or an office worker:

> My first dream is to finish a Bachelor's degree. It would be sad to stop studying as it can help you to succeed in life, not have so much hardship. The real future dream is to have a secure job. First I wanted to be a teacher but now I'm not sure, maybe I can get a job in an office. It's important to have money so if we have a problem we don't have a big hardship.

During her interview, Bee emphasized how hard she studied and stated that she was determined to do well at school in order to build a better future, although it was not easy to find the time or space to concentrate since she was primarily responsible for the day to day care of her adopted younger brother. Bee received a few small grants for her schooling through two slum-based NGOs, and drew mainly on her mother and her mother's network of friends and acquaintances in the slum to cover the cost of basic necessities such as food, shelter and clothes. She also worked, cleaning offices in the morning before school, and saved as much of her earnings as she could to put towards her future education.

Nan

Nan was fifteen when I met her and was living with her grandmother in a rented room in a three-storey concrete shop house that also housed nine other families. She worked full time making handicrafts at a small local NGO, where her grandmother also worked as a part time cook. Nan had high hopes for her future:

> When I come to be an adult I would love to be a tour guide using Japanese language. People are very rich in Japan and they tip well. Yes, I want something more than what I have now. This dream is a very big one! Will it come true? I think it depends on how well I can study.

In order to try and realize her dream, Nan planned to stop work and return to school to resume her studies. A few months before I met her, the NGO where she was working had agreed to sponsor her education from the beginning of the following academic year, and Nan's grandmother had agreed to support Nan while she studied. Nan was also waiting for her father to send some money to assist with her schooling. In the meantime, Nan was trying to teach herself Japanese using books that she had borrowed from the library of a Japanese NGO in the slum. At the time of fieldwork, Nan saw herself as very much in limbo, waiting for the next crucial step in her journey towards a better future:

> My life is very boring these days. Because I can't go to school I have to do something and earn some money to help my granny so I work. Someone at [a local NGO] offered me a job in the handicraft section and that's what I do. I would like to do a different job, but I don't know what I can do. Really, I want to be a tour guide. That's why I want to go back to school. Now I can see how important school is.

Jim

Jim was seventeen when I met him, and living in a two-storey, family-owned wooden soi house with a friend, his friend's parents and three younger sisters, as well as two other friends also in need of accommodation. Jim worked for his friend's mother, who ran a small street stall selling makeup and other beauty products at night in one of Bangkok's busiest nightlife spots. Jim's friends worked as casual labourers, his friend's sisters were at school, and his friend's father was unable to work due to liver failure and partial paralysis. Jim also had hopes of building a better material future:

> I would like to have a good job, one that earns good money, enough so I can live in a place of my own, not have to stay with [my friend's] family. There are too many people there. I would like to earn a lot of money. Maybe set up my own business selling things to tourists.

Although Jim spoke at different points in time about different ideas for his future, for example of becoming a stunt man or a gym instructor, these were united by a sense of searching for work that would allow him to secure a better material quality of life. He was aware that in order to get the good job he sought, he would have to resume his education, and to this end he enrolled in the community adult college at weekends to prepare for his lower secondary school exams. This entailed attending classes for two hours each on Saturdays and Sundays, and completing around five hours of homework each week. In order to cover the cost of this, he had borrowed money from his friend's mother and paid her back in weekly instalments from his earnings on her street stall. He also drew heavily on his friend's mother as well as his friends for food, shelter and extra money in order to get by.

Trying to Get Ahead

The notion of creating a better material future was a strong feature throughout fieldwork within the slum communities, both within everyday conversations and in interviews with young people and adult carers, and concerned the attempt to escape from material, and in particular financial, hardship and improve one's material quality of life, whatever measurable level of relative poverty was experienced by individuals. For those living in urban poverty, the notion of creating a better quality of life encompassed getting by as well as moving ahead – the former was necessary for the latter.

Hardship and attempts to escape it are multidimensional and can refer, for instance, to the social or relational realms as well as the material, and these multiple dimensions are interrelated. I focus here on young people's attempts to build better futures in the *material* realm, viewing their relationships with others in terms of their instrumental roles in shaping those attempts – fully recognizing, though not focusing on, the simultaneous inherent value of those relationships. During fieldwork, in broad terms material hardship entailed having insufficient money with which to pay for basic necessities such as nutritious food, adequate sanitation, clean water, secure and decent-quality housing and clothing, and for education and to repay debts. This hardship can be understood in the context of broader structures in the national and global context – socio-economic inequality, an inadequate welfare system, a highly unequal education system and labour market segmentation. However, such hardship is a relative concept.

Material hardship is relative in a national and local – city-wide – sense. In relation to an absolute, national poverty line, some of the young people and their families in this study may have fallen below it and some above it. In relation to the wealthy participants in Bangkok, the slum dwellers were all in positions of material disadvantage, in terms of housing, income, assets, investments, education and disposable income. In addition, within Khlong Toey slum, material hardship was also relative in a historical or generational sense, as well as in a geographical sense, with significant differences between slum communities. For adult carers who grew up in Khlong Toey, material experiences in childhood and youth were marked by a lack of physical infrastructure (an absence of paved walkways, water and electricity supplies and rubbish collection services), by a lack of educational opportunities, and for many young women by the enforced care of large numbers of younger siblings. For young people living in many of the Khlong Toey slum communities at the time of fieldwork, these aspects of life had changed, in light of the nationwide slum upgrading strategy that came in the wake of Thailand's economic boom and the inequality that gave rise to, and in light of the country's demographic transition to lower fertility rates (Baker and Phongpaichit 2005: 201).

The material hardship experienced by individual young slum dwellers was also relative to that experienced by other young people living in the same, neighbouring and more distant slum communities. For example, for some it entailed living in accommodation that was owned by the family but was extremely overcrowded, having adult carers who earned very little money, having insufficient food and having to work long hours in physically demanding jobs. For others it entailed living in rented accommodation with a single adult carer, having an adult carer who earned money but spent it on alcohol and/or gambling, having sufficient food only by virtue of outside assistance, and combining education and work. Others lived in family-owned houses with a small number of residents, had parents who earned enough money to pay bills and buy food, and were able to attend school full time. The focus here is on the *process* of attempting to build a better material future, whatever particular level of material hardship individual young people experienced at the time of fieldwork, which could, and did, change over time.

Material hardship was relative within individual young people's lives; periods of severe adversity were followed by periods of relative prosperity and vice versa, for example with a young person becoming homeless overnight due to the breakdown of family relationships, living with friends on a temporary basis then returning to live with relatives, or with a young person's fortunes changing within the space of a week as NGO funding became available to support their education. Again, here I focus on the *processes* of young people's attempts to build better futures, regardless of the particular level of hardship entailed in their material circumstances.

The desire to build better material futures is perhaps particularly pronounced in a context such as Khlong Toey slum, where poverty exists in such close proximity to staggering levels of material wealth. It can also be understood in the context of Thailand's focus on *pattana* (development), conceptualized within official discourse as economic growth and related advances in material standards of living. The Thai authorities have explicitly sought and advocated the country's economic development for centuries, and in 1961 the Thai government issued its first National Economic and Social Development Plan – characterized by the strive towards material advancement throughout the country. Since then, each five-year plan has been strongly oriented towards economic growth, with later plans also encompassing improvements in and access to education, health and housing. From the 1980s onwards, the notion of *pattana* found increasingly widespread expression within Khlong Toey slum communities, as prominent figureheads championed the causes of Bangkok's slum residents, as NGOs in receipt of national and foreign development aid proliferated, and as slum dwellers began to make public demands for improvements to their standards of living (Askew 2002). Since the 1997 economic crisis, Thai development discourse has expanded to include the notion of 'people-centred development', with the incorporation of Sufficiency Economy thinking into the country's latest National Economic and Social Development Plans, and with Thailand's 2007 Human Development Report focusing on the principles and application of the 'Sufficiency' approach. Within Sufficiency thinking, an exclusive focus on economic growth is rejected in favour of a 'human development' approach, which 'puts people and their wellbeing at the centre of development and provides an alternative to the traditional, more narrowly focused economic growth paradigm' (UNDP 2007: xvi). However, despite this discourse, economic growth and material advancement persist as the mainstays of 'development' in official policy and political decisions – and within the psyche of the urban poor and their rural counterparts – irrespective of attempts to expand the scope of alternative development models.

Despite the strong local and national historical orientation towards economic development, and despite being strongly oriented towards material advancement themselves, young slum dwellers were not consistently intent on forging futures free from the material hardship they knew. There were many times during fieldwork when people seemed defeated or deflated, when they engaged in self-destructive practices such as gambling, alcohol or drug abuse, and times when simply getting through the day seemed to be challenge enough for them. Other aspects of their lives in the present – trying to construct themselves as 'modern people' and to be 'good children' – were often counterproductive to their endeavours to create a springboard for material advancement. Nonetheless, the forging of better material futures was a key feature in their narratives and in the organization of everyday life.

There were three overarching, interrelated practices that young people engaged in, in their attempts to get by, get ahead and bring about the material futures they envisaged: studying, working to save money, and seeking support from others. The latter underpinned the former two – it was only with support from others that young slum dwellers were able to study and find work, and through these that they struggled to get ahead.

The majority of young people I met during fieldwork were involved in some form of study, reflecting the proximity of the fieldwork sites to NGOs whose core activities included educational sponsorship, to a community education centre and a slum-based school, and reflecting the widespread understanding of the role of education in achieving material advancement. Some of these young people were of compulsory school age (up to fifteen years) but some were older, engaging in studies to catch up with education they had missed out on when they were younger, to keep up with friends and try to qualify themselves to get jobs that were better paid than those they were currently doing. Some of these young people attended regular government-run schools – inside the slum for those enrolled at primary level and outside the slum for those enrolled at secondary level. Others attended vocational training colleges – some in the slum, others outside, depending on the choice of subject. Some were signed up to classes run by local NGOs, and only Ganya and Note – the two interpreters I worked with – were studying at university.

As well as studying, most of the young people I met during fieldwork were engaged in some form of paid work. Some of this was for family members, some was in the formal sector and some was in the informal sector, and any one person could be engaged in a mixture of these. The most common type of work was informal – serving on market stalls, street stalls and food stalls, preparing products such as fruit, spices and jasmine garlands for mobile street vendors, cleaning, collecting rubbish and labouring at the port. Some young people also engaged in less accepted money-generating activities, for example selling 'found'/stolen goods, but these mostly went under the radar – including mine – so were hard to capture properly and to do justice to here. The amount of time young people spent working varied greatly, depending largely on whether they combined work and study, and if they did, whether they studied full time or part time. This was linked in turn to family circumstances at the time. Remuneration was low, but whatever the details of work and earnings, young people were highly motivated by a desire to save for the future, or to pay for the education they hoped would bring them financial security later on in life.

In addition to studying and working, young slum dwellers turned to various people at different times in their lives, and to a range of people at any given time, as a key means of building the material futures they dreamed of. It was through support from family members, friends and patrons that young people were able to work and study. Young people sought assistance with various aspects of education, both financial and academic, with finding work and with procuring money and basic necessities such as food, shelter and clothing – all of which allowed young people to focus some of their efforts on securing the means of getting ahead.

Within the family, young people relied on their parents, grandparents, aunts, uncles and older siblings for assistance, and where they did not, it was because young people were themselves the main carers for others or were completely estranged from their families. Those who sought support from family members tended to be younger (below fifteen), and those who did not tended to be older. The kind of support they sought in connection with material advancement was mixed: for some it was limited to food, shelter and clothing; for others it consisted of work and remuneration; and for others it included schooling expenses as well as money and basic necessities. Young people also relied heavily on friends for money, food, shelter and help with coursework – or a combination of these.

One of the most pronounced methods by which young slum dwellers sought to improve their lot was through patronage originating outside the family, sometimes from individual patrons but also from a number of patrons at any one time. Young people drew on this patronage from a number of sources – through local NGOs, neighbours whose circumstances had taken a turn for the better or were generally more secure, partners who were considerably wealthier in material terms, and outsiders (usually accessed initially through NGOs) whose financial and social capital was widely understood to hold the key to future success. NGO patronage was by far the most popular, no doubt a result of the strong NGO presence in a number of slum communities, and this was widely used by young people of compulsory school age. Patronage from neighbours was also popular with young people of all ages, while those who had patrons in the form of partners or wealthy outsiders tended to be in their early twenties. The content of the patronage young people accessed varied. Those supported by NGOs on the whole received educational sponsorship, although this did extend to help with food, clothing and accommodation in situations of crisis. Where young people were supported by neighbours, they tended to receive food, shelter and access to work. Young people who received patronage from wealthy partners or outsiders received food, shelter, money and other material gifts, sometimes of considerable value, and occasionally employment.

Doing It Themselves

Young people's' narratives concerning the patronage they received were complex and sometimes contradictory. On the one hand, the cultural norm of *grengjai* (reluctance to impose upon others) found strong expression, and was offered readily in response to some of my offers to help young people in the small ways I could. The notion of reciprocity was a powerful one, and to accept patronage entailed binding oneself to one's patron and this – and the indebtedness it entailed – was seen as no small undertaking. On other hand, advancing one's material standard of living was a prevailing feature on the landscape of everyday life and dreams, and for those whose foundations in life were shaky, patronage was the only hope. On the one hand, young people readily sought and accepted support from others, firmly embedding themselves in networks of reciprocal exchange, yet on the other hand, their narratives around attempting to get ahead were marked by a strong sense of being alone in their endeavours. The support available to them, and in most cases that which had been available to them throughout their lives, was fragile.

Bee

As noted in the fieldwork notes at the beginning of this chapter, thirteen-year-old Bee dreamed of completing a Bachelor's degree and becoming a teacher or an office worker, and relied on her mother, her mother's network of friends and neighbours and two NGO-affiliated sponsors in order to try and fulfil her dreams. However, the sources of support open to her were far from reliable. In the year before fieldwork, Bee, her mother and sister were forced to flee their previous rented room and neighbourhood because their mother could not afford to pay the rent or to repay her debt to a local money lender whose interest rates were exorbitant. Fearing the consequences of non-repayment, they moved to a building site where Bee's mother had found work as a casual labourer, and they lived there in a corrugated iron hut for a couple of months. The sun beat hard, the rain poured in, the hut was hot and wet and life was extremely uncomfortable. Bee and her sister continued to attend school during this time. After two months, Bee's mother decided to leave the construction site because she was concerned about the girls' safety (most other construction workers were men), and they spent the following few months living on the street. During this time, Bee and her sister stopped going to school and did whatever casual work they could find to help their mother make ends meet. After a few months, Bee's mother managed to borrow enough money from a friend to pay the deposit for a rented room in a different community where they had been living for some months when I met them. Bee had returned to school but her sister had not. Despite providing shelter for her children, as well as the informally adopted son of one of her cousins, Bee's mother continued to struggle financially. She had not paid the money back to her friend for the deposit on the room, and she had borrowed more money from a local money lender in order to pay a telephone company for an enormous bill that Bee's younger sister had incurred, but had actually not paid the phone bill or the debt to the money lender because she had used the money for 'daily living'. At the time of fieldwork, Bee's mother faced prosecution by the telephone company, feared violent reprisals from the money lender and was considering fleeing the neighbourhood.

The precariousness of the support that Bee's mother, Mae Bee, was able to provide for her family was in part a reflection and extension of the insecurity that characterized her own past. Mae Bee was born in Khlong Toey slum to a single mother whose husband left before Mae Bee was born. She had to leave school after four years of primary education and worked in a local market in order to support her mother in the struggle for daily survival. The subsequent work opportunities open to Mae Bee were limited to the informal sector: street vending, construction work and cleaning – all menial jobs with low social status and inadequate pay. When she was young, Mae Bee and her mother were twice relocated from their home as part of the Thai government's shifting policy towards the 'problem' of urban slums – once to a different part of Khlong Toey and once to the outskirts of Bangkok where social networks and work opportunities fell away. She experienced frequent beatings at the hands of her mother's boyfriends, and went on to have violent relationships with the fathers of both of her children. Her first boyfriend, Bee's father, left her when Bee was a baby, and her subsequent boyfriend died several years ago. Low education due to childhood poverty and a concomitant reproduction of disadvantaged economic positioning, an absence of adequate social security nets and gendered violence all contributed to making the support that Mae Bee was able to provide for Bee very fragile. After returning from fieldwork, I learned that Bee was doing well at school, although one of her sponsors had withdrawn support for her education, and she continued to work as a cleaner every morning, doing longer hours to try and compensate for the loss of sponsorship. She was living with an aunt and her aunt's family on a temporary basis because Mae Bee was working very long hours in order to try and repay her debts and felt that she was not able to provide the care necessary for her children.

Nan

As also discussed in the opening fieldwork notes, fifteen-year-old Nan dreamed of returning to school, learning Japanese and becoming a tour guide. She relied in particular on her grandmother and a small local NGO in her attempt to realize her dreams, and also held out hope for the financial support promised by her father. However, by the end of fieldwork, each of these forms of assistance had all but evaporated. By the time I met her, Nan's grandmother (Ba Lek) had been suffering from diabetes for a number of years and, despite taking medication, found that she was unable to work the hours demanded by her job. The NGO that employed her as a cook agreed to let her work part time, but this meant a reduction in income and she found it increasingly difficult to support Nan financially, especially since her husband's recent death had already diminished her own financial security. In addition to and connected with the financial hardship that Ba Lek experienced, she had begun to suffer with the emotional strain of being Nan's primary carer.

She worried constantly about Nan staying out late and would scour the neighbourhood at night-time looking for Nan when she wasn't home by her curfew of 10 p.m., and she found Nan's spending habits unsustainable. Ba Lek found it increasingly difficult to cope and the two of them began to argue frequently.

As with Mae Bee, the fragility of the support that Ba Lek was able to provide for Nan can be understood in part in the context of vulnerability that has marked her own life. Ba Lek was born in the north-east of Thailand into a rice-farming family. Her father died when she was young and her mother struggled to raise her family of six children and keep the farm going. Ba Lek attended school for four years and left in order to help her mother on the farm, but when she was fifteen she decided to move to the nearest town to work as a waitress, as repeated crop failures meant there was insufficient money coming into the household and a desperate need for it. It was in the town to which she relocated that Ba Lek met her first husband, with whom she had two children. However, he left when Ba Lek was twenty-three, and at that point she moved to Bangkok where she undertook an array of informal jobs, leaving her children with their grandmother in the countryside. Ba Lek met her late husband when she was in her thirties, and she moved to Khlong Toey where he worked in a chemical factory and where she continued to work in various casual, informal sector jobs. Again, low education due to childhood poverty and a concomitant disadvantage within the labour market, as well as inadequate social security nets, all contributed to the fragility that characterized the support Ba Lek was able to provide for Nan.

In addition to the faltering support available from her grandmother, the NGO that had earlier agreed to support Nan in resuming her studies withdrew their offer, as it transpired to be conditional on Nan's conversion to Christianity. The NGO was affiliated to a community church and directed by the church pastor and his wife, and in return for their patronage, Nan was urged to attend church every Sunday and undertake the bible study set for young people in the congregation and discussed in study groups after Sunday services. Nan did not want to do these things, and following the rules laid down by the pastor and his wife was very uncomfortable for her. After a short period of deliberation, she determined that the conversion expected of her in return for educational sponsorship was a price that she could not pay. While this may be a rather extreme example, it illustrates the phenomenon of young people refusing NGO-organized patronage because of the conditionality attached to it – becoming morally indebted to the NGO and obligated to respond to the requests made of them.

As well as the fragility that characterized the support available from her grandmother and the local NGO, the financial assistance that Nan hoped for from her father did not materialize, at least during fieldwork. Nan's parents broke up when she was three years old and her mother moved out of the family home. Nan does not know where her mother went, but was told by her grandmother that her father was an alcoholic and her mother could not tolerate the behaviour born of his drinking. A few years later, Nan's father lost his job and took Nan with him to live in the basement of an apartment building, where they stayed for about a year. During this time, Nan's father earned small amounts of money collecting rubbish for recycling and Nan started school, but left to help her father work. For the next four years, Nan and her father moved back and forth between the streets and various forms of temporary accommodation, and Nan was in and out of school. When Nan was eleven, her father began a new relationship, but Nan did not get on with her father's new partner and left for Bangkok, to live with her grandmother in Khlong Toey slum. Nan's father had promised he would support her financially by providing money for her schooling, but he did not have the money at that time. After a year, Nan's grandmother sent her back to the north-east of Thailand to live with her father and his partner, and in turn they sent Nan back to Bangkok to live with an aunt and uncle, also in Khlong Toey slum. Nan found life with her aunt and uncle unbearable; she was not allowed to go out in the evenings and if she did she was beaten on her return. She left her aunt and uncle's house, this time to stay with a friend whose parents ran a street food stall, where she worked in return for food and a place to sleep. When Nan was thirteen, she moved back in with her grandmother and when she was fourteen she began working at the local NGO. Shortly after I met Nan, her father announced that he and his partner were expecting a baby and that he would be unable to provide the money for Nan to return to school as his financial commitments were now elsewhere. Shortly after returning from fieldwork, I learned that Nan had left her job at the NGO, had not yet returned to school, and was dividing her time between her grandmother's room and several friends' houses, doing whatever work she could find to earn a little money.

Jim

As we have seen, seventeen-year-old Jim dreamed of getting a good job, earning good money and living independently, and drew heavily on his friend's mother (Mae Goi) for accommodation, work, money and assistance with college fees in order to try and turn his dreams into reality. However, it transpired that this source of support, so central to Jim's endeavours, was also highly precarious. During fieldwork, Mae Goi fled the neighbourhood because of considerable debts to a community savings group and a local money lender, which she was unable to repay. Initially Jim continued to stay at her house and run her makeup stall, but later moved in with his step-grandmother while deciding what to do next, and he withdrew from the community college course on which he had enrolled. An interview with Mae Goi's son revealed that this was not the first time Mae Goi had been forced to accrue such substantial and unsustainable debts in order to support her family. Six years previous to fieldwork, Mae Goi and her husband had been forced to leave their old neighbourhood and take their son out of school because of debts to local money lenders. Since moving to Khlong Toey slum, Mae Goi's husband became ill with liver failure and was paralysed on his left side and unable to work, adding further pressure to the considerable financial hardship that Mae Goi already experienced. For Jim, it transpired that the material support she was able to give was short-lived.

Jim neither sought nor received support from his birth family. He was born in Khlong Toey and had lived with his mother and father there until he was two years old, when his parents split up and his father left. Shortly after this, his mother remarried and Jim, his mother and stepfather moved to an upgraded slum community. His mother and stepfather were both in work and things went well for a while. Jim went to school until he was ten, but at this point his mother had a row with her sister and had to leave Khlong Toey. She took Jim with her and left Jim's stepfather behind. Jim and his mother moved to the outskirts of Bangkok and Jim left school to work with his mother as a labourer in a fruit and vegetable market. When Jim was twelve, his mother's new boyfriend moved in with them, and life at home gradually became intolerable, as he was regularly beaten for reasons that he struggled to understand. When he was fifteen, Jim ran away and lost contact with his mother. He returned to Khlong Toey to find his stepfather, to whom he had been very close. His stepfather had just been evicted from the community where he had been living as it was being knocked down to make room to expand the port, and was renting a room in another community. Jim stayed with him for a while, but his stepfather worked as a long-distance lorry driver for the Port Authority of Thailand and was often away. While on a job driving back from Laos, Jim's stepfather was involved in a road accident and was sent to prison for eighteen months. During this time, Jim stayed alternately with his step-grandmother and with friends, and struggled to find work to support himself. He stole or begged for food and did whatever casual work he could find, collecting rubbish for recycling and running errands for neighbours and local businesses. The year before I met Jim, his stepfather was released from prison and moved back to Khlong Toey slum, but died during fieldwork. After returning from fieldwork, I learned that Jim went to the north of Thailand to seek out relatives who run a family business there. He returned to Khlong Toey slum because the relationships deteriorated, and returned to work as a casual labourer at a local fruit and vegetable market.

The young people discussed here, while distinctive in the details of their lives, were united by a great deal of turbulence due to the precariousness that marked the assistance available to them, and in this they were not alone. Every young slum dweller in this research experienced some loss of support during fieldwork, or had done previous to it, and there was nothing in their situations to indicate that this would not happen again. This is not to say that people did not succeed in reaching the goals to which they aspired – gaining educational qualifications, getting jobs, even finding decent-quality housing outside of the slum. Rather, the point is that if successes were achieved, it was in spite of the considerable instability that marked the support open to young people, despite the precariousness that marked their journeys. Sometimes things would go well for individuals for a while, even a relatively long while, but sooner or later the support mechanisms that enabled this seemed to falter: family members lost their jobs, became ill, died, were forced to flee their neighbourhoods, moved upcountry, went to prison or (re)turned to alcohol abuse. NGO scholarships did not always work out. Friends had very limited resources with which to support each other, and the wealth of community patrons might be the result of unsustainable debts which resulted in the threat of violence from money lenders and the end of patronage. Patronage from wealthy partners always ceased when relationships broke down. For young slum dwellers, the journey towards a better material future was easily disrupted, the potential for derailment always lurking round the corner.

It is true that Thailand has systems that mean, in theory, that the attempt to build a better life in material terms is undertaken with public assistance for those who cannot depend on support from private or family networks. Universal education provision means that all children are given a 'free' school place until the age of fifteen. However, the hidden yet necessary costs involved, such as those incurred in purchasing study materials and school uniforms, and the loss of potential earnings from young people, effectively preclude many in low socio-economic positions from participating unless they can access financial assistance outside their families, or unless those families become severely indebted. Thailand also has a social security system, but this only provides minimal benefits to those working in the formal sector and is therefore not available to the majority of those I met during fieldwork, who were engaged in informal work.

So it would seem that, with inadequate official support and such precarious assistance from those around them, young slum dwellers really were forced to forge their own futures, made ultimately responsible for bringing about the material advancements they aspired to. It may be true that 'the Thai way to power and resources is to seek patronage, to attach oneself to a superior power … and to become the protégé … of somebody who has more resources' (Mulder 1990: 4), but for many of the young people in this study, consistent and reliable patronage was not something they felt they had access to.

Doing It Ourselves

The way in which young slum dwellers struggled to get ahead with little consistent assistance was strongly reflected in their narratives, which spoke not only of a sense of being responsible for their own material futures, but of a sense in which this was as it *should* be. Young people referred to the process of building a better material future as something over which they had choice and control, and in connection with this they spoke of the material futures they envisaged in terms of a model of adulthood characterized by self-reliance and independence. Here, the felt sense of agency was strong. Many stated that if they studied hard enough, they would be able to get good jobs, and that if they worked hard enough, they would be able to earn enough money to have a good standard of living. The following excerpt is taken from a conversation I had with Or, a young mother in her early twenties who ran a street food stall, in which she spoke of her dream to move to a 'beautiful' neighbourhood and open an international restaurant:

> Yes, this is a big dream. Will it happen? If I work hard at the noodle stall then I think I can make it work. Let's say eighty per cent. For this I have to work every day and take no rest. But it's worth it, to make a better life for me and my son.

Similarly, when I asked seventeen-year-old Jim early on in fieldwork if he thought he would succeed in his dream of earning a lot of money, he spoke in terms of personal effort:

> As I said, I study at the community college now, I am studying for my lower secondary exams. I have two more years left. It is very, very difficult for me to study, I'm not a clever person, and sometimes I am lazy to study too, but I keep trying, keep trying. I believe if I study hard I will get the qualifications and I can start to improve my life.

Note, a young man in his early twenties, gave the following response to my question about whether he thought he would achieve his goal of running his own business: 'as long as I keep focused on the goal, even if I go off track I always come back to the goal, so I believe I can be successful, yes'. Since returning from fieldwork, continued correspondence with Note revealed an entrenched belief that his achievements were, to a large extent, the product of his own hard work:

> You think I have what I have today because of luck? No, luck has nothing to do with it. It's because I work hard. Luck is nothing. When I was on the streets I worked hard, even when I was a kid. Now I want to improve myself right, go up, up, up in the social, but it's not luck that lifts me, it's working hard.

Despite acknowledging and feeling grateful for the assistance they received, the notion of succeeding – or not – through personal effort was prominent. Those who did not consider themselves to be on track to securing better material futures explained why this was the case with reference to their own behaviour, for example referring to being 'lazy' or spending their time in 'nonsense' ways – not working or studying enough. Many also located the reason for their lack of success in the personal choices and behaviour of those in their immediate families. For example, thirteen-year-old Bee explained the current precariousness of her situation with reference mainly to her younger sister:

> Now my family is having a very difficult time about money. My sister made a problem ... She called her friend many times on the mobile, and it cost so much ... a lot compared to mum's income. Well, I do what work I can but I don't get paid very much, not enough to fix the problem. And mum doesn't earn much money. Compared to the cost of the phone bill mum earns just a little. She borrowed some money from a money lender but that didn't pay the phone bill so we still have the debt. Now I am so worried because there is a notice from the court saying that if we don't pay we are in trouble. And we have to pay the money lender too. My stupid sister! I don't want to go back to the hardship we had before, I feel my life is just starting to get better.

Similarly, many adult carers attributed young people's apparent failure to improve their lives to personal choice and behaviour, bemoaning what they saw as a wilful destructiveness in a context of increased opportunity. The father of a seventeen-year-old girl, in talking about the differences he perceived between his life as a young person and his daughter's, said:

> My girl has the chance to make a better life. Her mother and I are poor, but she has the chance to improve her life and not know the hardship as we do. She has the opportunity for education, which we never had, but she chooses to spend all her time with her friends instead of studying. How can she improve her life in this way?

The sentiments in this narrative were common among adult carers; young people could achieve upward mobility if they tried hard and made the right decisions, and it was ultimately their responsibility to bring about their own material advancement, albeit with gratefully acknowledged support from others. If they did not succeed in improving their lot, it must be down to personal choice – assistance was there for the taking and opportunities existed that never did before.

Linked to the understanding of the journey towards a better material future as their responsibility, young people also spoke of the destination – the future itself – in terms of self-reliance and independence. When I asked Jim what the most difficult things about his life were, he replied:

> The most difficult thing now is about the new beginning. I am not a kid any more, I am becoming an adult and I am trying to improve my life. Going back to school and working, I wonder can I do these things? Can I study again? Will I get a good job? I believe I can but it's very scary. In Thailand we become an adult when we can take care of ourselves, stop relying on others and look after ourselves. I am coming to be an adult so I should rely only on myself.

Other young people echoed this emphasis on self-reliance in their narratives about the upward mobility they endeavoured to realize, and adult carers frequently cited self-reliance as one of the main hopes they had for the young people growing up in their charge. Nan's grandmother, Ba Lek, offered the following when I asked about her hopes for Nan in the future:

> One thing is that I would like to see Nan be able to take care of herself. She only has me to look after her now but I am old and sick. Although she has her father and stepmother upcountry, she will not live with them so she must learn to take care of herself, be independent and not rely on others to help her.

There is a strong resonance between the sense of self-reliance and individual responsibility that characterized slum dwellers' experiences and narratives, and the ideals promoted within certain elements of the context in which they were located. While it is impossible to identify an unequivocal, straightforward, causal or one-way relationship between grand-level principles and people's practices or interpretations of them, I highlight a few widely promoted ideals here, as it was by virtue of acting and thinking in accordance with them that young slum dwellers' attempts to succeed were ironically so readily thwarted.

Despite the characterization of Thailand as an affiliative society 'in which people greatly depend upon each other and thus find their security in dependence and patronage rather than in "individualism"' (Mulder 1990: 60), elements of the discursive frameworks in which participants were located celebrated the notions of self-reliance and personal responsibility.

First, there was the broad cultural script that widely condemned the practice of 'scrounging', evident in the narratives of poor and wealthy participants. The following excerpt is taken from a conversation I had with a university professor and is illustrative of a general disdain for what was understood as a tendency among poor people towards an over-reliance on others. In this particular conversation, the university professor was explaining why she was opposed to the Thai (Thaksin) government at the time and what she dismissed as its 'populist' initiatives to make money available to poor communities:

> Thaksin, we believe he just wants votes. This is why he gives money to poor people, to make them vote for him. Like the one million baht fund, yes the people like having the money, of course they do, but we believe this doesn't really help them as they won't learn to stand by themselves. In Thai we say *kee kaw*, like a scrounger. How can these people really improve themselves deep down if they always rely on other people to drop money onto them?

Second, and related to the disdain for *kee kaw*, slum dwellers' narratives of self-reliance and personal responsibility resonate with one of the key principles of Theravada Buddhism. As noted in Chapter 1, this holds as one of its central tenets the concept of *kamma*, which roughly translates as intentional action that brings about consequences: 'Actions which are willed, deliberate, accompanied by volition, are kamma; these are potentially productive of a future result' (L.K. Mills 1999: 31). According to Theravada Buddhist philosophy, it is through one's intentional actions in the past that people's current conditions have come about, and through their intentional actions in the present that people determine their conditions in this and future life cycles, and in spiritual terms whether or not they reach *Nibbana* or complete the journey towards Awakening. The law of *kamma* contends that 'unwholesome' intentional actions bring about painful results and that 'wholesome' intentional actions bring about pleasant results (ibid.: 32).

So, the cultural religious framework within which young slum dwellers were located places considerable emphasis on personal responsibility for one's circumstances. With reference to the relationship between *kamma* and socio-economic positioning, Mulder (1990: 4) notes the following historical perception, which continues to prevail in present-day Thai society:

> … a man's position in this world logically followed from the karma … that he had built up in previous existences. If he happened to be poor and powerless in this existence, he somehow deserved it … To question the social order or one's place within it was to doubt the justice of Karma.

The concept of *kamma* was an important orienting principle for participants in their everyday lives, frequently invoked as the reason to behave in certain ways and not in others, and as the explanation for a good or bad turn of events. While the relationship between abstract philosophical or religious principles and everyday practice and belief is highly complex, the emphasis that participants placed on personal responsibility for building better futures echoed this feature of the context in which they lived their lives and attempted to forge their futures.

Third, slum dwellers' narratives of self-reliance resonate with common interpretations of Sufficiency Economy philosophy. The Sufficiency approach contends that 'individuals need a certain measure of self-reliance to deal best with the market' (UNDP 2007: xv), and people in this study referred quite often to Sufficiency Economy thinking. One afternoon, I went on a neighbourhood walk with fifteen-year-old Bew, and during our walk, as she was showing me where her extended family lived, we passed through a particularly deprived area. She explained that Loi, her informally adopted younger brother, had lived in the area previous to moving in with Bew's family, and this led to a conversation between Bew and myself about the events leading up to his informal adoption. When I asked Bew if her family received any assistance in looking after Loi, she replied that they didn't, and went on to say: 'Well, we have Sufficiency Economy now'. When I asked what she meant, she said, 'We do things ourselves'.

Fourth, the notions of self-reliance and responsibility resonate with the view, suggested in the emerging youth and development discourse, that as long as young people take responsibility for their own development through making the 'right' decisions and taking the 'right' courses of action, their futures will be bright.

Finally, the notions of self-reliance and personal responsibility resonate strongly with neoliberal economics and the particular form of subjectivity that this promotes. The period spanning the 1940s to the 1960s in Thailand has been labelled by commentators as the American era (Baker and Phongpaichit 2005), a period in which the foundations of neoliberalism were laid down with substantial backing from the United States, and a period characterized by the promotion of a particular model of development. At the end of the Second World War and the dawn of the Cold War, Thailand embarked on a rapid journey towards a free market economy, characterized by the promotion of economic growth in the private sector, foreign investment and the condemnation of state-led development policies (ibid.: 151). This free market ideology has been further promoted in the Thai context through the structural adjustment loans given to the Thai government by the IMF at the beginning of the 1980s and in the wake of the Asian financial crisis in the late 1990s.

At the heart of the free market agenda, pressed upon Thailand by the US government and multilateral institutions, and pursued internally with vigour, lies a model of the human subject as a decision-making individual who is personally responsible for their own development or lack thereof. According to this model, 'action and responsibility for action reside with the person of the individual' (Preston 1996: 253):

> The free market comprises atomistic individuals who know their own autonomously arising needs and wants and who make contracts with other individuals through the mechanism of the marketplace to satisfy those needs and wants.

This notion, of the human subject as a decision-making agent responsible for his/her development, underpins the 'blame the victim' approach to urban poverty that rose to particular prominence in the United States in the 1960s following Oscar Lewis's description of a culture of poverty within marginalized communities. As noted in Chapter 2, the culture of poverty thesis, which – in its widely interpreted form – sees the persistence of poverty as a result of the intergenerational transmission of certain negative attitudes and behaviours, continues to inform thinking and policy around inner-city marginalization to this day (Bourgois 2001).

In their personal endeavours to get ahead, and in their valorization of self-reliance and personal responsibility, the young slum dwellers in this research map neatly onto the prominent discourses outlined here, and these discourses together provide something of a culture of legitimacy for participants' narratives. And yet, ironically, it is precisely by virtue of being ideal subjects in terms of each of these discourses that participants' journeys towards a better future were so very insecure. By operating in accordance with the rules of the game – by assuming ultimate responsibility for forging a better future – urban poor youth emerge as the losers. With little in the way of reliable support, a future of higher education, decent work, liveable incomes and secure housing remains on the distant horizon.

During fieldwork, those who seemed to be on track to securing, or maintaining, a high material standard of living were the few in receipt of substantial and consistent backing from people who wielded considerable financial and social power.

Note was born in Khlong Toey but was sold at birth to a foster family outside, with whom he lived until he was thirteen, when his relationship with family members began to break down and eventually prompted him to leave home. He had run away for the first time at the age of eleven, staying at friends' houses and on the streets, and continued to run away every time his domestic situation became unbearable for him, but each time his foster family tracked him down. When Note was thirteen, he ran away for good and lived on the streets for two years, stealing food and money from shops, begging, racing motorbikes, working at a paper factory and working at a street food stall in a struggle to survive. During his time on the streets, Note became addicted to gambling and when his gambling debts got out of control he returned to his foster family's house and stole their money. He was caught by the police and sent to a youth correction unit, where he stayed for six months, until a lawyer from a slum-based NGO whose remit included working with juvenile offenders approached him and asked if he would like to apply to their orphanage and resume his studies. His application was successful and he moved from the youth correction unit into the orphanage. After a few months, Note was sent to the north of Thailand, where the foundation runs an agricultural school for young people deemed to be at risk of returning to the streets if they remain in Bangkok. There he completed his compulsory education and returned to Bangkok to study computing for three years at vocational school. After this, he won a scholarship to study for his International Baccalaureate in Europe, and having successfully completed this he was awarded a further scholarship to study for a Bachelor's degree in America. Through the NGO that supported him in his early studies, Note was later introduced to a wealthy American businessman who provided him with considerable amounts of money and accommodation in America and Bangkok, and who arranged several stints of paid work experience in his US-based company. This patron also agreed to employ Note, on completion of his degree, in another of his US-based companies, in order that Note could gain the two years' work experience necessary to embark on an MBA course.

Note was not on course to realizing his dreams of material advancement by virtue of being self-reliant or personally responsible, despite his intermittent vision to the contrary; he had the backing of a powerful slum-based NGO and, more importantly, through this, of an extremely rich sponsor whose patronage proved, for the most part, to be reliable. In this he was unusual, and a source of considerable jealousy among his peers in the slum. Before I met Note, I had heard about him through other young people who told me of his pending return from studying in Europe and of their envy of, among other things, the sponsorship he received and the opportunity this gave him to make something of his life. Once he arrived in Khlong Toey and began hanging around in some of the same places as Ganya and I, our encounters were invariably strained, Note telling of his experiences abroad and Ganya responding by emphasizing her seniority – she was a few months older than him – to elevate her status to match his.

The wealthy young people in this research relied heavily on their families and networks of affiliates and acquaintances to provide the dependable and unswerving support that young slum dwellers were so badly in need of but did not have. And these families and extended networks were, by definition, well positioned to assist in a multitude of ways, providing the inputs necessary for the accrual and preservation of material wealth. It was by virtue of having such a head-start in the game that these wealthy young people were rewarded by it.

Not only was the dream of material advancement something of a mirage for many, but through their attempts to build better material futures in the only ways available to them, young slum dwellers inadvertently undermined their attempts to look wealthy and modern. The very need for assistance from outsiders in the first place speaks of a considerable level of poverty, and indeed having to turn to NGO-affiliated patrons was widely recognized as one of the markers of poverty and low status. In addition, young slum dwellers further weakened their claims to the status of good children in their attempts to get ahead. In turning to family members for assistance – although this assistance may not have been adequate or reliable – young people were seen as taking from, rather than giving to, the family. As P Yom, a mother of a thirteen-year-old girl, commented:

When I was young I had to work to pay for my study. I left school when I was ten to help get money for my mum, but I went back to school when I was fourteen, to night school, and paid for it myself. I worked in the day and studied at night. And I didn't ask my mum for anything. Nowadays, no. Just taking and no giving.

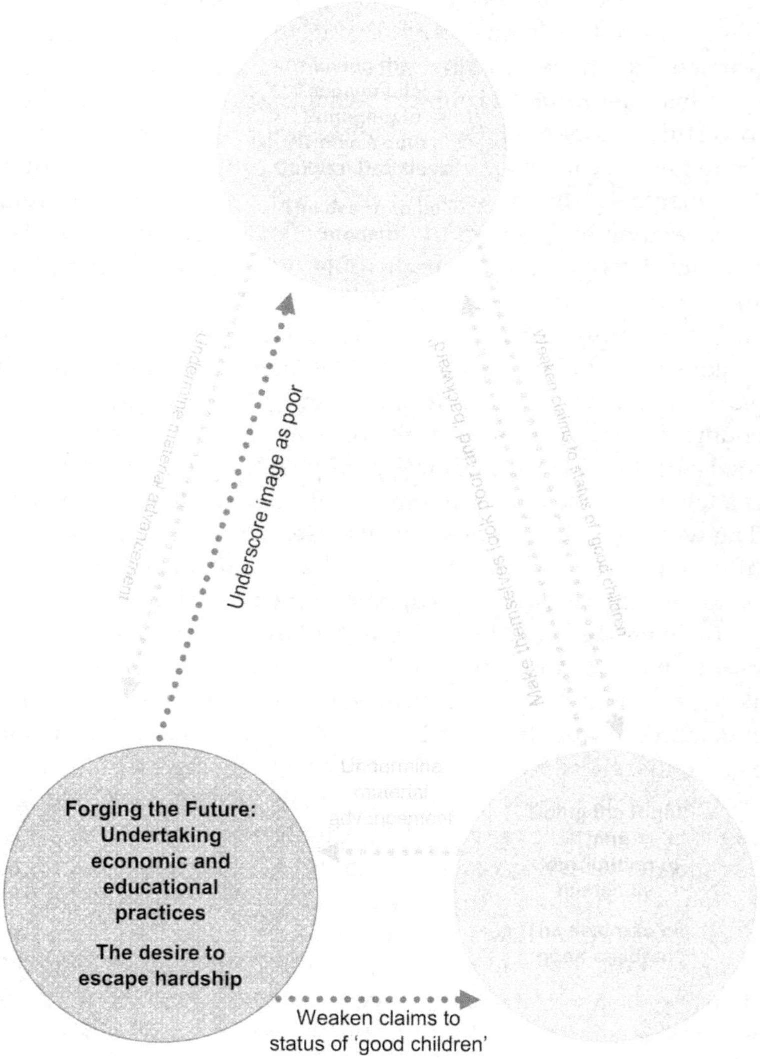

Figure 6.1. Diagram showing that building a better material future can be precarious and have unintended, negative outcomes.

The Adverse Outcomes of Agency

The notion of working towards a better material future was a strong orienting principle for young slum dwellers, whatever objective material conditions they were living in. Despite being firmly embedded within personal and social networks and receiving help from various people to build better material futures, they were forced to take ultimate responsibility as individuals for their attempts at material advancement due to the precariousness of the support available to them. The notion of individual responsibility was strongly reflected in slum dwellers' narratives, both in terms of how things *were* and how things *should be*, and this notion of being individual agents responsible for their own success or failure resonated strongly with the ideals promoted in certain prominent elements of the local, national and global context in which their lives were nested. However, it was by virtue of exercising agency in accordance with these very ideals that young slum dwellers found the journey towards material advancement so arduous, the destination so hard to reach. Those born into relative wealth could depend on others and had a relatively smooth journey towards maintaining material success. For those who had no choice but to strive for development by doing it themselves, the journey was unstable, their efforts to succeed easily undermined.

In their endeavours to build better material futures, young slum dwellers also – unwittingly – undermined their attempts to construct themselves as wealthy, modern subjects *and* good children. The need to rely heavily on outsiders for assistance points to poverty, and turning to family members for support easily became conceived of as a neglect of filial duty. These processes are illustrated in the highlighted elements of the theoretical framework diagram (Figure 6.1).

Part III

Conclusion

This book has explored the lives of young people living in slum communities in Bangkok. It has examined their search for a better life, investigating what this means for people, how they go about trying to secure certain elements of it and the consequences of their endeavours. In this concluding chapter, I give an overview of the key findings and discuss what they might contribute to the literatures outlined in Chapter 2. I then draw attention to one of the main methodological issues that arose in this study, but which does not often receive attention in scholarly work. The chapter closes with some broad ideas about what might be done to support young people living in adversity, in their search for a better life.

Summary of Findings

The three empirical chapters in this book (Part II) each explored a different sphere of everyday practice: attempts to *live the teenage life*, attempts to *contribute to the family*, and attempts to bring about *material advancement*. In the first empirical chapter, we saw how young slum dwellers were actively oriented towards a lifestyle characterized by conspicuous consumption of the commodities of the global youth culture industry and related practices of embodiment, representation and interaction. In this, we saw how young people were actively attempting to distance themselves from associations with poverty, parochialism and old fashioned, rural ways, and how each element of the teenage life discussed was strongly endorsed by market forces. In that chapter, I highlighted the way in which, as young people attempted to present themselves as modern, global subjects, they inadvertently weakened their attempts to achieve 'good child' status, through diverting energy, time and money away from the family, and in light of related narratives concerning wayward youth. In attempting to live the teenage life, young people also undermined their chances of material advancement, through diverting time and money away from education and paid work and the potential opportunities these bring to access decent jobs and save money respectively, and thereby improve material standards of living. In addition, I highlighted the way in which the dream of being and being seen as wealthy, global and modern itself remained out of reach for participants, in light of the absence of adequate resources, in light of the constant arrival of newer branded commodities into Bangkok's landscape of intense commercialization, and in light of the difficulty young people experienced in maintaining their images outside the slum environment. Discussion of living the teenage life also pointed to the way in which young slum dwellers held themselves responsible when their attempts to create their desired images did not succeed.

In the second empirical chapter we saw how young slum dwellers were also actively oriented towards contributing to their families, through direct and indirect financial support and through the performance of domestic and care work. In this, we saw how they were actively attempting to construct themselves as good children, and how this was necessary if they were to make viable subjects of themselves according to the local cultural script of filial obligation. In that chapter, I highlighted the way in which, as young people attempted to demonstrate their moral worth, they inadvertently weakened their attempts to look wealthy and modern (in light of the widespread association of assisting the family with poverty and old fashioned ways) and further undermined their attempts at material advancement – again through diverting time and money away from education and paid work. Further to this, I highlighted the way in which dreams of augmenting moral status were themselves somewhat elusive to participants, due to the absence of resources with which to support their families to the degree required and the related narrative of the 'uncaring/unhelpful teenager'. Discussion here also illustrated the way in which young slum dwellers blamed themselves when they failed to fulfil their filial obligations in the eyes of their adult carers.

In the third empirical chapter, we saw how young slum dwellers were, in addition, actively oriented towards future material advancement, and how they worked towards this through studying and working and by turning to others for assistance with these. In this, we saw how they struggled determinedly to escape the material hardship that characterized their life experiences, and how the notion of material development was both promoted and problematized in their surrounding context. In that chapter, I highlighted the way in which dreams of material advancement also seemed elusive, in light of the fragility of the support available to participants. Furthermore, I pointed to the way in which, in their endeavours to build better material futures, young slum dwellers weakened their own chances of success in building images of wealth and modernity, as the very need for assistance in the first place, coupled with the fragility of that assistance, underscored their poverty and undermined their attempts to construct themselves as good children; they required support *from* their families instead of giving *to* them. This chapter emphasized the way in which young slum dwellers held themselves to account for their apparent inability to pave the way for future material advancement.

Throughout these empirical chapters, I have placed an emphasis on the unintended, negative consequences of young slum dwellers' practices, in particular on the ways in which attempts to build a better life in each sphere of practice remain somewhat elusive and – importantly – result in significant compromises to their endeavours in the other two spheres. The theoretical framework diagram introduced at the beginning of the book, explicated in Chapter 2 and referred to in each empirical chapter, represents how the young people in this study are caught in a cycle of unintended consequences, exercising agency within a given sphere but always contending with the ways in which this seems to perpetually undermine their endeavours in other spheres. This issue – of the unintended consequences of exercising agency from positions of structural disadvantage – has a number of implications for the literatures discussed in Chapter 2.

Implications of Findings

First, the findings in this book highlight the importance of addressing multiple spheres of life in the study of marginalized youth in the Global South and in the policies directed towards them. If research and policy are restricted to one sphere of practice or element therein, they are likely to overlook the interconnections between multiple spheres, and it is within these interconnections that counterproductive tendencies can occur. As it stands, the literature on youth in Thailand is comprised of studies that tend to focus on one aspect of life – health, leisure or illicit pursuits – and anyway is largely silent on the issue of agency and its outcomes, which would be an analytical precursor to exploring the ways in which agency 'bumps up' against itself in different realms of activity.

The youth and development literature such as that encapsulated in the World Bank's 2007 report *Development and the Next Generation* is also out of touch with the multi-faceted nature of the lives, dreams and efforts of marginalized youth. Here it appears to be less a matter of having ignored the voices of youth and more a matter of having focused so selectively on one aspect – that of productive economic activity – that other salient elements of their lives are side-lined.

If different spheres of life were recognized in these literatures, then the adverse interconnections between them – the nuanced ways in which practices in one area adversely affect endeavours in others – could be acknowledged, and policy and programming could be built on a more holistic understanding of the complexities that young people face in their search for a better life.

Second, considering the unintended consequences of young slum dwellers' agency helps to remind us of the ways in which structures such as market forces, cultural norms and expectations surrounding gender and generational relations and poverty, to name a few, constrain and are constitutive of marginalized agency. In some ways, the unintended consequences of the practices emphasized in this study are a product of these structures; participants look 'bad' by virtue of trying to live the teenage life partly because of their low positioning within an unequal socio-economic structure and the strain this places on their scarce resources. Participants look 'poor' and 'backwards' by virtue of trying to construct themselves as good children, again in part because of their low positioning within the socio-economic structure and the restricted options this leaves them for repaying the debt of gratitude into which they are born. Participants' efforts in working towards material advancement are continually thwarted due to their low positioning within an unequal socio-economic structure and the resulting fragility of support available to them.

The literature on Thai youth is largely silent on the issue of social structures, tending instead towards viewing individual and group behaviours as if they are isolated from the contexts in which they transpire. The youth and development discourse is also insufficiently attuned to the structures that constrain and constitute agency; it seems to assume that young people's efforts to bring about development, along with state and private sector support for those efforts, will be sufficient to achieve the outcomes intended. And yet, as we have seen, those efforts are made within – and made extremely difficult by – the constraints of socio-economic inequality as well as other structures. If research and policy relating to the lives of marginalized youth in the developing world are to understand and benefit those young people, then they must be more attuned to the multiple structures that surround agency and the unintended consequences these give rise to.

Third, the empirical chapters in this book serve as a reminder that unintended consequences can ensue from the process of *participating* in dominant cultures as well as resisting them. Many of the studies that emphasize the contradictory, ironic or counterproductive outcomes of youth cultural practice focus on the unintended consequences of practices of resistance – implicitly or explicitly. The empirical chapters in this book show how, even when young people from marginalized communities attempt to participate in dominant cultures, their actions still entail some profoundly counterproductive outcomes. Even when they embrace dominant notions of wealth, sexuality, global connection and modernity, even when they enact the dominant cultural norm of filial obligation, and even when they strive for the dominant goal of material development and assume personal responsibility for it, still they undermine their own endeavours.

My attention to the unintended consequences of participants' practices points to a methodological conclusion that I would like to revisit here. It has been by virtue of withdrawing from participants' lives, both physically and emotionally, and engaging with critical theories about them as opposed to their own understandings, that I have been able to acknowledge and analyse the unintended outcomes of their endeavours and the structures that inform these. While in the field and aligned with participants' own interpretations and with the new social studies of childhood and its emphasis on agency, my analysis was much more strongly oriented towards the positive outcomes of agency, towards seeing the positive through its mere exercise. Once I returned from fieldwork and as time passed, I became increasingly distant from participants, albeit still in contact with some, and increasingly aligned with other literatures, and the 'successes' began to appear more as instances in longer life courses whose trajectories would rise and fall over time. My analysis shifted to place more of an emphasis on some of the structures that constrain as well as enable agency and the complex interactions between these through everyday cultural practices. This points not only to the importance of ensuring a degree of detachment from participants following fieldwork (should over-attachment have been an issue), but to the potential for multiple and shifting interpretations of data and the related task of social research in bringing these, and the contexts in which they are produced, to light.

Recommendations

This book is not intended as a policy or programming study. However, there are some policy and practical recommendations arising from it. Institutions such as the World Bank must re-evaluate their assumptions and recognize that it is not, and nor should it be, solely up to you(th) in the developing world – or anyone struggling to get by – to develop themselves. The vehement promotion of neoliberal, free market ideology that entails a reduction of state support is harmful to those who start out with very little in life, in the way in which it provides a culture of legitimacy for policies that are ultimately damaging to the most vulnerable groups in society, and in the symbolic violence it engenders as people come to believe that they really are and should be responsible for their lot.

The Thai government has made some moves towards instituting some of the state support necessary for allowing all of its citizens the chance to achieve a better life, for example through the universal healthcare scheme and the universal pension scheme, and it is essential that these are built on and not retracted in the frenzy of economic and political upheaval. It is also essential that this kind of support is extended to other arenas beyond healthcare and pensions, so that, for example, education is not only compulsory for all up to the age of fifteen, but actually accessible. This might entail supporting some young people with the hidden costs of schooling and with compensating their families for the loss of earnings that they would otherwise be providing. It is also vital that slum upgrading programmes are rolled out and properly financed and, related to this, that tenants are afforded security of tenure. Housing needs to be truly affordable for those who happen – through no fault of their own – to be unable to meet the cost of inner-city rent prices.

Thailand instituted a national minimum wage in 2013 (although this may become a variable minimum wage according to the particular economy and cost of living in each region). This again may look like a step in the right direction for those in low-paid work, but it has been recognized that millions of workers are still not receiving the minimum wage, and that anyway this is not enough to allow people to do anything beyond pay for absolute basic necessities ('TDRI Says Floating Minimum Wage Is a Disadvantage for Workers' 2013). It also does nothing to help those who work in the informal sector, as many slum residents do, who do not earn a wage but make their money ad hoc, directly from their customers.

Despite the relative lack of support available to them, and despite the unintended outcomes that can ensue in the search for a better life, the participants in this research were remarkable in their determination and persistence, and especially in their persistent and determined *hope* in the face of continual setbacks. To me, there appeared at points to be little reason for hope, and yet each time their goals eluded them or produced some negative outcome they would pick themselves up, dust themselves down and start over, somehow managing to retain a sense of hope that one day things would get better, and perhaps even stay that way. Here, hope – an example of what Durham refers to as 'the increasingly interesting field of sentiment' in the new anthropology of youth (Durham 2008: 946) – appears less a matter of audacity (Obama 2007) and more a matter of cruel necessity, a much-needed companion to those whose attempts to build a better life are defined by struggle and negative repercussions. As 21-year-old Or stated during one of our last encounters:

> Well, yes, I hope that I can make things work for me, my boyfriend and especially for my son, I want him to have a comfortable life. Keep hoping! If we don't have hope we have nothing, right?

Bibliography

Abouharb, M.R. and D. Cingranelli. 2007. *Human Rights and Structural Adjustment*. Cambridge: Cambridge University Press.

Abu-Lughod, L. 1990. 'The Romance of Resistance: Tracing Transformations of Power through Bedouin Women', *American Ethnologist* 17(1): 41–55.

Allen, D.R., et al. 2003. 'Sexual Health Risks among Young Thai Women: Implications for HIV/STD Prevention and Contraception', *AIDS and Behavior* 7(1): 9–21.

Amit-Talai, V. 1995. 'Conclusion: The "Multi" Cultural of Youth', in V. Amit-Talai and H. Wulff (eds), *Youth Cultures: A Cross-Cultural Perspective*. London: Routledge, pp. 223–33.

Anderson, W.W., and D.D. Anderson. 1986. 'Thai Muslim Adolescents' Self, Sexuality, and Autonomy', *Ethos* 14(4): 368–94.

Anon-DPF. 2006. *Bangkok Housing*. Bangkok: Publisher Unknown.

Ansell, N. 2005. *Children, Youth and Development*. Abingdon: Routledge.

Askew, M. 2002. *Bangkok: Place, Practice and Representation*. London: Routledge.

Baker, C., and P. Phongpaichit. 2005. *A History of Thailand*. Cambridge: Cambridge University Press.

Benveniste, L. 2008. 'Thailand Social Monitor on Youth: Development and the Next Generation'. PowerPoint Presentation, 11 March, Bangkok. Retrieved 5 August 2016 from http://www.worldbank.or.th/WBSITE/EXTERNAL/COUNTRIES/EASTASIAPACIFICEXT/THAILANDEXTN/0,,contentMDK:21684702~pagePK:141137~piPK:141127~print:Y~theSitePK:333296,00.html.

Boonyabancha, S. 2002. *Urban Community Development Fund, Thailand: The Experience of the Urban Community Development Office (UCDO), (Community Organizations Development Institute – CODI)* London: University College London.

Bourgois, P. 1989. 'Crack in Spanish Harlem: Culture and Economy in the Inner City', *Anthropology Today* 5(4): 6–11.

Bourgois, P. 1995. *In Search of Respect: Selling Crack in El Barrio*. Cambridge: Cambridge University Press.

Bourgois, P. 2001. 'Culture of Poverty', in N.J. Smelser and P.B. Baltes (eds), *International Encyclopaedia of the Social and Behavioral Sciences*. Oxford: Pergamon, pp. 11,904–907.

Bucholtz, M. 2002. 'Youth and Cultural Practice'. *Annual Review of Anthropology* 31: 525–52.

Caputo, V. 1995. 'Anthropology's Silent "Other": A Consideration of Some Conceptual and Methodological Issues for the Study of Youth and Children's Cultures', in V. Amit-Talai and H. Wulff (eds), *Youth Cultures: A Cross-Cultural Perspective*. London: Routledge, pp. 43–62.

Carrier, J.G. 1996. 'Sociology', in A. Barnard and J. Spencer (eds), *Encyclopedia of Social and Cultural Anthropology*. London: Routledge, pp. 524–27.

Cash, K. 1999. 'Understanding the Psychosocial Aspects of HIV/AIDS Prevention for Northern Thai Single Adolescent Migratory Women Workers', *Applied Psychology: An International Review* 48(2): 125–37.

Chestnut, L.G., B.D. Ostro, and N. Vichit-Vadakan. 1997. 'Transferability of Air Pollution Control Health Benefits. Estimates from the United States to Developing Countries: Evidence from the Bangkok Study', *American Journal of Agricultural Economics* 75(5): 1,630–35.

'Councillor Slams Immoral Generation'. 2005. *The Nation*, 20 August.

Damrongchai, P. 1998. 'Statement by Mr. Prasit Damrongchai Permanent Secretary, Office of the Prime Minister, Head of Delegates from the Royal Kingdom of Thailand', *Address to the World Conference of Ministries Responsible for Youth, Lisbon, 11 August*. Retrieved 2 April 2010 from http://www.un.org/events/youth98/speeches/118thay.htm.

Duang Prateep Foundation. 1995. *History of Khlong Toey Slum*. Video. Bangkok: Duang Prateep Foundation.

Duang Prateep Foundation. 2003. *Duang Prateep Foundation 25th Anniversary Journal*. Bangkok: Duang Prateep Foundation.

Durham, D. 2008. 'New Horizons: Youth at the Millennium', *Anthropological Quarterly* 81(4): 945–57.

Dyson, J. 2008. 'Harvesting Identities: Youth, Work and Gender in the Indian Himalayas', *Annals of the Association of Human Geographers* 98(1): 160–79.

Dyson, J. 2010. 'Friendship in Practice: Girls' Work in the Indian Himalayas', *American Ethnologist* 37(3): 482–98.

Ford, N., and S. Kittisuksathit. 1996. *Youth Sexuality: The Sexual Awareness, Lifestyles and Related Health Service Needs of Young, Single Factory Workers in Thailand*. Bangkok: Institute for Population and Social Research (IPSR 202).

German, D., et al. 2006. 'Motivations for Methamphetamine Cessation among Young People in Northern Thailand', *Addiction* 101: 1,143–52.

Griffin, C. 2001. 'Imagining New Narratives of Youth: Youth Research, the "New Europe" and Global Youth Culture', *Childhood* 8: 147–66.

Hall, S., and T. Jefferson (eds). [1977] 2006. *Resistance through Rituals: Youth Subcultures in Post-War Britain*. London: Routledge.

Hall, T., and H. Montgomery. 2000. 'Home and Away: "Childhood", "Youth" and Young People', *Anthropology Today* 16(3): 13–15.

Hammersley, M., and P. Atkinson. 1995. *Ethnography: Principles in Practice*, 2nd edn. London: Routledge.

Harvey, D.L., and M.H. Reed. 1996. 'The Culture of Poverty: An Ideological Analysis', *Sociological Perspectives* 39(4): 465–95.

Hecht, T. 1998. *At Home in the Street: Street Children of Northeast Brazil*. Cambridge: Cambridge University Press.

Hewison, K. 1999. 'Thailand's Capitalism: The Impact of the Economic Crisis', *UNEAC Papers* 1 [online]. Retrieved 30 March 2010 from file:///C:/Users/user/AppData/Local/Packages/Microsoft.MicrosoftEdge_8wekyb3d8bbwe/TempState/Downloads/Thailands_Capitalism_The_Impact_of_the_Economic_C.pdf.
Hewison, K. 2000. 'Resisting Globalization: A Study of Localism in Thailand', *The Pacific Review* 13(2): 279–96.
Hoechner, H. 2015. 'Mobility as a Contradictory Resource: Peripatetic Qur'anic Students in Kano, Nigeria', *Children's Geographies* 13(1): 59–72.
Holden, T.J.M. 2006. 'The Social Life of Japan's Adolechnic', in P. Nilan and C. Feixa (eds), *Global Youth? Hybrid Identities, Plural Worlds*. London: Routledge, pp. 72–90.
International Organisation for Migration. 2016. *Global Migration Trends Factsheet 2015*. Geneva: International Organisation for Migration.
Jeffrey, C. 2010. 'Timepass: Youth, Class, and Time among Unemployed Young Men in India', *American Ethnologist* 37(3): 465–81.
Jeffrey, C. 2012. 'Geographies of Children and Youth II: Global Youth Agency', *Progress in Human Geography* 36(2): 245–53.
Jeffrey, C., and S. Young. 2012. 'Waiting for Change: Youth, Caste and Politics in India', *Economy and Society* 41(4): 638–61.
Kaboski, J.P., and R.M. Townsend. 2012. 'The Impact of Credit on Village Economies', *American Economic Journal: Applied Economics* 4(2): 98–133.
Kamat, S. 2007. 'Populism Repackaged: The World Bank's Perspective on Equity and Youth', *Development and Change* 38(6): 1,209–18.
Kanato, M., and K. Saranrittichai. 2006. 'Early Experience of Sexual Intercourse: A Risk Factor for Cervical Cancer Requiring Specific Intervention for Teenagers', *Asian Pacific Journal of Cancer Prevention* 7: 151–53.
Kaplan, M., and J.D. Kelly. 1994. 'Rethinking Resistance: Dialogics of "Disaffection" in Colonial Fiji', *American Ethnologist* 21(1): 123–51.
Katz, C. 2004. *Growing Up Global: Economic Restructuring and Children's Everyday Lives*. Minneapolis, MN: University of Minneapolis University Press.
Khlong Toey District Office. 2005. *Basic Information for Khlong Toey District*. Bangkok: Khlong Toey District Office.
Kittiprapas, S. 2001. 'The Extended Bangkok Region: Globalization and Sustainability', in F. Lo and P.J. Marcotullio (eds), *Globalization and the Sustainability of Cities in the Asia Pacific Region*. Tokyo: United Nations University Press, pp. 364–96.
Kritayanavaj, B. 2008. 'Global Financial Crisis 2008: A View from Thailand', *GH Bank Housing Journal* 4(2): 36–43.
LaRocco, T. 2011. 'Neoliberalism and Thailand's Class Struggle', *Foreign Policy Association*. Retrieved 20 August 2015 from https://foreignpolicyblogs.com/2011/06/08/neoliberalism-and-thailands-class-struggle/.
Liechty, M. 1995. 'Media, Markets and Modernisation: Youth Identities and the Experience of Modernity in Kathmandu, Nepal', in V. Amit-Talai and H. Wulff (eds), *Youth Cultures: A Cross-Cultural Perspective*. London: Routledge, pp. 166–201.

Lewis, O. 1968. *La Vida: A Puerto Rican Family in the Culture of Poverty – San Juan and New York*. London: Panther.
Luttrell-Rowland, M. 2007. 'Gangs, Soldiers and "Idle Girls": Constructions of Youth and Development in World Bank Discourse', *Research in Comparative and International Education* 2(3): 230–41.
Maier, Fr. J.H. 2005. *Welcome to the Bangkok Slaughterhouse: The Battle for Human Dignity in Bangkok's Bleakest Slums*. Hong Kong: Periplus Editions.
Malhotra, A., et al. 2005. 'Masculinity and Risk Behavior among Youth in Thailand', *XXV IUSSP International Population Conference*, Tours, July 2005.
Manopaiboon, C., et al. 2003. 'High Rates of Pregnancy among Vocational School Students: Results of Audio Computer-Assisted Self-Interview Survey in Chiang Rai, Thailand', *Journal of Adolescence* 26: 517–30.
Mead, M. [1928] 1943. *Coming of Age in Samoa: A Study of Adolescence and Sex in Primitive Societies*. Harmondsworth: Penguin.
Miles, S. 2000. *Youth Lifestyles in a Changing World*. Buckingham: Open University Press.
Mills, L.K. 1999. *Buddhism Explained*. Chiang Mai: Silkworm Books.
Mills, M.B. 1997. 'Contesting the Margins of Modernity: Women, Migration, and Consumption in Thailand', *American Ethnologist* 24(1): 37–61.
Mills, M.B. 1999. 'Migrant Labour Takes a Holiday: Reworking Modernity and Marginality in Contemporary Thailand', *Critique of Anthropology* 19(1): 31–51.
'Ministry Bans Tank Tops for Songkran'. 2003. *The Nation*, 29 March.
Mitchell, A. 2006. 'Youth and Development'. *All Party Parliamentary Group on Overseas Development Event, London, 5 December 2006*. London: ODI.
'Monks to Rent Mall Space in Thailand'. 2005. *Australian Broadcasting Corporation*, 26 November. Retrieved 5 April 2010 from http://www.abc.net.au/news/2005-11-26/monks-to-rent-mall-space-in-thailand/749208.
Montgomery, H. 2001. *Modern Babylon? Prostituting Children in Thailand*. Oxford: Berghahn Books.
Montgomery, H. 2007. 'Working with Child Prostitutes in Thailand: Problems of Practice and Interpretation', *Childhood* 14(4): 415–30.
Moore, D. 1999. '"Sail On, O Ship of State": Neo-liberalism, Globalisation and the Governance of Africa', *Journal of Peasant Studies* 27(1): 61–96.
Moore, K. 2006. '1.3 Billion Youth: Is the Research and Policy Community Prepared?' *Notes of the Round Table Discussion Co-hosted by the Chronic Poverty Research Centre, Overseas Development Institute and Peace Child International, 21 November 2006, London*. London: ODI. Retrieved 12 June 2007 from http://www.odi.org.uk/events/2006/11/21/362-meeting-report.pdf.
'Morality Losing Ground'. 2005. *The Nation*, 30 June.
Morrison, L. 2004. 'Traditions in Transition: Young People's Risk for HIV in Chiang Mai, Thailand', *Qualitative Health Research* 14(3): 328–44.
Morrow, V., and M. Richards. 1996. 'The Ethics of Social Research with Children: An Overview', *Children and Society* 10(2): 90–105.
Mulder, N. 1990. *Inside Thai Society: An Interpretation of Everyday Life*. Bangkok: Editions Duang Kamol.

Nayak, A. 2003. *Race, Place and Globalization: Youth Cultures in a Changing World*. Oxford: Berg.

Nelson, K.E., et al. 2002. 'HIV Infection in Young Men in Northern Thailand, 1991–1998: Increasing Role of Injection Drug Use', *Journal of Acquired Immune Deficiency Syndromes* 29: 62–68.

Niang, A. 2006. 'Bboys: Hip-Hop Culture in Dakar, Senegal', in P. Nilan and C. Feixa (eds), *Global Youth? Hybrid Identities, Plural Worlds*. London: Routledge, pp. 167–85.

Nilan, P. 2006. 'The Reflexive Youth Culture of Devout Muslim Youth in Indonesia', in P. Nilan and C. Feixa (eds), *Global Youth? Hybrid Identities, Plural Worlds*. London: Routledge, pp. 91–110.

Nilan, P., and C. Feixa. 2006. 'Introduction: Youth Hybridity and Plural Worlds', in P. Nilan and C. Feixa (eds), *Global Youth? Hybrid Identities, Plural Worlds*. London: Routledge, pp. 1–13.

Obama, B. 2007. *The Audacity of Hope: Thoughts on Reclaiming the American Dream*. Edinburgh: Canongate Books.

Ockey, J. 1999. 'Creating the Thai Middle Class', in M. Pinches (ed.), *Culture and Privilege in Capitalist Asia*. London: Routledge, pp. 230–50.

Parnwell, M.J.G., and D.A. Arghiros. 1996. 'Introduction: Uneven Development in Thailand', in M.J.G. Parnwell (ed.), *Uneven Development in Thailand*. Aldershot: Avebury, pp. 1–27.

Peleggi, M. 2002. *Lord of Things: The Fashioning of the Siamese Monarchy's Modern Image*. Honolulu, HI: University of Hawai'i Press.

Perlman, J.E. 1976. *The Myth of Marginality: Urban Poverty and Politics in Rio de Janeiro*. Berkeley, CA: University of California Press.

Phongpaichit, P., and C. Baker. 1998. *Thailand's Boom and Bust*. Bangkok: Silkworm Books.

Podhisita, C., P. Xenos, and A. Varangrat. 2004. 'The Risk of Premarital Sex among Thai Youth: Individual and Family Influences', *Journal of Population and Social Studies* 12(2): 1–31.

Pornchokchai, S. 2003. *Global Report on Human Settlements: City Report, Bangkok*. Bangkok: Thai Appraisal Foundation.

Preston, P.W. 1996. *Development Theory: An Introduction*. Oxford: Blackwell.

Ruland, J., and M.L.B. Ladavalya. 1996. 'Managing Metropolitan Bangkok: Power Contest or Public Service?', in J. Ruland (ed.), *The Dynamics of Metropolitan Management in Southeast Asia*. Singapore: Institute of Southeast Asian Studies, pp. 30–70.

Sansone, L. 1995. 'The Making of a Black Youth Culture: Lower-Class Young Men of Surinamese Origin in Amsterdam', in V. Amit-Talai and H. Wulff (eds), *Youth Cultures: A Cross-Cultural Perspective*. London: Routledge, pp. 114–43.

Sattah, M.V., et al. 2002. 'Prevalence of and Risk Factors for Methamphetamine Use in Northern Thai Youth: Results of an Audio-Computer-Assisted Self-Interviewing Survey with Urine Testing', *Addiction* 97: 801–808.

Scheper-Hughes, N. 1992. *Death without Weeping: The Violence of Everyday Life in Brazil*. Berkeley, CA: University of California Press.

Schor, J. 2008. 'Understanding the Child Consumer', *Journal of the American Academy of Child and Adolescent Psychiatry* 47(5): 486–90.

Sethapramote, Y. 2014. 'The Economic Consequences of Thailand's Political Crisis', *The Nation Multimedia*, 28 March.

Shahabi, M. 2006. 'Youth Subcultures in Post-Revolutionary Iran: An Alternative Reading', in P. Nilan and C. Feixa (eds), *Global Youth? Hybrid Identities, Plural Worlds*. London: Routledge, pp. 111–29.

Slagter, R., and H.R. Kerbo. 2000. *Modern Thailand*. Bangkok: McGraw Hill.

Tangmunkongvorakul, A., R. Kane, and K. Wellings. 2005. 'Gender Double Standards in Young People Attending Sexual Health Services in Northern Thailand', *Culture, Health & Sexuality* 7(4): 361–73.

'TDRI Says Floating Minimum Wage Is a Disadvantage for Workers'. 2015, *Thai PBS*, 9 June.

'Thais Increasingly Dissolute'. 2005. *The Nation*, 31 August.

Thato, S., et al. 2003. 'Predictors of Condom Use among Adolescent Thai Vocational Students', *Journal of Nursing Scholarship* (Second Quarter): 157–63.

Thaweesit, S. 2004. 'The Fluidity of Thai Women's Gendered and Sexual Subjectivities', *Culture, Health and Sexuality* 6(3): 205–19.

Thianthai, C. 2004a. 'A Glance into the Life of a Computerized Generation: A Case Study on Thai Teenagers Living in Bangkok', *MANUSYA: Journal of Humanities* (Special Issue No. 8): 1–21.

Thianthai, C. 2004b. 'Gender and Class Differences in Young People's Sexuality and HIV/AIDS Risk-Taking Behaviours in Thailand', *Culture, Health & Sexuality* 6(3): 189–203.

Thomas, N., and C. O'Kane. 1998. 'The Ethics of Participatory Research with Children', *Children and Society* 12(5): 336–48.

Thorbeck, S. 1987. *Voices from the City: Women of Bangkok*. London: Zed Books.

Trnka, S., and C. Trundle. 2014. 'Competing Responsibilities: Moving beyond Neoliberal Responsibilisation', *Anthropological Forum: A Journal of Social Anthropology and Comparative Sociology* 24(2): 136–53.

United Nations Children's Fund (UNICEF). 2011. *The State of the World's Children 2001. Adolescence: An Age of Opportunity*. New York: United Nations.

United Nations Development Programme (UNDP). 2007. *Thailand Human Development Report 2007: Sufficiency Economy and Human Development*. Bangkok: United Nations.

United Nations Division for Social Policy and Development. 2005. *World Youth Report: Young People Today, and in 2015*. New York: United Nations.

United Nations Economic and Social Commission for Asia and the Pacific (UNESCAP). 2000. *Youth in Thailand: A Review of the Youth Situation and National Policies and Programmes*. New York: United Nations.

Van Esterik, P. 2000. *Materializing Thailand (Materializing Culture)*. Oxford: Berg.

Viratkapan, V., and R. Perera. 2006. 'Slum Relocation Projects in Bangkok: What Has Contributed to Their Success or Failure?' *Habitat International* 30: 157–74.

Vuttanont, U., et al. 2006. '"Smart Boys" and "Sweet Girls" – Sex Education Needs in Thai Teenagers: A Mixed-Method Study', *The Lancet* 368: 2,068–80.

Wacquant, L. 2002. 'Review Symposium. Scrutinizing the Street: Poverty, Morality, and the Pitfalls of Urban Ethnography', *American Journal of Sociology* 107(6): 1,468–532.

Willis, P. 1977. *Learning to Labour: How Working Class Kids Get Working Class Jobs*. Farnborough: Saxon House.

World Bank. 2007. *World Development Report: Development and the Next Generation*. Washington, DC: World Bank.

World Bank. 2008. *Thailand Social Monitor on Youth: Development and the Next Generation*. Washington, DC: World Bank.

Wulff, H. 1995. 'Introduction – Introducing Youth Culture in Its Own Right: The State of the Art and New Possibilities', in V. Amit-Talai and H. Wulff (eds), *Youth Cultures: A Cross-Cultural Perspective*. London: Routledge, pp. 1–18.

Young, S., S. Kumar, and C. Jeffrey. 2017. 'Beyond Improvisation? The Rise and Rise of Youth Entrepreneurs in North India', *Transactions of the Institute of British Geographers* 42: 98–109.

Index

CPSIA information can be obtained
at www.ICGtesting.com
Printed in the USA
JSHW021348111019
1894JS00007B/70

9 781789 205350